BEYOND RISK IN ADOLESCENT SAFEGUARDING

Creating Conditions for Young People to Flourish

Carlene Firmin, Kristine Langhoff,
Delphine Peace, Michelle Lefevre,
Nathalie Huegler and Roni Eyal-Lubling

AF769198

First published in Great Britain in 2026 by

Policy Press, an imprint of
Bristol University Press
University of Bristol
1–9 Old Park Hill
Bristol
BS2 8BB
UK
t: +44 (0)117 374 6645
e: bup-info@bristol.ac.uk

Details of international sales and distribution partners are available at policy.bristoluniversitypress.co.uk

© Carlene Firmin, Kristine Langhoff, Delphine Peace, Michelle Lefevre, Nathalie Huegler and Roni Eyal-Lubling 2026

DOI: 10.51952/9781447378839

The digital PDF and ePub versions of this title are available open access and distributed under the terms of the Creative Commons Attribution-NonCommercial-NoDerivatives 4.0 International licence (https://creativecommons.org/licenses/by-nc-nd/4.0/) which permits reproduction and distribution for non-commercial use without further permission provided the original work is attributed.

British Library Cataloguing in Publication Data
A catalogue record for this book is available from the British Library

ISBN 978-1-4473-7881-5 paperback
ISBN 978-1-4473-7882-2 ePub
ISBN 978-1-4473-7883-9 OA PDF

The right of Carlene Firmin, Kristine Langhoff, Delphine Peace, Michelle Lefevre, Nathalie Huegler and Roni Eyal-Lubling to be identified as authors of this work has been asserted by them in accordance with the Copyright, Designs and Patents Act 1988.

All rights reserved: no part of this publication may be reproduced, stored in a retrieval system, used to train or develop an artificial intelligence system, or transmitted in any form or by any means, electronic, mechanical, photocopying, recording, or otherwise without the prior permission of Bristol University Press.

Every reasonable effort has been made to obtain permission to reproduce copyrighted material. If, however, anyone knows of an oversight, please contact the publisher.

The statements and opinions contained within this publication are solely those of the authors and not of the University of Bristol or Bristol University Press. The University of Bristol and Bristol University Press disclaim responsibility for any injury to persons or property resulting from any material published in this publication.

Bristol University Press and Policy Press work to counter discrimination on grounds of gender, race, disability, age and sexuality.

Cover design: Nicky Borowiec
Front cover image: Unsplash/Jon Tyson
Bristol University Press and Policy Press use environmentally responsible print partners.
Printed and bound in Great Britain by CPI Group (UK) Ltd, Croydon, CR0 4YY

FSC
www.fsc.org
MIX
Paper | Supporting responsible forestry
FSC® C013604

Bristol University Press' authorised representative in the European Union is:
Easy Access System Europe, Mustamäe tee 50, 10621 Tallinn, Estonia,
Email: gpsr.requests@easproject.com

Contents

List of figures, tables and boxes

Figures

Table

Boxes

About the authors

Carlene Firmin is Professor of Social Work and Director of the Global Centre for Contextual Safeguarding, Durham University. Since 2008 she has used research to reimagine protection for young people beyond their front doors.

Kristine Langhoff is Professor of Social Work at the University of Sussex. She trained as a social worker; her practice and research have focussed on youth, safety and harm.

Delphine Peace is Research Associate in the Global Centre for Contextual Safeguarding at Durham University. Through action research she works alongside young people and practitioners to transform child protection systems.

Michelle Lefevre is Professor of Social Work at the University of Sussex. She previously trained and practised as a social worker and arts psychotherapist, particularly in the context of safeguarding.

Nathalie Huegler is an independent Associate Researcher (Research in Practice, University of Sussex) and Senior Research Fellow, University of East Anglia.

Roni Eyal-Lubling is Lecturer at the School of Government and Society at The Academic College of Tel-Aviv – Yaffo. She is trained as a sociologist and social worker; her research and practice have focused on youth, young adulthood and intergenerational relations.

Acknowledgements

We the authors of this book would like to begin by thanking all the Innovate Project team and participants – including young people, their families and practitioners – for helping us reimagine what safeguarding, and safety, could mean for young people: this book, and the vision it sets out, would not have been possible without you.

Carlene would also like to thank God for His guidance, peace and love. I would also like to thank my co-authors on this book from both Sussex and Durham University for all they have done to enable us to share this book together. I'd like to acknowledge the wider team at the Global Centre for Contextual Safeguarding at Durham University, for their boundless support, energy, insight and important challenge, that have helped me to see where we needed to be more imaginative and ambitious in our vision for safeguarding systems; as well as the hundreds – if not thousands – of practitioners, young people, their families and wider communities who have been the foundation of my research for nearly two decades. On behalf of my younger self, I also would like to thank my secondary school history teacher Mr Whelpdale and my primary school teachers Mrs Donnington, Miss Harris and Miss Gaffney – teachers were a significant safety net throughout my childhood and, along with my wonderful mum – Anita Pearson, my extended family and my church community, provided me with contexts in which I could flourish including during moments of profound loss. And finally, I'd like to acknowledge my husband, Obinna, and our two boys, Ziora-Blue and Kambili-Bey, whose love and patience create the conditions in which my work is possible.

Kristi would like to thank the young people and professionals who have participated in research over the years – who have inspired, influenced, changed, taught and cared for me. Thank you to my Durham and Sussex colleagues for having endlessly interesting ideas and my wise Action Learning Set mates: Anna, Catherine and Ericka. I am endlessly grateful to my brilliant and kind son, Jack, who reminds me daily how hilarious and wonderful young people are. For Willa, who is hope and light, for Harry and the friends who have become family since moving an ocean away from my home. On behalf of my teenage self: I'd like to thank my mum who introduced me to coffee, my dad who took me to the theatre even though he hates theatre and my high school art teacher Mrs Lynch, for letting me hang out in her classroom whenever I wanted and making me feel like I was a creative and interesting person.

Delphine would like to thank the young people and professionals she has learnt so much from over the years, for their dedication to creating more humane systems. Thank you to my colleagues from the Global Centre for

Contextual Safeguarding at Durham University and to University of Sussex colleagues, for their invaluable guidance and encouragement. It is a privilege to be part of a team where we support one another to flourish. Thank you to my loving family, my wonderful friends and the caring adults who have held and nurtured me through my teenage years and made me feel valued. And thank you to my husband, David, and to our sons, Adrien and Charles, for making each day a joy.

Michelle would like to express her endless gratitude to the young people, families, practitioners and researchers she has worked with in practice and academic settings over the years. You have taught me, in particular, how funny, creative, wise and resilient young people are in the face of adversity, and about the centrality of authentic engagement and trust-building. My teenage self wants to thank those special schoolfriends who brought such love and care into my daily life, the teachers who constantly gave me hope and encouragement, and my sister, Lorraine, to whom I could always turn in difficult times. Finally, to Claire, who has co-created such a loving and safe home for us and our genealogy of playful, adored, naughty felines – thank you every day!

Nathalie would like to thank all the young people she has met throughout her social work practice and research work, along with many wise and supportive family members, friends, mentors and colleagues, across organisations and countries, whose help, care and constructive challenge continue to enrich her lifelong learning journey. Among many long relationships and some much briefer encounters, as a young person, E. sticks out – a probation social worker who not only made me and friends welcome as chatty teenage 'creative disruptors' of our local Amnesty International activism group but also allowed me to graffiti paint her car (and then continued to drive it to her work appointments for months afterwards).

Roni would like to thank all the brilliant colleagues on the Innovate Project who introduced me to new ways of thinking about safeguarding young people in the UK and beyond. To the adolescent girls and young women I worked with at the Rotem Centre and to Dr Michal Komem who together taught me to listen closely and trust 'life knowledge'. To my parents, Ila and Eli, who created a loving home that was always open, always full of people and grounded in giving to others; and to my husband, Yaniv, and my children, Uri and Amalia, for being partners in keeping the tradition going.

1

Introduction

At various points in the 1998 album *The Miseducation of Lauryn Hill* we hear audio from a classroom. A teacher is asking a room of students about the word 'love'. What it means for them, if they have ever felt loved or been in love. At one point a young man says you love someone when 'You are willing to do everything for that person'; and later in the album a young woman describes the feeling of 'taking that person for what he or she is, no matter what he or she look like or no matter what he or she do'. Hill used their accounts to punctuate songs on one of the greatest hip hop albums of all time; but here we take their ideas as a starting point to conjure up (new) feelings about safety and safeguarding.

What would it take for all young people to feel this way about the people in their lives; if they believed their families, friends and professionals who came into their lives were willing to do everything for them, for exactly who they were? What would our safeguarding systems look like if they were designed to foster these types of relationships; if safety, enacted through love, was the goal? What if we lived in societies that framed young people's lives through a lens of flourishing and freedom, more than crime and containment? If we started from a place where we saw youth far more as a gift to nurture, rather than we did a risk to be mitigated? We use this book to begin this reimagining, reweighting and reorientating of safeguarding systems – and ask ourselves, and data from a project we worked on together – to move beyond thinking about safeguarding young people and towards creating conditions in which they are safe and loved. In doing so, we offer ways to reshape how we understand, and provide, what young people need and want to live full and safe lives.

But why?

We live in a world where a lot of adults spend a lot of time worrying about young people. We also live in a world where many are scared of young people. Every generation has had its reason to be worried, its reason to be scared. In the last 30 years alone we have seen concerns about death due to recreational drug use in nightclubs (Moore and Miles, 2004; BBC, 2017), the threat of 'anti-social behaviour' with young people wearing 'hoodies' (BBC, 2005; Robinson, 2009; Millie, 2014), violence incited by computer games (Ferguson, 2011; DeLisi et al, 2013) and music lyrics (Richardson and Scott, 2002; Roberts et al, 2003), risks posed by strangers in public spaces, and now online (Benavente et al, 2022; Finkelhor et al, 2023; Child Safeguarding Practice Review Panel, 2024).

We come to this book at a time of equal concern. There is a growing recognition that the idea of 'stranger danger' oversimplified the harms young people face online – with many encountering harassment and abuse online by people they see physically in educational and neighbourhood settings (Finkelhor et al, 2023). Around the world over 193,000 homicides occur among youth aged 15–29 years annually (WHO, 2024). In 2022, the World Health Organization estimated that up to 1 billion children aged 2–17 years experienced physical, sexual or emotional violence or neglect. Child abuse inquiries around the world show that many of these children, particularly during adolescence, are harmed by other young people and adults who are unrelated to them. This abuse occurs in a range of public contexts that should be safe, from sports clubs and churches to fast-food outlets and schools. For example, the Australian Maltreatment Study in 2023 found that 10 per cent of Australians had experienced peer-sexual harassment, and that those reporting sexual victimisation in childhood were more likely to report abuse by a peer than abuse by an adult family member (Hunt et al, 2024). Over ten years earlier, a UK study found similar patterns (Radford et al, 2011), as have wider studies on young people's experiences of street-based victimisation and violent crime (Office of National Statistics, 2018). More widely, an estimated 400+ million children around the world are exposed to child sexual exploitation and abuse annually (Economist Impact, 2022), and there is also now a growing concern regarding the criminal exploitation of young people (Marshall, 2024; Sheehan et al, 2024; de Vries et al, 2025). International communities have called for comprehensive preventative and protective measures that address these forms of harm (UNDOC, 2022), and countries have responded via a range of practices – including online youth work provision in the Netherlands (Todorovic et al, 2025), redesigned trauma courts focused on exploitation in the US (Musto, 2022) and the creation of child-safe institution standards in Australia (Royal Commission, 2022).

In the UK, services providers, policy makers and regulators have undertaken a decade-long period of reform in a bid to provide protection. This reform has gone through three broad phases.

The UK journey to date: a local response to global challenges

Between 2009 and 2016, Phase 1 focused on better implementation of systems as they had been designed. This operated generally via a 'continuous improvement' model whereby changes stimulated by evolving research and policy would be introduced and tested for efficacy within existing administrative systems and practice paradigms (Bason, 2018, p 291). Government guidance was updated, and local area partnerships were tasked with developing action plans for implementing that guidance, initially in response to child sexual exploitation (Pearce, 2013). A range of resources were introduced to local areas to assist with implementation including training and bespoke risk assessments and checklists (Franklin et al, 2018), and the children's social care inspectorate undertook themed inspections on child sexual exploitation to offer another view into progress (Ofsted, 2015). In the midst of this phase, the then UK Prime Minister threatened sanctions for local areas that failed to effectively implement the system (Prime Minister's Office, 2015).

However, over time, people, ourselves included, began to see that ineffective practice was not simply the result of poor implementation. When the Prime Minister threatened sanctions, he was tasking social workers to respond to harms using systems that were never designed for that purpose (Gorin and Jobe, 2013; Hanson and Holmes, 2014; Firmin and Knowles, 2022). Consequently, state intervention via social work often either had limited effectiveness or, on some occasions, made things harder for young people. Challenges included the fact that social workers operated in systems designed to assess parenting as a route to protection, whereas issues such as sexual and criminal exploitation were rarely instigated by parents and were often beyond their control (Shuker and Ackerley, 2017; Lloyd and Firmin, 2019; Pike and Langham, 2019). Commissioned interventions often focused on educating young people to make 'safer choices' but failed to address the unsafe situations in which their choices were constrained (Weston and Mythen, 2020). Youth work provision had been decimated in the UK, reducing the availability of services with a reach into the community and extra-familial contexts where harm often occurred (Villa, 2024). Young people impacted by these harms often committed criminal offences in the context of their own abuse and so were viewed as both a victim and a perpetrator, while trying to access services that did not straddle those binaries (Cockbain and Brayley, 2012). In the absence of a clear and consistent youth strategy, policy frameworks held young people criminally responsible from the age of ten, for non-consensual sexual behaviours they couldn't consent to until they were 16; and for most support stopped on their 18th birthdays even though the harms they faced did not. It became clear, then, that practice problems stemmed from system inadequacies; hence, iterative tinkering about with incremental improvements, inside existing frameworks, would be insufficient.

From 2018 until about 2023, we entered into Phase 2, the phase of redesign. In this phase policy makers, researchers and services providers, recognised that they needed to go beyond better implementation of existing systems and instead looked to transform elements of these systems. This phase was characterised by increased political investment in innovation (Department for Education, 2022) and interest in an emergent loose grouping of harms, often viewed distinctly, under the banner of 'extra-familial harm' or 'risks outside of the home'. These extra-familial risks and harms (EFRH) included sexual and criminal exploitation, street-or-community-based interpersonal violence (sometimes referred to as 'knife crime' or 'serious youth violence'), abuse in young people's own romantic/dating/intimate relationships and peer-sexual abuse and harassment – both in person and online (HM Government, 2023; Action for Children, 2024; Wroe et al, 2025). The rationale for this grouping was a recognition that the child protection and wider safeguarding systems being leveraged in response to these harms were designed with the idea that risk/protection for young people under-18 sat within families (Featherstone et al, 2018; Lloyd and Firmin, 2019), whereas for these harms, this was *rarely* the case. Yes, there were occasions when parents or carers exploited their children, but these were in the minority. For the remainder, young people were either living in safe and protective homes but came to harm in extra-familial contexts/relationships; or they had experienced abuse, neglect or other challenges at home which increased their exposure to extra-familial harms. In both these scenarios, using systems predominantly focused on parental (in)action as a source of harm was unlikely to create safety in the extra-familial contexts where young people had been abused, or for young people who were aging into adulthood and relative independence from their families. This grouping also grew out of increasing concerns around criminal exploitation, and latterly serious violence, and warnings that lessons learnt for responding to sexual exploitation were not being employed for young people impacted by these issues (Ofsted, 2018; Action for Children, 2024), as well as a national outcry about sexual harassment in English and Welsh schools (Estyn, 2021; Ofsted, 2021).

In some ways the UK has been viewed as unique in this phase of its journey (Shawar et al, 2022), as political will, national scandals and mounting advocacy coalesced to create rapid policy and service development in a short period of time. However, many matters we were trying to resolve in the UK were also challenging systems in other counties around the world. In various parts of Europe, the US, Australia, Chile and Canada, systems:

- often rely on out-of-home and residential care to remove young people from community-based harms (for example, Clawson et al, 2009; McKibbin and Humphries, 2019);
- criminalise young people in need of protection (for example, Miller-Perrin and Wurtele, 2017; Palmer, 2019; Pullmann et al, 2020);
- are designed to focus on individual, and in many cases parental, responsibility, for young people's protection (Fong and Cardoso, 2010; Musto, 2022);
- reduce protections for young people beyond the age of 18, and often beyond the age of 16.

These challenges have meant that the systems social workers are operating in, and/or alongside, have required (sometimes radical) transformation to be effectively leveraged in response to risks and harms beyond families.

In the UK, Phase 2 reforms focused on such redesign, and emerging practice or system innovations were drawn upon to facilitate this. These innovations have included: trauma-informed approaches to build safety, choice, empowerment, trust and collaboration into all elements of service delivery (DeCandia and Guarino, 2015; Christie, 2018); Contextual Safeguarding to radically reorient services focused on individual young people and families towards the social conditions of extra-familial contexts where EFRH occurred (Firmin, 2020); Transitional Safeguarding as an emerging systems change approach to promote more developmentally attuned and fluid approaches to safeguarding young people and young adults across transition to adulthood (Holmes and Smale, 2018); Public Health Approaches to violence reduction, to identify and address population-level drivers of violence across primary, secondary and tertiary prevention efforts (WHO, 2017); and culturally competent, latterly rephrased as culturally sensitive, approaches to youth intervention, that recognised localised, historical, structural and contextual needs of young people impacted by violence and responded accordingly (Lindsay et al, 2022). In different ways these approaches, among others, sought to disrupt existing ways of working in response to the challenges outlined previously. Once no longer restricted by conventional practice paradigms and design idiosyncrasies, the core features of those systems that failed to address, and in some cases exacerbated, young people's exposure to EFRH or its impact could be reimagined and transformed.

The study underpinning this book

We undertook the ethnographic research that inspired this book during this second period of reform. From 2019 to 2023, the Innovate Project (Lefevre et al, 2024) sought to uncover the contingent and overlapping geographic, cultural, temporal, economic, social and political spaces and discourses that were influencing social policy, welfare systems and the law in respect of EFRH. We were interested in the policy priorities, statutory practice guidance, and performance and quality assurance indicators that services must evidence to demonstrate accountability, transparency, effectiveness and compliance with legal and professional standards. These requirements, additionally modulated by the availability of funding and resources, govern professional values and the organisational cultures and climates within which day-to-day practice with young people affected by EFRH is locally determined and (often invisibly) shaped (Lefevre et al, 2025).

We worked as a team, in collaboration with practitioners and service leaders, to track efforts at system innovation over three years in six research sites; these were local authorities, social care organisations and multi-agency safeguarding networks which were seeking to introduce new ways of working based on trauma-informed practice, Contextual Safeguarding and/or Transitional Safeguarding. We also worked iteratively through that period with a wider network of service leaders in the UK and internationally to help us understand the relevance and prevalence of what we were uncovering. We observed meetings (making extensive reflective fieldnotes), reviewed social work assessments and plans, conducted focus groups, interviews and reflective workshops with practitioners and leaders, interviewed young people and parents, and reviewed local policy documents in our six sites (see Table 1.1).

We analysed this extensive dataset primarily using the theoretical framework of Institutional Ethnography, which is concerned with detailing how everyday lives and practices within organisations and systems are arranged, and identifying how discourse and forms of governance ('ruling relations') influence and direct these processes, often outside the awareness of those involved (Smith, 2005, p 68). This in-depth qualitative approach required us to continually scrutinise our own positionality and subjectivities – the ways in which our personal, academic and/or professional histories, cultures and values shaped not only our theorisations of data but how we viewed young people and their everyday lives, their cultures and networks, and the nature of safeguarding and welfare systems. While all currently in academic roles, or in research and learning, as a team our backgrounds have included social work practice in the safeguarding field (Lefevre, Huegler, Eyal-Lubling and Langhoff), psychotherapy training (Lefevre), designing and delivering trauma-focussed group interventions (Langhoff), practice and policy development in the third sector (Peace, Huegler and Firmin) and statutory organisations (Firmin), including social justice advocacy. Some of us grew up and have worked in countries with different socio-legal frameworks (USA – Langhoff; Germany – Huegler; France – Peace; Israel – Eyal-Lubling) or grew up in local communities directly impacted by serious violence (Firmin).

These diverse influences have all profoundly shaped our perspectives on what has been needed at a systems level to transform young people's experience of professional intervention and its outcomes and, as a team, we have encompassed a range of views – for example, on the ethical appropriateness of professionals privileging a young person's autonomy when their choices may compromise their safety or well-being. Rather than seeing the tensions this inevitably evokes as problematic, something to be hidden, we found a way to embrace reflexivity relationally through the psychosocial containment offered by psychoanalytic theory and process-orientated methods. Our regular 'Many Minds' analytic groups (Thomas et al, 2025), where we immersed ourself in data excerpts, for example, provided

Table 1.1: Data collected for Innovate Project across six sites

Data collection method	Site 1 Trauma-informed practice	Site 2 Trauma-informed practice	Site 3 Contextual safeguarding	Site 4 Contextual safeguarding	Site 5 Transitional safeguarding	Site 6 Transitional safeguarding
Observations of meetings	30	30	16	22	23	24
Professional interviews	23	15	16	24	22	25
Professional focus groups	6	6	0	0	3	1
Documentary review	20	56	11	45	34	8
Case file reviews	13	10	8	5	0	0
Surveys	115	169	60	80	0	0
Engagements with young people	6	0	1	6	0	0
Engagements with parents	0	0	35	0	0	1

a co-present space with agreed boundaries and commitments to openness and mutual care; here, we were able to make transparent and contain the 'profound ontological, ethical, emotional and intellectual dilemmas' that are raised by questioning norms and 'certainties' (Lefevre et al, 2019, p 1837).

During our fieldwork we observed and analysed the challenges that practitioners and leaders in our research sites were experiencing as they tried to improve services for young people. As these challenges persisted, we found ourselves wondering less whether the approaches they were seeking to implement were useful and more whether it was actually *possible* to do so; particularly in ways that enabled services to more effectively respond to situations in which young people were at risk, or being harmed, beyond their family homes. We increasingly felt this was unlikely within prevailing system conditions without disrupting the status quo of social care organisations and the partnerships in which they worked.

As we ran this project, many of us were also working on additional studies in national and international responses to EFRH. These projects included: how safety for refugee young people in Germany could be improved through contextual perspectives, and identifying opportunities to develop contextual approaches with asylum-seeking and refugee youth in other European settings (Peace, Wroe and Huegler, 2025); how creative and participatory methods help reimagine the acts and practices of resistance among young survivors of sexual violence and exploitation (Warrington, Langhoff and Warnock, 2024); and co-developing child protection pathways designed specifically with EFRH in mind (Firmin, 2024). For some of us, coming at the issue of EFRH from different angles reshaped our own views on what may be needed in response. In addition to questioning whether innovations were feasible in existing service conditions, we also recognised how system conditions were compromising ideas we had previously championed. For example, Firmin and Peace, alongside other researchers with whom they were working recognised the ethical risks of 'mapping' young people's friendships in the name of 'Contextual Safeguarding' and the way that their own work had contributed to these practices. As with the innovations we were studying, we had failed to appreciate the ways in which recommendations such as 'consider young people's peers when assessing their experiences of harm' would result in the mapping, dispersal and potential criminalisation of young people in need of protection (Firmin and Wroe, 2021; Lloyd, Manister and Wroe, 2023; Firmin et al, 2025). More broadly we recognised how structural redesign had often been prioritised at the expense of cultural organisational reform; and that all the innovations we were interested in required the latter as well as, if not more than, the former (Firmin et al, 2026). In another example, Langhoff's (for example, Hickle, 2016) earliest writing on trauma-informed practice references the importance of creating trauma-informed organisational contexts but over-emphasised the role of front-line practitioners in creating safety and stabilisation through trauma-informed care, without sufficiently acknowledging (1) the way in which traumatised systems might pass responsibility to front line professionals for creating contexts of safety that are outside their control and (2) the potential for a focus on trauma-informed direct practice to detract from challenging the systems and structures that might actively traumatise young people.

Critically, these shortfalls meant that, while we had seen some progress in safeguarding White British young women from sexual exploitation, serious and increasing concerns remained for young men, racially minoritised young people, those who were neurodivergent or had additional learning needs, older young people and those who existed at the intersections of these protected characteristics (Firmin and Wroe, 2021; Davis, 2022; Wroe, 2022; Franklin et al, 2024). So many features of our system were stacked against these young people, who continued to be viewed as a-risk, rather than at-risk, of harm, and who were hyper-visible to exclusionary and criminalising processes but often invisible in protective and welfare-orientated ones.

These ideas began to crystalise for us collectively in the final year of the Innovate Project when we held a two-day analysis session to identify the key messages we wanted to share from across the entire project. In 2024 we published a paper detailing what we learnt about the progress made during this period of reform and setting out why a fundamental shift in thinking and action at macro and meso levels would be necessary if micro level practice improvements were to be possible (Firmin et al, 2024). In short, we argued that while some features of service improvement were evident in the six sites who participated in the Innovate Project, all struggled to fulfil the disruptive potential of the innovations they utilised. In some cases, the innovations were even compromised during the implementation period. Rather than redesign systems, innovations took on the features of the systems they were due to disrupt. Attempts at Contextual Safeguarding with young people's peer groups resulted in individualised interventions with different young people who shared a friendship or the labelling of young people's friends as 'risky'. Services adopting a trauma-informed approach recognised the impact of interpersonal harms on young people but often struggled to see how the systems of which they were a part could also be trauma-inducing. In our Transitional Safeguarding sites, professionals struggled with ongoing binary victim/perpetrator and child/adult framings, as part of early efforts to change systems.

In 2024 we concluded therefore that a further phase of reform – Phase 3 – was required. Not one that redesigned how systems were delivered but one that fundamentally reimagined the foundations upon which those systems were built, and reorientated practices accordingly.

Looking forward – beginning to reimagine

In this book, therefore, we contribute to a growing Phase 3 chorus: one that is challenging fundamental features of conventional safeguarding systems (Billingham and Irwin-Rogers, 2022; Wroe, 2022; Cocker et al, 2024). Using the UK as our system(s) case study, we move beyond the constrictions imposed by the challenging features of existing systems and reimagine them, drawing upon our Innovate Project data to illustrate shortfalls in redesign and to build upon green shoots of reimagining. We situate these results with reference to literature from various countries around the world which are mobilising responses to EFRH. In doing so, we offer a vision for any country seeking to go 'Beyond Individuals, Risk and Justice' in safeguarding young people affected by EFRH, and weight responses 'Towards Collective, Safety and Care' for all young people in contexts beyond their front doors.

To achieve this, we set out our vision in three parts. Part I of this book redefines system foundations; Part II reimagines system relationships; and Part III resets system goals. Notably, we do so by relying less on literature about the nature of EFRH but instead by drawing upon a wider conceptual evidence base that brings us back to the roots of key concepts that characterise, or are missing from, our existing systems. Whether it is literature on the responsibilisation of the deserving or undeserving poor (Chapter 4), developmentally expected behaviours during adolescence (Chapters 3 and 6) or philosophical debates on the nature of love (Chapter 2) and so on, we use broader concepts to make sense of the data we gathered during the Innovate Project, and invite readers to look beyond evidence on EFRH to begin transforming how systems support young people impacted by it.

In Part I, we start with the system foundations: the values, priorities and concepts upon which to build systems that promote, and protect, young people's safety.

The first foundation we select – 'Love and care' in Chapter 2 – is one that is too often absent from current system design and delivery. Using concepts of ethical care (Noddings, 1984; Tronto, 2005), radical empathy (Givens, 2021) and revolutionary love (Porto, 2025), we ask what it would look like if systems responded to EFRH from a place of 'radical love', in which young people impacted by EFRH felt loved and cared for by those who tried to keep them safe.

In the following two chapters we consider two concepts that, unlike love, already characterise safeguarding systems – 'Respect' (Chapter 3) and 'Responsibility' (Chapter 4) – and we then reimagine them. In terms of 'respect', we propose a move away from conditional forms of respect, in which young people earn respect through compliance with systems (systems which often seek to control them and on occasions have caused them further harm); and a move towards systems based on 'Recognition–respect' – in which young people are recognised as whole human beings, and young people's sense of self-worth and self-esteem is facilitated. When it comes to 'responsibility', we reflect on changes already underway, and which began in the Phase 2 period of system reform in the UK summarised previously. From 2015 onwards in the UK there have been gradual changes in who is considered responsible for responding to EFRH, and what exactly they are responsible for – with systems gradually reducing the burden placed on the shoulders of young people under 18 and their families to protect themselves from EFRH, while simultaneously increasing responsibility for the state (and professionals working in statutory systems) to respond to EFRH. In Chapter 4 we propose moving beyond this pervasive account of responsibility and recommend systems that focus less on changing *who* is responsible and focus more on *how* that responsibility is enacted. In doing so, we offer a system foundation that moves towards professionals, and the state more widely, holding responsibility for creating the conditions in which young people can be safer, have their needs met and flourish, within an overall paradigm of collective responsibility that is shared with young people, families, communities and societies; and away from professionals enacting individualised responsibilities to change young people's behaviours in persistently unsafe contexts.

In the final chapter of Part I, Chapter 5, we approach a theme that currently characterises safeguarding systems – 'information-sharing' – but do so through the concept of 'Privacy'. We suggest that privacy should be valued in protective systems as one route to providing young people with safety. Thus, any actions that uphold or breach privacy should be done so in a way that is purposeful, proportionate and participatory, in pursuit of safety as the overarching goal.

Part II of the book builds upon these foundations and applies them over three chapters to the relationships that characterise the pursuit, and provision, of safety.

In Chapter 6 we begin by considering young people's relationships with their parents, carers, family and kin more widely. As is the case with our account of 'Responsibility' (Chapter 4), in this chapter we chart the changing position of parents/carers within developing UK responses to EFRH and note the implications of this for how parents/carers featured (or were absent) in the evidence we collected during the Innovate Project. We propose systems that appropriately value families for the safety they afford young people impacted by EFRH, in the context of young people's changing relationships with caregivers during adolescence, so as to ensure that their contribution is valued, and the context in which they seek to make that contribution is appropriately recognised. Reflecting the values introduced in Part I, we illustrate the potential for systems to value the ways that parents/carers and wider families contribute to young people's safety, by promoting relationships of love/care over relationships of control/punishment in which the value of privacy is valued rather than ignored; supporting parents to respect and encourage young people's growing independence and autonomy, while also recognising and upholding their responsibilities to be partners – alongside others – in the provision of safety.

In Chapter 7 we draw attention to young people's friendships with peers, informal community relationships and romantic relationships as central to their experiences of safety. We note that in many ways our systems have been designed to either ignore the (increasing) role of young people's extra-familial relationships in providing safety, or to recognise them solely as a risk to be disrupted or dispersed. We therefore propose systems that move beyond this, respecting young people's friends and partners through processes of positive regard and recognition, acknowledging the importance of privacy as characterising many of these relationships and valuing the ways in which young people show love and care for each other in wider contexts of EFRH. We argue that such an approach creates the conditions in which the power of friendship can be leveraged for good, and ensure young people have access to safe and protective relationships that can outlive professional 'interventions' and grow with them into adulthood.

We round up Part II of the book with Chapter 8, young people's relationships with professionals. We highlight two features of these relationships which require a rethink: casework-based relationships and information-gathering-based relationships. We outline how professional relationships with young people can move beyond these restrictions and create conditions for building safety, if social workers, youth workers and others in caring professions are situated in community with young people and the people who matter to them. Such relationships can be ones in which young people seek safety by sharing their concerns with professionals, rather than being ones in which professionals monitor young people and worry about the things young people feel unable to share. We also note that not all professional relationships are equal – and that in the system we imagine, those that are enforcement or criminal-justice-based would reduce in dominance and those that are welfare or care-orientated would take a primary position. In this way, we do not imagine safeguarding systems with more professional relationships – instead we focus on systems with better, appropriate and proportionate relationships.

Having detailed the ways we would reorient the foundations of safeguarding systems (Part I), and the relationships those systems produce or interact with (Part II), we close the book by outlining the goals of the safeguarding systems we propose (Part III). Part III is made up of two chapters. In Chapter 9 we outline the goals of safety and justice, and the relationship between the two. In terms of 'safety', we reflect on the various ways that safety can be provided to or built around young people impacted by EFRH, and the ways safety can be withheld or compromised in risk-averse or risk-dominated safeguarding systems. We argue that while in many ways the care ethic running through this book is viewed as contrary to a justice ethic, the pursuit of social and epistemic forms of justice can facilitate the forms of safety we promote. As such we propose safeguarding systems that pursue safety over (and as a way of mitigating) risk, and social/epistemic justice over criminal justice goals – noting that criminal justice can be subsumed within wider goals of safety so as to ensure its proportionate place in systems that all too often criminalise young people in need of support.

We use Chapter 10 to detail systems goals for young people that extend beyond EFRH – goals for young people to flourish and have their needs understood and met. We consider what young people need access to, and how systems might prioritise what young people need to feel and live safely instead of what the safeguarding systems they encounter might need in order to maintain perceptions of safe processes, procedures and multi-agency working arrangements. We then imagine systems that move with young people, beyond just meeting needs to ones that are attuned and responsive, capable of creating spaces for flourishing.

We conclude our book by arguing that, collectively, these system foundations, relationships and goals offer a framework for systems that move beyond 'safeguarding adolescents from EFRH' and instead are geared to 'providing safety for, and meeting the needs of, all young people'. In this framework, systems are weighted towards collective safety and care, over-and-above (not as opposite or in competition with) individualism, risk and justice. Such a framework is not only relevant to the UK. It speaks to the relationships, everyday lives and goals that matter to all young people and disrupts paradigms familiar to many countries around the world – particularly those that have been influenced by Anglophone and/or neo-liberal policy frameworks. We demonstrate that, by disrupting the foundations upon which current protective systems are built, we can reimagine what objectives systems might alternatively pursue, and what relationships could make that pursuit a reality. This collective offering provides a new way of conceiving of and designing systems that would be able to deliver what young people need to live full lives while also keeping them safe in the process.

Illustrating and practising our vision

Chapters 2–10 each conclude with a diagram to illustrate the shift we are recommending, followed by a set of reflective questions that may assist organisations in considering the implications of these recommendations for transforming practice methods and systems. In addition, we link readers to a key resource developed through the Innovate Project, which will assist services in planning and implementing innovations at a local level.

Chapters 2–5 illustrates the four ways in which we propose that safeguarding systems could be (re)orientated. Rather than depicting binaries, the diagrams are intended to illustrate 'system weighting'. At present, our data suggest systems are orientated towards risk management, individual responsibility, conditional forms of respect and the undermining of privacy under the banner of 'information-sharing'. This orientation is expressed through the priorities of systems, what they measure as success, the language they use and how professionals within those systems view young people. Through these diagrams, we will illustrate what priorities, measures, language and view of young people might exist in the reimagining we offer; namely one in which systems are orientated towards love and care, recognition-based respect, collective responsibility and the protection of privacy. In this vision these system foundations dominate, and as a result risk is mitigated through a pursuit of love/care, and information is shared in systems that protect and respect privacy. It is not that we do one or the other – more that we flip the influence of these different orientations and subsume things as we know them within things as they could be.

In Chapters 6–8, we illustrate what these reorientated foundations would mean for young people's relationships. As with the figures in Part I of the book, we present these ideas as a matter of weighting rather than as a binary; for example, leading with the love and care that families can and do provide to young people and, in this context, considering their role in risk management and their potential to pose 'a risk', rather than seeing families through a lens of risk-management first.

In Chapters 9–10, we present figures that summarise how the goals of safety and justice, and needs and flourishing, can be expressed through the system foundations and relationships detailed in Part I and Part II of the book. By breaking down diagrams in this way we articulate what sits underneath the final visuals offered in Chapter 11, which summarise the ways in which foundations, relationships and goals would interact in transformed safeguarding systems (Figure 11.1), and three key ways such systems would facilitate practices weighed towards care, collectivism and safety (Figure 11.2).

Some elements of what we propose in this book may cause discomfort; as authors, we too have had to work through those feelings as we composed the book, asking ourselves why we each struggled to let go of certain practice principles or system features that others felt free to deprioritise. There is much about where we get to that removes elements of certainty, protection and holding that help those who research and/or deliver systems feel safe. However, we have recognised that, while conventional safeguarding systems may address *some* aspects of risk and protection for *some* young people, they do not guarantee safety for *all*, nor do they necessarily promote young people's broader welfare needs, respect their rights or enable them to flourish. As such, we invite practitioners, system leaders and policy makers to lean into the discomfort and lack of certainty that is unavoidable when working with the realities of risk (Munro, 2019) and ask whether it might be worth it to move beyond those aspects which are undermining positive transformation. The framework that unfolds through this book is one to be put to the test and we hope that, by the time readers reach Chapter 11, you will see it as a basis upon which a practical transformation of safeguarding systems can commence.

Box 1.1: Reflective questions for leaders and practitioners raised by Chapter 1

1. How confident are you that the approach taken by your service promotes young people's needs, rights and preferences as well as their safety, and enables them to flourish in their lives? If not, what factors and processes get in the way of this?
2. If you could imagine a new and better system, what might this look like at macro level (national policy, governance and regulation), meso level (organisational culture and climate, local guidance, networks and resources) and in everyday practice (micro level)?
3. What kind of change process might be needed to achieve the better system you envisage? A better implementation of existing guidance and models, carefully paced, incremental improvements or a more radical shift in thinking and transformation of systems?

Resources to support innovation

To support you in determining what kind of process is most appropriate for making your aspired changes, you may find it helpful to read Chapter 4 'Deciding between innovation and practice improvement measures' in Lefevre et al (2024).

PART I

System foundations

2

Love and care

Introduction

'Love' and 'care' are emotionally and ethically charged terms with multiple and layered meanings and fuzzy boundaries. They are counterposed in this chapter to explore their role and relevance for public policy, system design and interpersonal practice with young people affected by extra-familial risks and harms (EFRH). We begin the chapter by exploring the varied ways these terms are conceptualised and how they shape the formal 'carescapes' (Bowlby and McKie, 2019) that are provided for young people by practitioners and service systems. We move then to consider a meeting we observed during our ethnographic research in the Innovate Project. Through its analysis, we explore how the 'ruling relations' (Smith, 2005, p 68) of professional discourse, public policy and statutory guidance govern (inter-)organisational resources, cultures and practices and, in turn, affect the extent to which young people feel loved and valued by keyworkers, Government and wider society. Drawing on the concepts of ethical care (Noddings, 1984; Tronto, 2005), radical empathy (Givens, 2021) and revolutionary love (Porto, 2025), we end by proposing a carescape governed by a sensibility of 'radical love'.

Being cared for and loved

'Care', as a phrasal verb, refers to an act or process that involves another: caring *for* or *about* someone. Caring might be enacted at a role and task level within a loving familial or romantic relationship, such as when raising a child or if a partner or elderly parent is sick. In this sense, caring for someone embodies affectional love. In such scenarios, obligation and accountability within practices of relational care commonly evolve over time and context; for example, a parent has to adapt from providing significant and intimate physical care in early childhood, to a more 'hands-off' form of caring in adolescence that is nonetheless emotionally and psychologically demanding (Coleman, 2011). The balance of authority for day-to-day decisions, including managing risk, similarly shifts incrementally from primarily being the parents/guardians' responsibility towards the battleground of adolescence, where young people want – and developmentally need – much more privacy and choice around their self-care, self-presentation and social engagement (Huegler and Ruch, 2022).

If they are to develop and flourish physically, psychologically and socially, children need to be cared *about* by, as well as receive consistent, emotionally attuned and sensitive care *from*, people to whom they matter and who demonstrate their love through manifestations of warmth, affection and unconditional positive regard (Cicchetti, 2016). While such loving care is most often provided through family relationships (including wider kin and community), supplemental or remediating social care services may need to be provided when safeguarding harms have occurred. Here, the use of 'care' as a noun may take on additional meaning as a legal status – 'in care' – when a threshold of harm has been reached whereby state actors intervene and make decisions regarding where, and by whom, their care needs are met. Local authorities are said to be in a 'corporate parenting' role for such children, with the expectation that they act 'as any good parent would do by supporting, encouraging and guiding their children to lead healthy, rounded and fulfilled lives' (Department for Education, 2018, p 8).

Caring about someone may imply particularity, that is, a personalised fondness that has been generated through interaction over time. This most commonly occurs through familial bonds or friendships, but sometimes such affectional connections may develop naturalistically within the context of a professional role and task, for example, a practitioner spontaneously liking a particular young person with whom they are working over weeks or months and sometimes even years. However, such 'natural caring' (Noddings, 1984, p 79) is serendipitous and cannot be mandated. As the Scottish Independent Care Review (2020, p 8) noted, 'A legislative framework for love would be driven by an institutional view of love that could not possibly reflect the experience of being loved and cared for.'

In this chapter, we are concerned rather with 'disinterested love' – a more generalised benevolent tenderness and concern towards other people, in the absence of any relational or transactional connection, that is rooted in an underpinning philosophy that all human beings deserve to be cared about (Meehan, 2003, p 102). Such an inclusive and 'compassionate love' (Sprecher and Fehr, 2005, p 629) for other humans, might be intensified into 'ethical caring' (Noddings, 1984, p xv) towards unrelated others following recognition of suffering, need or oppression. Here a commitment is made to action, prompting, for example, volunteer or charitable work or state aid for the 'distant countries' made vulnerable by political conflict or humanitarian catastrophes (Glanville, 2016, p 339). It might well play a role, too, in not only what brings professionals into social care work initially but how they relate to and act towards young people in contact with services due to EFRH.

Loving and active commitment to the betterment of others, without the inducement of personal affectional connections, and 'without distinguishing between worthy and unworthy people, friends and enemies, neighbours and strangers, likeable and unlikeable creatures' has been defined within the

Aristotelian philosophical concept of agape (Chabot, 2008, p 811). The deliberative and sustained practice of 'love that is in service to others' that agape implies is said to have the potential to advance connectivity, empathy, harmony and respect between peoples (Enright et al, 2022, p 234). Porto (2025, p 16), for example, describes how education practices and systems rooted in agape may foster empathy rather than hate and anger between individuals and societies. The attitudes of non-violence, social cohesion and social justice promoted at a community level are potentially transformational, leading Porto to describe agape as 'revolutionary love' (Porto, 2025, p 4). We go on now to consider why a revolution in attitudes to, and practice of, love and care, at both a professional and a societal level, is necessary if we are to proactively address the needs of young people facing safeguarding risks beyond the home and family.

The carescape of young people affected by EFRH

Our institutional ethnography enabled us to surface how policy priorities, statutory practice guidance and performance indicators shaped the availability of service funding and resources, professional values and attitudes, and organisational cultures and climates. The formal 'carescape' (Bowlby and McKie, 2019) that is produced fundamentally shapes how young people receive and interact with universal services and targeted interventions, such as healthcare, schooling, social care and youth support, and the extent to which they feel cared *for* and *about*.

Government funding priorities for services during the years of adolescence are orientated around the tripartite concerns of addressing safeguarding risks, promoting young people's engagement in education, employment and training, and reducing likelihood of involvement in criminality. These public investments, designed to support pro-social behaviour, promote healthy development and maximise young people's future economic and social contributions, could be considered part of the social contract between citizens and the state, designed to improve the experiences of all through promoting social cohesion and economic prosperity (Coote, 2023). However, it has been argued, this social contract is now breaking down in the wake of years of cuts to public services and welfare spending, which 'have left our public services and social safety net in tatters' (Bhadani et al, 2023, p 66).

The impacts of this 'desiccated public sector' (Boddy, 2023, p 137) have been profound for young people in the UK, who recently reported the lowest levels of life satisfaction across Europe (Children's Society, 2022). Levels of school attendance and engagement are dropping; many young people describe the school setting as unwelcoming and disaffecting with some feeling lonely and unsafe in this space (Department for Education, 2023a). Suspensions and exclusions are used too often when young people's behaviour is perceived and experienced as challenging, disruptive or dangerous by school staff, and this is disproportionately true for Black Caribbean boys, Gypsy, Roma and Traveller children, young people with special educational needs and disabilities and those eligible for free school meals (Graham et al, 2019). Access to state-registered alternative provision that is timely and effective in re-engaging young people in meaningful education is limited (Children's Commissioner, 2025). Support for those with special educational needs and disabilities has reached a crisis point, with long waiting times for assessments and support within an 'often chaotic and adversarial system' (Public Accounts Committee, 2025, p 1). It is perhaps unsurprising, then, that marginalised and structurally disadvantaged young people do not feel loved by society when they see no prospect of the meaningful educational and employment, affordable housing and community regeneration that might offer them a route out of inequality and poverty towards a fairer standard of living – which they arguably have a right to expect in the social contract (Nakkan, 2025) – or worse when some of these systems, such as education, actively cause them harm.

Billingham and Irwin-Rogers (2022) write compellingly of the central importance to humans of 'mattering' – having significance and worth to other people, both interpersonally within social and familial relationships, and as a member of society. Young people vulnerable to EFRH seem often not to have had their basic human needs for this existential recognition and connectivity met to a sufficient degree, such that it impedes the growth of their internal sense of self-identity, self-worth and self-efficacy (Sroufe et al, 2005). For some, this may be fundamentally rooted in earlier developmental trauma, such as abuse, neglect, witnessing violence, or family disruption, which has affected their well-being, psychosocial development and resilience in diverse ways (D'Andrea et al, 2012; Gregorowski and Seedat, 2013). But, alternatively or additionally, young people caught up in EFRH commonly experience a marginalisation and precarity wrought by poverty, social exclusion and structural discrimination that significantly impacts their sense of social significance and agentic power (Billingham and Irwin-Rogers (2022) – and indeed the capacity of their parents, carers or wider family to provide nurturing care for them (Featherstone et al, 2018).

'Mattering' does not seem to be equitably distributed through society. As noted previously, these structural impacts can be particularly malign for young people who are minoritised and racialised; identify as LGBTQ+; have special educational needs; live in areas of high socio-economic deprivation; are refugees or seeking asylum; and/or exist at the intersections of these identities. Social attitudes towards these young people, including through the media, can be extremely negative and this is particularly true where they are involved in, and often disproportionately viewed through a lens of, (sometimes serious) offending such as interpersonal physical violence, weapon-carrying or drug distribution, including in the context of being exploited or abused, in a context where they are afforded little space to portrayed as complex, joyful, talented, loved and valuable human beings in their own rights. Bearing in mind the tendency by policy makers, media and professionals to individualise problems and responsibilise those who experience social harms and precarity (Chapter 4), we argue that such structural impacts and social attitudes need themselves to be addressed as a priority if young people are to be loved and flourish.

Young people experiencing EFRH commonly need more specialist forms of care and support, and they are clear that they want it to be person-centred, relational, youth-relevant, collaborative, anti-oppressive and rights-respecting (Lefevre et al, 2019; Warrington and Larkins, 2019). Yet both their needs and perceived vulnerabilities, and the policy objectives, service priorities and interventions designed to respond to them, are generally defined and framed by government, professionals and academia rather than young people themselves (Holmes and Lefevre, 2024). Those affected by EFRH do not always share professional constructions of vulnerability, societal definitions of risk or government expectations of their conduct and feel alienated by interventions dominated by mechanisms of surveillance and control (Williams, 2018). Young people prefer youth-centred, self-referral, therapeutically orientated services to address anxiety, depression or trauma (Children's Commissioner, 2022) but mental health services tend to be time-limited and are severely rationed by eligibility criteria, accessible only once a particular threshold of risk or harm has been reached (Children's Commissioner for Wales, 2020; Royal College of Paediatrics and Child Health, 2020). Given these inadequacies, it is unsurprising that many young people affected by EFRH experience systems and practices as alienating and intrusive which then fail to engage them – paradoxically increasing risk and need (Lefevre et al, 2019).

Love and care in the English policy and practice context

Social policy fundamentally shapes service delivery and professional practice, with ebbs and flows between different governments and over time and space. In this section we draw attention to how recognition by government of its responsibility in ensuring that public policy reflects the right of young people affected by EFRH to feel loved and cared for by the state has been slow to come, particularly in England, although it is now enshrined in Scottish legislation and procedures (Scottish Government, 2024). Important developments were instigated through the flagship *Every Child Matters* programme of public sector reform by the New Labour Government in the earlier part of this century, which finally recognised that young people who were being sexually exploited were not prostituting themselves, how serious welfare concerns should be addressed even if young people were simultaneously involved in behaviour considered 'criminal' and/or 'anti-social behaviour', and that 'the system' should 'tackle the underlying causes of such behaviour' (Chief Secretary to the Treasury, 2003, p 33).

However, while the role of government and public services in 'valuing children, protecting them, promoting their interests and listening to their views' was acknowledged (Chief Secretary to the Treasury, 2003, p 14), it seemed that only parents were tasked with loving and cherishing children. The aspired outcomes of public investment were rather on young people 'growing up able to look after themselves ... making a positive contribution ... not engaging in anti-social or offending behaviour ... [achieving] economic wellbeing' (Chief Secretary to the Treasury, 2003, pp 6–7). The *Care Matters: Time for Change* White Paper a few years later, took important steps to improve the quality of care and consistency of support for children in state care (Department for Education and Skills, 2007), but it also paved the way for deregulation and subsequent marketisation creep which, it is argued, has had a detrimental effect on democratic oversight and direct accountability by contracting safeguarding and the provision of care placements 'to unregulated, unregistered and uninspected organisations ... undermin[ing] accountability, and add[ing] complexity and fragmentation' (Jones, 2015, p 463) – none of which seems designed to promote young people feeling adequately cared for or about.

The potential for professionals to provide reparative healing for developmental trauma experienced by young people at-risk, through relationally engaged communication and care, has also received inadequate attention until more recently (Hickle and Lefevre, 2022). Throughout the 1990s and 2000s, the dominant managerialist, technical–rational paradigm in social care had downgraded recognition of the importance of the emotional and relational when working with abused, neglected and marginalised young people and their families (Lefevre, 2018). In particular, it had over-burdened social workers with bureaucracy and had deflected their attention away from interpersonal direct work with young people and towards the fulfilment of routinised administration (Munro, 2011). The succession of reports recognising the nature and prevalence of EFRH in the 2010s, however, started to call attention to the needs of this group, particularly those experiencing sexual exploitation. It emphasised the key role that practitioners had in engaging young people productively with support through building relationships of trust (Berelowitz et al, 2013; Cossar et al, 2013). The All-Party Parliamentary Group for Runaway and Missing Children and Adults (2016, p 4) drew attention to how contemporary systems gave young people the message that 'no-one cares' and argued that 'we need to show as a society that we do care'.

The practice realities

We discuss now a practice observation from one of our Innovate Project research sites in 2021 in England which, we feel, illustrates some of the complexities of demonstrating an ethic of care within contemporary systems. One of the project researchers observed a multi-agency panel held monthly in the locality to consider risks and strengths for young people where concerns about EFRH had risen, and to review and advise on support and intervention plans. Box 2.1 summarises the panel discussion about a Black British young man whom we have called Jay. Italicised text represents verbatim text noted down by the researcher. Text in single speech marks are the researcher's own words. The remainder of the text comprises subsequent paraphrasing by this book's authors.

Box 2.1: Multi-agency panel observation

17-year-old Jay is discussed at a multi-agency panel meeting after having been missing from care for three to four weeks. The panel has had previous case discussions regarding Jay, with concerns stretching back a year. This is not Jay's first 'missing episode' but his '*longest so far*'. He took '*no money, clothes or other belongings*', and there has been '*no real sighting*' *of him*'. In fact, professionals had previously been under the impression that he was '*settling down and making plans*'. The Youth Offending Team (YOT) worker seems to know him best, describing Jay as '*having a positive relationship with his foster carers*', but the 'looked-after child' social worker 'seems to have barely met him'.

The police officer at the panel meeting is asked to provide an update. He emphasises Jay's age and states that Jay '*couldn't be bothered to stick to his curfew*'. Jay is described as a '*gang nominal*' who had '*made that decision*' to miss a court date'. Because Jay had cut off his electronic monitoring 'tags' prior to disappearing, this meant that '*for us [the police], he's wanted, although he's also missing*'. There is a likelihood of a custodial sentence given the breaches of his order. A discussion ensues about the level of investigation which the officer feels he can '*invest*', with this seeming to be a low priority within his workload. Jay is classed as medium '*not high risk*' by the officer.

A discussion follows during which the YOT worker and social worker challenge this perspective of Jay as a gang nominal. They state concerns that, when arrested, Jay had a '*burner phone as well as class A drugs inserted in his rectum*'. They fear Jay was likely being 'exploited by an older gang member' and might have gone missing because of being 'in debt following an arrest for drug possession with intent to supply'. These workers provide further background information on Jay's vulnerabilities, including 'a history of physical and emotional abuse' during his childhood and concerns that he might have an 'undiagnosed learning disability – possibly autism'. Jay is described as having been 'lacking adult protection and support throughout his life'.

The police officer is asked if this changes his assessment of Jay's risk and vulnerability, but while he 'fully appreciate[s] the stance of professionals from children's social care', he 'doesn't have the resources/time to look in detail for one missing young person' who is '*making lifestyle choices*'.

There is a degree of acknowledgement from the chair of the different perspectives of the professionals present regarding the level of risk to Jay. What all were able to agree on was the necessity to articulate clear plans in the meeting to promote Jay's welfare as soon as he made contact. These included ensuring the usual social worker was alerted in the event of Jay's arrest. The panel would review Jay in four weeks' time.

Reflection

The polarised discussion of Jay in the panel resonates, for us, with so many other 'cases' of young people at risk of criminal exploitation. The officer's use of language ('lifestyle choices', 'can't be bothered') makes it quite clear that he disagrees with the framing of this young man's absence from his placement as an indication he might be 'at risk'. Instead, Jay is constructed by the officer solely as a risk to society, agentically responsible for his own difficulties; there is no acknowledgement of the possibility of victimisation. We have noted this type of 'battling out' of the binary conceptualisations of vulnerable victim and adultified perpetrator in a number of other studies and publications (Lefevre et al, 2019; Firmin et al, 2022). Jay's positioning within this binary needs to be understood in the context of the intersecting effects of race, age and gender. As a Black adolescent male, Jay is implicitly adultified and responsibilised, with his vulnerability obscured by racialised constructions of dangerous masculinity and criminality. These intersectional dynamics shape professional risk assessments, thresholds for concern and the allocation of care and protection (Davis and Marsh, 2020). What is also striking here is remembering that, as someone in foster care, Jay has a particular entitlement to care and consideration by the state – his 'corporate parent' should act as a 'normal parent' would in circumstances of vulnerability such as this. However, Jay is discussed in a rather distanced and unemotional way, even by those workers who know him and his story best. Were Jay to have listened in surreptitiously, would he have felt *cared about* by these professionals at a personal level? To what extent might the outcomes of the decisions and plans at this meeting ensure Jay is meaningfully *cared for* by society – boundaries provided in the context of loving care – rather than being just labelled, restrained and punished? We caution against directing blame towards the individuals involved for potential inadequacies. The police officer named a key constraint: the lack of resources, underpinned by strict risk prioritisation criteria, which meant he had insufficient time to spend responding to and working with young people like Jay. While the youth justice worker and social worker did seek to foreground Jay's welfare in the meeting, they lacked the positional power over procedures or resources to do anything far-reaching or meaningful which might make a significant difference to the next stages of Jay's journey through the system.

English social policy continues to shift. *Stable Homes, Built on Love*, the strategy and consultation document published by the Conservative government in response to recommendations from the Independent Review of Children's Social Care, had proposed creating 'a children's social care system which priorities love and stability for children and families relentlessly' (Department for Education, 2023b, p 3). This resonated with the ethos of the Scottish Government's 'promise' to children, which explicitly stated that all children and young people should 'grow up loved, safe, and respected' (Independent Care Review, 2020, p 1). Since then, however, there has been a change of Government. A Children's Wellbeing and Schools Bill, seeking to improve child safeguarding and raise educational standards in England, is progressing through Parliament at the time of writing. While there is much to be hoped from new legislation that says it will put children first, support care-experienced young people to thrive and requires 'everyone working in children's social care to build lasting relationships with children and families' (Department for Education, 2025, p 5), it is feared that 'the sufficiency challenges facing councils at the moment, could mean the promised supports for young people do not materialise' (Sacks-Jones, 2024, cited in Long et al, 2025, p 141). Practice is always shaped by the ruling relations of macro systems. Rather than lay blame on individual practitioners who struggle to ensure young people's needs and rights are adequately met within resource constraints, non-youth-centred systems and toxic public debates, we argue that transformation of public policy and societal discourse about young people affected by EFRH is necessary, if a young person like Jay, who is experiencing intersectional disadvantages, is to receive the kind of care that might make a real difference to his current experiences and life trajectory.

Transforming carescapes for young people affected by EFRH

So, how do we create a more supportive and loving care ecology (Bowlby and McKie, 2019) for young people affected by EFRH, what would it look like and what would it take to get there? We propose three strategies.

First, we emphasise that a just society starts from the humanistic stance that every young person has value and matters as a human being. At a structural level, the state needs to show that it is serious about its intention for *all* young people to grow up feeling loved and cared for, including when they act in a way that is dangerous or harmful to others. It then follows that public policy and services for young people affected by EFRH should be driven by principles of social recognition (Barry, 2016), reparative care (Hickle and

Lefevre, 2022) and restorative justice (Givens, 2021), rather than surveillance, restraint and punishment. Aspirational policy will remain lip service if not matched by adequately resourced services and youth-centred performance indicators, a rights-informed 'social guarantee' for this is needed, 'backed by investment and regulation' (Coote, 2023, p 71). Moreover, Government must make the well-evidenced case for the long-term social and economic benefits of timely and effective (but costly) preventative and reparative services for young people affected by EFRH (National Audit Office, 2022). In so doing, too, it must robustly challenge noxious populist discourse in the press, social media and parliamentary debate about the marginalised youth who find themselves on the receiving end of society's disregard, disdain or apathy – such as young people who are racialised, are seeking asylum, have refugee-status or are affected by other intersectional inequalities, as well as young people impacted by peer violence and abuse, and those who display behaviour considered 'anti-social' or 'criminal'.

Second, for professional carescapes to embody a stance of loving care towards young people in intention, process and outcomes, they must be orientated around an ethic of care (Gilligan, 1982; Tronto, 2005), informed by psycho-social, relational and contextual principles (Hickle and Lefevre, 2022; Firmin et al, 2025). Building the kind of trusting relationships that encourage young people to engage with support requires that professionals be available to spend unhurried, person-centred time with young people. Conveying that they are valued at a human, personal level requires professionals to interact consistently with young people in a warm, friendly, attentive, patient manner, balancing authority with compassion and remaining congruent, even when a young person's behaviour or actions provoke feelings of irritation, fear, shock or disgust. Such ethical caring 'requires an effort that is not needed in natural caring' (Noddings, 1984, p 80) and demands a degree of 'love labour' (Purcell, 2024, p 154) that could result in practitioners defending against young people's own emotions and experiences and becoming distanced or punitive. Managing this cannot – and should not – be the responsibility of the individual. Structures and procedures need to be in place organisationally to ensure that manageable workloads and reflective supervision are in place to support the mentalisation of young people's lives and experiences, the planning and execution of this work, and the emotional processing of its impact.

Finally, the organisational and professional carescapes produced through welfare institutions and public policy must work collaboratively and productively with the informal caringscapes offered by young people's families, friends and local communities (McKie et al, 2002; Nagy and Horkai, 2021). The dynamic discursive interaction between these socio-relational spaces, interwoven with histories and cultures, has a potential to support a young person's sense of self and mattering over time in ways that go far beyond what standard interventions could achieve. We will develop these ideas further in Chapters 6 (Parents and families) and 7 (Friendship, partners and community).

Creating a more supportive and loving care ecology for young people therefore requires systems orientated towards the provision of love, over and above the mitigation of risk. Present efforts and service improvement attempt to create care and kindness within systems that prioritise risk mitigation; in short, they continue to see young people as a risk to be managed, more than young people to be cared for but to manage that risk kindly. Such a weighting, we argue, does not go far enough; instead in this chapter we propose a system foundation of love, in which we continue to identify and mitigate risk. Figure 2.1 illustrates this; summarising the priorities, measures, language and view of young people within a system orientated to love. Shifting the dial towards such system orientation is a fundamental feature of the reimagining we propose.

Conclusion

Through this chapter, we have considered how services might look different if they were built on a system foundation in which all young people affected by EFRH were cared about, even loved, in both the process and outcome of any professional response. We have noted that not only would this be impossible for an individual practitioner to achieve in isolation, but that services will struggle to concretise loving care within organisational cultures and climates without the support of a public policy that challenges toxic public discourse and resources services adequately. Borrowing from Givens' (2021) concept of 'radical empathy' to build trust and understanding at a community and social level, we propose a movement of 'radical love' which would commit government, services and professionals to transformative action.

Figure 2.1: Features of safeguarding systems orientated to love

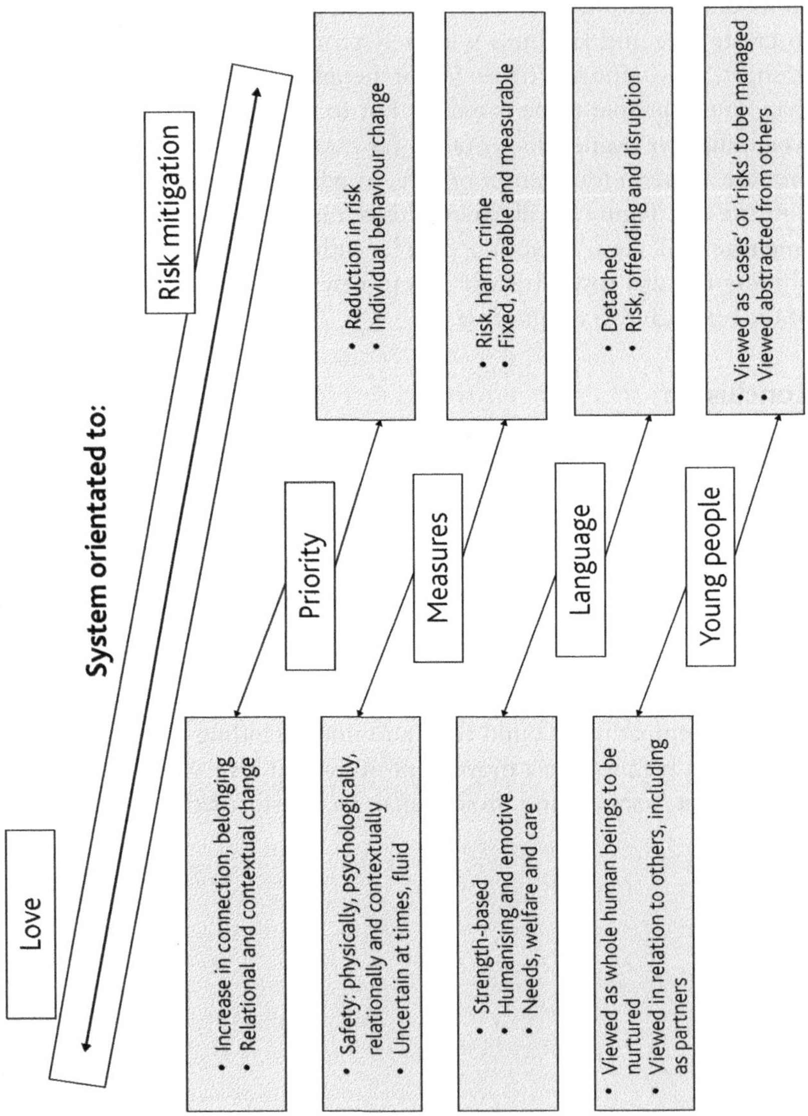

Box 2.2: Reflective questions for leaders and practitioners raised by Chapter 2

1. Do young people affected by EFRH feel loved and cared for by you/the overall service? What kind of service data would need to be collected and how, for you to feel really confident of your response?
2. What aspects of practice guidance, organisational culture or system structure would need to develop or change to ensure service delivery consistently demonstrates an ethic of care, particularly towards those young people affected by intersectional disadvantage?
3. This chapter proposes a movement of 'radical love' which would commit government, services and professionals to transformative action. How might you contribute your ideas, voice and actions towards this movement?

Resources to support innovation

We suggest using the Promoting Ethical Innovation in Social Care (PEISC) Framework to support your reflections. This tool, which was developed through the Innovate Project, can be freely downloaded at: www.theinnovateproject.co.uk/practice-tools/.

3

Respect

The idea of '(dis)respect' has been associated with UK policy responses to extra-familial risks and harms (EFRH), particularly that which is characterised as violent or anti-social, for decades. Yet, the ways in which respect is shown, given and received is often relatively absent from discussions about safeguarding, protection and young people's access to safety. This is interesting as despite the term 'respect' having multiple meanings, and being difficult to define (Gaskell, 2008), it is perhaps easy to reach one clear consensus about it: everyone wants respect, no one wants to be disrespected. Feeling disrespected is uncomfortable, frustrating, even sometimes enraging. It can be paralysing (leading to disconnection and disengagement) or catalysing – compelling us to act out, respond and confront the disrespect. For all of these reasons, creating the conditions in which young people feel and are respected is foundational to the provision of safety.

The English word 'respect' has its roots in the Latin '*respicere*', which means 'to look back at' (Malti et al, 2020). This suggests it is something requiring reflection and consideration – respect develops or grows in response to an interaction or observation of someone's behaviour or character. It has a 'motivational component' (p 10); we have to want to respect someone, and our respect for them is evidenced in our attitude towards (and/or treatment of) them. Respect is an other-orientated feeling; it is often accompanied by feelings like kindness, admiration and liking (Malti et al, 2020) and aligns with concepts such as prosociality, fairness, justice and feelings of regret or sadness over wrongdoing. It makes sense that if we respect someone, we like them, perhaps admire them, and we would feel bad if we did something that harmed or disappointed them.

In this chapter we explore the potential of foregrounding ideas of respect, in developing systems, services and practices that increase young people's access to safety. We start with an overview of how respect has been understood over time, both as a general concept and in relation to work with young people, and work from this using data from the Innovate Project to reflect upon the presence or absence of respect in professionals' work with (and on behalf of) young people. Through this process we identify where notions of who deserves respect, how we demonstrate or communicate feelings of respect, and precisely why it matters for work with EFRH, have been up for debate; and will work with that debate to craft the foundations of respectful safeguarding systems.

What is respect, who is respected and why does it matter for young people?

Who deserves respect – and why – has been a subject of philosophical debate for centuries. It has largely been conceptualised in relation to power and authority, and offered more freely to those who hold a particular role or status in society (Giselsson, 2012). It has also been stretched and extended, for example, during the Enlightenment, with its focus on expanded rights, freedoms and our ethical obligation to fellow humans. Immanuel Kant championed this perspective, foregrounding respect as a fundamental task for just and ethical societies (Hill, 1998). Nearly a century later, revolutionary and decolonial writer Frantz Fanon (1952) spoke more expansively of respect via the recognition of others' full humanity and the need to dismantle oppressive structures that deny recognition, dignity and freedom.

This way of thinking has embedded itself into contemporary philosophical and psychological understandings of respect, though distinctions have been made between the nature and quality of respect we offer to others. In the late 1970s, Darwall (1977) coined terms to frame these different types of respect, using the phrase '*appraisal–respect*' to describe the kind of respect we have for people whom we admire due to their personal qualities/traits or accomplishments. In appraising who they are, we consider (and perhaps instinctually feel) they are worthy of respect. He used the phrase '*recognition–respect*' to describe the kind of respect Kant spoke of; when it is a decision you make, rather than a feeling you have, it is perhaps a cognition first, preceding respectful feelings or behaviours (Peplak and Malti, 2017).

These two types are not mutually exclusive; Malti et al (2020, p 14) suggest that perhaps recognition–respect '*provides the foundation for experiences of appraisal–respect*'. This means that feeling respected for who we are, as people, contributes to social conditions where we are acting in prosocial ways that engender the further respect of others. In other words, we have to feel respected for who we are before we can act 'respectably'.

Whom we respect, and the rationale we might provide for this, changes throughout childhood. Developmental theorists have suggested that, from middle childhood, we begin to consider who is deserving of respect (that is, appraisal–respect) in relation to fairness, reciprocity and prosociality (Piaget, 1965; Audley et al, 2020). As we grow and become developmentally capable of thinking about others and considering their perspectives, our understanding of respect becomes more nuanced, along with all other aspects of social and emotional development and identity formation (Malti et al, 2020). Feeling respected is an essential component in learning how to form and maintain relationships throughout adolescence and into adulthood; it is woven together with how we engage cooperatively with others (Hsueh et al, 2005) and feel a sense of belonging within social groups (Huo et al,

2010). If we think back on our own adolescence, many of us can probably relate to the mixed feelings of wanting to be seen as a unique and distinct individual, capable of making our own decisions, while also wanting very much to feel the approval of others and an authentic connection to the people we care about and admire.

The relationship between giving and receiving respect is one that young people are perhaps particularly sensitive to, notably the difference between being expected to 'act respectfully' towards someone in authority and the feeling that accompanies having respect for someone that is also respectful of them (Deutch and Jones, 2008). The latter (that is, bi-directional respect) is not always distinct from the former; where young people feel respected by an adult in authority, that mutually respectful relationship can enable the adult to act authoritatively without communicating disrespect or losing the young person's respect.

Establishing bidirectional respect requires attunement to how young people feel respected in their personal relationships while also recognising cultural and structural conditions that influence how they experience respect. Experiences of discrimination and the daily, cumulative impact of structural and historical disenfranchisement can influence young people's expectations and their perceptions of how adults (in positions of authority) feel and behave respectfully towards them (Deutsch and Jones, 2008). In these instances, establishing bidirectional respect also requires attunement to the structural and historical factors that might inhibit some groups from being perceived as worthy of respect or who are made to work harder for the appraisal–respect that others are automatically granted. For example, we know that respect has often been withheld from women and girls (Wolfram et al, 2007; Arnot and Swartz, 2018), people from economically disadvantaged and/or minoritised ethnic/racial communities (Miller and Savoie, 2002) and from people who are neurodiverse or disabled (Chapman and Carel, 2022).

EFRH and respect: respecting authority or respectful authority?

When we look for respect in responses to EFRH, notions of 'authority' loom large. The relationship between respect and authority is both an interpersonal one, as adults' use of authority over young people is (whether they like it or not) largely dependent upon how young people decide to participate in that authority (Noddings, 2004); but it is also a political one. Respect has long been linked to anti-social behaviour and violence within the context of communities where people experience structural and political powerlessness and disenfranchisement (Irwin-Rogers and Billingham, 2022). Feeling powerless can be deeply humiliating (Frost, 2016), and when shame follows, it can paralyse (that is, leading to disengagement) or mobilise, sometimes through engagement in violence.

The relationship between violence (or other forms of 'anti-social behaviour') and disrespect is multi-faceted; while feeling disrespected might lead someone to act violently, these violent acts themselves can be interpreted by others as a form of disrespect. For example, in the UK, New Labour's 'Respect Agenda' of the early 2000s framed young people's engagement in 'anti-social behaviour' as the 'most visible example of disrespect' (Gaskell (2008: 224). This can feel like an intractable problem, particularly when the political solution to dig our way out of this cycle of violence and disrespect is to demand behaviour from young people (that is, rule following) that seems respectful – as the only pathway available for young people to receive respect from adults and the wider society in which they live.

The potential cost to de-emphasising respect for young people is high. We know that when young people feel disrespected, it can lead to feelings of shame (Munford and Sanders, 2020), and shame is a 'powerful force in limiting human agency, capacity, and potential' (Frost, 2016, p 432). This is perhaps particularly true for young people in communities where structural harms such as poverty and educational exclusion accumulate, leading them to feel looked down upon and misrecognised (Irwin-Rogers and Billingham, 2022).

Being recognised in our relationships with others enables us to feel love and a sense of belonging, and having access to equal rights in our communities and the wider society in which we live enables us to feel dignity and respect (Honneth, 1996). Conversely, being misrecognised is deeply harmful to us all as it erodes self-confidence, isolates us, makes us disconnected from others. That disconnection makes us feel like we do not matter (Irwin-Rogers and Billingham, 2022) and what we have to offer the world is not valuable (Munford and Sanders, 2020). When Munford and Sanders (2020) explored the concept of misrecognition with young people who had received statutory services (for example, child welfare and criminal justice), they found that young people described misrecognition as shame, unworthiness and disrespect. If misrecognition is disrespectful, then recognition is respectful – and young people described feeling respected when professionals listened, made an effort to understand what the young person felt they needed, advocated for them, valued fairness and involved them in decision-making. This seems intuitively true: when we are disrespected, we feel unseen and misunderstood, we are isolated, experience shame and our confidence diminishes. When we are respected for who we are (that is, recognition–respect), we feel seen and understood, we feel like we belong, like what we have to offer is valued, and our confidence grows.

What does this mean for where respect is currently found when innovating new responses to EFRH, and what could it mean in the future? To begin answering this question, we return to one of the Innovate Project sites, where we gained access to various sources of data related to a multi-agency piece of work focussed on a group of peers identified as at risk of harm.

How is respect designed in (or out) of practice responses to EFRH and the young people affected?

Many services that are innovating responses to EFRH, are trying to move beyond one-to-one 'casework' models of intervention, and towards practices that engage young people's friends and wider communities (explored in greater detail in Chapter 7), and this was the case for three sites that participated in the Innovate Project. In one of these sites, we were collecting data at a time where professionals were particularly focused on trialling approaches that assessed and intervened with whole groups of young people impacted by EFRH, rather than solely working with them each individually. We were given permission to attend five multi-agency meetings related to this work and had access to seven documents in which professionals recorded information about the group and the situation they were in (for example, assessments and reports). Similar to the other concepts explored in this book (such as privacy in Chapter 5), the language of respect was not directly used in meeting or case documents, whether in a positive or negative way (that is, feeling disrespected or acting disrespectfully). As such, our curiosity was drawn to the absence of respect as a consideration at any point in discussing young people's lives and behaviours, even as we observed professionals' deep commitment, care and consideration for young people's safety.

When we looked at this work through the lens of respect, we identified two insights about how 'systems' (as it is enacted through typical meeting protocols, structured reporting documents and shared language around assessing risk) give or withhold respect:

1. Professionals are looking for ways to offer appraisal–respect, and they want to feel respected in return.
2. The system is designed to offer young people appraisal–respect but not recognition–respect, even if research indicates that young people respond better to the latter.

Professionals' appraisal–respect for young people was present when they inserted examples of young people taking up sports or a part-time job as evidence of their capacity for good, safe or prosocial behaviour. In other words: they deserved the respect of others because they were capable of acting respectably. These examples were sparse across the data and, in other instances, even when the format of written documents prompted professionals to identify positive traits or strengths, professionals struggled when there were not clear examples of 'respectable behaviour' to identify. This was particularly true in one written assessment of a peer group where concerns centred around substance misuse and potential criminal exploitation related to drug supply. The assessment form had several sections, including one to summarise what was discussed about the group and another section for identifying 'resilience and strengths'. The summary section of the form included a lot of details on potential risk and on the perception of the group within the community, such as: 'The group have been known to be rude and abusive to police and shopkeepers; it has been known that shopkeepers don't report crime or [Anti-Social Behaviour] committed by the group due to fear of repercussions' (Social work assessment, case file).

However, it also included information that struck the research team as an important, inherent strength: 'The group have well established connections with each other, with some knowing each other prior to secondary school ... It has been noted that the group is very loyal to each other' (Social work assessment, case file).

Loyalty, connection and belonging are incredibly powerful and respectable traits. However, this was not noted in the section of the form allocated for 'resilience and strengths'. Instead, the only information provided in that section said: 'It is felt by professionals that most of the group have been offered support ... although it could be challenged that a higher level of support could be offered' (Social work assessment, case file).

The inability to recognise loyalty as a strength, and a resource therefore to work with, demonstrates why it is critical to examine, and reimagine, the foundations of our systems – as we are attempting to do in this book. Including a section on 'strengths' in a practitioner assessment form will not necessarily facilitate practice that recognises and builds upon young people's strengths, if disrespect, or at least a lack of respect, underpins how that form will be used. In this example, the focus on professional action as a strength, over the inherent resilience and strength of young people, made it difficult for professionals to choose recognition–respect as a starting point for planning any intervention. We identified this difficulty at play in various ways in our data including:

1. A new member in a multi-agency meeting noted that while she had only recently taken on a new role, she had 'seen signs of work and it's really refreshing'. The phrase 'signs of the work' is far removed from the fragile, sticky, gritty, human interactions between professionals and young people – the kind of interactions that actually compose 'the work'. It also foregrounds professional action over any consideration for the real difficulty some young people might face in choosing to show-up and open-up to a professional.
2. A professional described another multi-agency meeting forum as 'fundamental in highlighting and addressing the needs of any exploitation risks in my team'. Here, the risks seem to float about in space, connected tangentially to the team of professionals who 'hold' the risk, but are otherwise separated from the lives of young people who are waking up to dangerous lived realities.

3. In a discussion of concerns about the peer group at school, including 'toxic masculinity' and bullying of a transgender child, the troubling behaviours were attributed to the nature of the peer group and the influence of the group's leader. One professional noted 'their minds become like one and it's just unpleasant'. 'Unpleasant' is a word that conjures up distance and sensory removal – no one wants to be close to an unpleasant smell or sight or sound. It's also very difficult to imagine respecting or empathising with someone that you find 'unpleasant'. Discussion of potential interventions remained removed from the real, live boys enacting this behaviour. They wanted to 'see some empathy' and discussed how to identify who might have capacity for empathy (implying that the other young people are – by default – perhaps incapable of empathy), but without connecting the problem they were worried about to the boys who were behaving in truly problematic ways.

Perhaps the professionals were not being given the space to acknowledge that seeing the boys' cruel treatment of other children made them feel angry and sad, or made it hard to have empathy for them, or to remain curious about why they were behaving this way. Throughout, professionals' own experiences in the work remained absent. However, we did notice how their own implicit desire to be respected by young people shaped their understanding and interpretation of the 'risks' posed by young people. For example, in one discussion of the peer group who were described as 'a bit anti-social' in a meeting, professionals appeared frustrated that the group seemed to find the adults' concerns about drug-use 'amusing', as they chanted 'ket, ket, ketamine in the school playground'. Here, perhaps, the implication is that professionals want to be respected by young people – they want to be *treated respectfully,* and they want young people to *act respectably*.

Within these practices, statements and actions of disrespect, or a professional desire for respect, we also identified green shoots of respect. In one meeting, a practitioner prompted other colleagues to reconsider the language that they were using, stating: [social worker] 'we have a vulnerable 15-year-old missing or homeless and the size of his cannabis bags are increasing each week' (Researcher observation, multi-agency panel).

We noticed many such interventions across the meetings observed throughout the Innovate Project. On each occasion, by holding onto vulnerability professionals offer a bridge to thinking differently. While such a bridge is not a direct line to designing-in respect as foundational to developing support for/with young people, in our project it perhaps offered a necessary route to maintaining curiosity about the situations young people were in. Such curiosity mitigated the potential that practitioners would make decisions, often ones that were restrictive, punitive or stigmatising (Chapter 8) because of the legitimate fear of the potential violence or harm that young people faced; decisions in which opportunities for safety within young people's relationships and communities were under-recognised.

Data we collected during the Innovate Project demonstrated to us just how difficult it was for professionals to operate in systems in which respect had been given such little consideration – particularly when making decisions for, and about, young people whom they were very worried about but knew little about. Yet, if anything, the gaps in professional knowledge about young people, and the situations they faced, meant making respect visible in system foundations even more important. We have started to wonder if respect could be thought of like a banister: something that professionals can choose to hold onto as the terrain changes, and perhaps whatever is happening, it can provide support as they take their next step. However, to have such an effect we need a system that can move beyond being designed upon appraisal–respect, which requires young people to engage and act first before being deemed worthy of respect; and instead move toward the a system intentionally designed to offer recognition–respect – one in which young people feel and are valued and understood regardless of how they act. Wider work on EFRH would suggest that such respect would, in any case, create conditions in which young people are more likely to respond to or positively interact with professional offers of support. In this sense 'engagement' in services is the by-product of respect, rather than respect being a by-product of engagement.

Envisioning what could be: systematic respect, recognition and pride

In an earlier study completed by some of us, two years before the Innovate Project, a young person commented:

> I think just like manners just from both sides, because it's just like, say for example if I've been out and a person comes and says to my friends kind of calmly, like 'you guys are being a bit loud, please can you leave', they're like 'oh yeah, yeah, yeah, sorry, sorry Miss, sorry Miss', and then we're kind of more like obliged and just kind of want to do the right thing. Because it's like, you know, all most guys, I mean obviously it is girls too, but all most people want is to feel like they're the top person, so if they feel like the top person for like doing something good.

Their view chimes with decades of research into young people's development, flourishing and well-being, which indicates that young people behave 'respectably' when they feel and are respected. Data collected for the Innovate Project illustrate that UK safeguarding systems have not been well designed to do this; they do not create the conditions in which respect is feasible, nor are they built upon foundations in which respect is foregrounded. Systems designed upon ideas that respect is earned and conditional upon a young person's compliance with systems, rather than provided by systems intended to facilitate their safety, do not reflect what we know about adolescent development.

So where then do we start in building the foundations of a respect-full system? Honneth's (1996) concept of recognition holds some promise. Applying it could mean we design systems intended to make young people feel recognised, and in the process offer support and services that facilitate young people's sense of self-worth and self-esteem. In some services this is already more feasible – for example, much of youth work is provided through this lens, and this is probably one of the reasons why youth workers manage to forge relationships with young people more easily than professionals who operate in statutory services. However, in other services and systems this will be more challenging; particularly in systems (and services within them) that are leveraged due to concerns related to young people's safety or the harm they are experiencing/displaying. As data from the Innovate Project suggest, recognition–respect needs to be an intentional choice when attempted in systems/services mobilised around risk and worry.

In Figure 3.1 we illustrate what a system orientated towards recognition–respect, over and above conditional (that is, 'appraisal') respect, might look like. We summarise the priorities, language and measures that would characterise such a reorientation, and the implications for how professionals in such systems might view young people. Rather than young people needing to 'meet professionals in the middle' in order to be respected, professionals would view all young people as deserving of respect and care, in recognition of their whole humanity, and come towards them therefore, reaching out even further in moments of distress.

To be intentional in weighing our systems towards recognition–respect, we need to resolve the issues of misrecognition in our systems, and to do so we need to put respect at their roots. Recognition–respect in a system used to respond to EFRH would create the conditions in which young people are respected for who they are as people. This, in turn, requires an active choice both by the system ('this is how we are going to design services for this cohort of young people' and 'what evaluation and impact measures have been built into the system that might tell us how respect is prioritised?') and the professionals ('what can I do to ensure this young person feels respected by me?' and 'how will I know they feel respected?'). Such work will offer space for mutual recognition, or multi-way recognition across young people, families, their wider communities, professionals and so on, in which conditions for respect are favourable. Such foundations are ones in which the strengths of 'loyalty' for example, can be visible and harnessed

Figure 3.1: Features of safeguarding systems orientated to recognition–respect

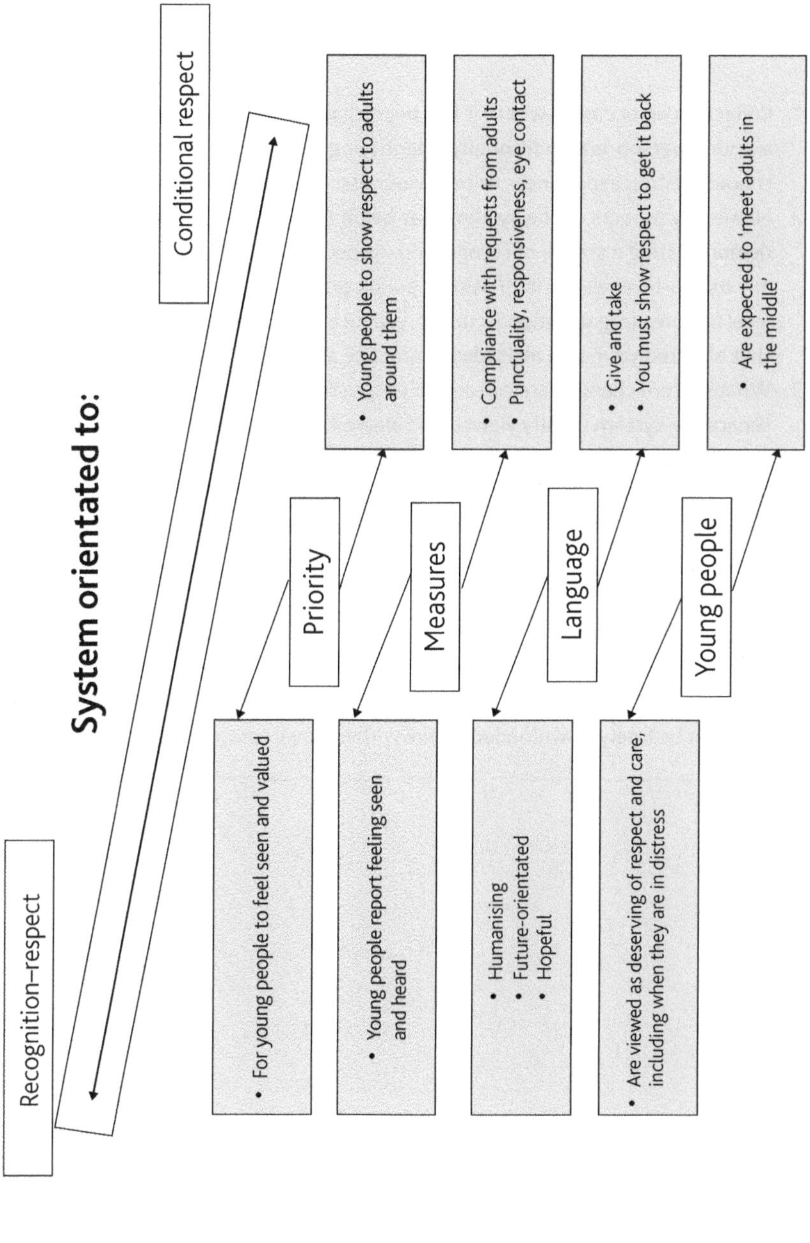

to develop routes to safety for young people; routes that will likely outlive any professional intervention.

Box 3.1: Reflective questions for leaders and practitioners raised by Chapter 3

1. Reflect on an occasion where it has been challenging for you to value and respect a young person unconditionally, identifying any aspects of the young person's characteristics, experiences or behaviour associated with this response.
2. Name any aspects of the system that helped or undermined you in developing or demonstrating a stance of recognition–respect towards this young person. Include any macro-level elements (national policy, governance and regulation) and meso-level features (organisational culture, practice guidance and supervisory processes) that affected your own attitudes or practice at the micro-level.
3. What system changes are needed to ensure that young people involved with your service are systematically viewed and worked with in a fair and respectful way? Are the principles and structures in place to achieve this, and just need to be implemented more effectively, or is fundamental reform of attitudes and policy required?

Resources to support innovation

We suggest using the DEISC tool for Doing Ethical Innovation in Social Care to help you reflect on how to ensure practice and service innovations are ethically appropriate as well as practically feasible. This tool, which was developed through the Innovate Project, can be freely downloaded at: www.theinnovateproject.co.uk/practice-tools/.

4

Responsibility and responsibilisation

Who is responsible for young people's flourishing, safety and protection? In what ways is this responsibility apportioned, and what exactly are individuals, groups, organisations, the state or society overall responsible for? In the UK, the story has often gone something like this. When things go wrong for young people either they, or their parents, are responsible for making it better. Young people have either made 'wrong' or 'risky' decisions, or their parents/carers have failed to fulfil their duty to keep their young people safe. The state is responsible for stepping in, via criminal justice and social work agencies, when parents, carers or young people fail; and they are responsible for building the capacity of young people or their parents/carers (if they are under 18) to stay safe in the future. In this perspective, responsibility is commodified risk (translated into costs) that is 'owned' either by individual actors (young people, parents) or corporate entities such as state agencies (local authority service departments, schools, health trusts, police forces and so on).

In this chapter we seek to rewrite this story – reimagining what responsibility means in the context of responding to and preventing extra-familial risks and harms (EFRH), whom it concerns and in what ways. Using our project to reflect on where system innovations got to, and where they got stuck, we trouble old and current stories of responsibility and responsibilisation, and set out how relational considerations of responsibility, based on ethics of care, may help us reimagine safeguarding in ways that promote well-being and flourishing for young people, families and communities.

Framing responsibility and responsibilisation

Before we consider, critique and later reimagine stories of responsibility and responsibilisation in relation to safeguarding and EFRH specifically, it is important to first summarise the meanings and framings of these two key concepts more generally. Responsibility has become an often used (and at times over-used) feature of socio-political discourse in neoliberalist societies, conjuring up ideas of 'good' or 'active' citizenship (Juhila et al, 2016; King et al, 2021). Trnka and Trundle (2014) outline its etymological roots, from medieval Christian congregational 'responses' to liturgy through to the advent of the modern 'responsible' citizenship based on suffrage rights from the 18th century onwards. 'Responsibility', therefore, is an indication of accountability and obligation to self and others in relation to action and inaction – but can also extend to the apportioning of moral blame.

Policy makers and politicians are persistently concerned with managing the 'irresponsible'. From concerns about 'feckless' and immoral 'underclasses' in Victorian England that influenced the Poor Law and subsequent welfare policies, through to a pre-occupation with 'problem', 'troubled' and 'socially excluded' families and individuals that persisted throughout successive post-war governments in the UK and elsewhere, this continues in different guises to date (King et al, 2021). For example, UK 'New' Labour policies during the late 1990s and early 2000s called for linking 'rights with responsibilities' for people considered 'anti-social', targeting specifically young people and communities in poor neighbourhoods (Clarke, 2005).

Levitas (2005) delineated three distinct discourses in policy responses and framings of 'social exclusion'. Two focused on *individual* behaviour and responsibility: the openly blaming 'moral underclass' discourse, and the ostensibly more reformist 'social integrationist' discourse, aimed at 'activating' and 'engaging' the unemployed. Only the more rarely applied 'redistributionist' discourse was primarily concerned with redressing structural inequalities, pointing towards *collective* responsibilities within societies.

Over recent decades the UK and other welfare states have seen public spending austerity alongside spiralling wealth inequalities, with individuals, families and communities still individually responsibilised for their experiences of poverty, exclusion, precarity and marginality. In neoliberal societies such as the UK (Juhila et al, 2016; King et al, 2021), such mechanisms of responsibilisation focus on the choices and capabilities of individuals, shifting burdens of associated risks and costs away from larger collective entities (particularly states but also, increasingly, multinational corporations) and on to individuals, families and smaller communities. Such an approach creates conditions which reify individual freedom and independence while neglecting how dynamics of entanglement and interdependence influence, and often unequally constrain, the very choices which 'free markets' purport to provide. Thus, individuals, families and communities who are already marginalised by inherently structural and intersecting inequalities, are also subjected to moral blame for their apparent failure to comply with notions of 'independent', 'active' and 'responsible' consumer citizenship.

What has this framing meant for the development of system responses to EFRH – and the young people, families and communities impacted?

Divided responsibilities: the state, young people and families

The commodified perspectives on responsibility that focus on identifying bearers of risk, cost and blame outlined previously are visible in designs and divisions of contemporary child protection, and wider safeguarding systems in general, and in their application to EFRH specifically.

In England and Wales, legislation of the 1980s and 1990s divided responsibility for addressing or preventing abuse and harm between the state, parents and young people themselves. As per the design of the Children Act 1989, the state was to hold parents accountable for child abuse and neglect (of children and young people up to their 18th birthdays) that was attributable to their own (in)action; and it was to hold young people accountable for behaviours which led them to fall into 'bad associations' or be put in 'moral danger'. EFRH largely fell into the latter scenario, a position reinforced through the Crime and Disorder Act 1998 which underpinned the design of the Youth Justice System, defining the age of criminal responsibility. Up to the late 1990s it was presumed that children under 14 were not generally criminally responsible, although for children aged ten and over this was 'rebuttable' if prosecutors could demonstrate a child's awareness of their serious wrongdoing. This doctrine ('*doli incapax*') was abolished following the murder of two-year-old James Bulger by two ten-year-old boys, leading to most of the UK retaining the lowest age of criminal responsibility in Europe, bar Scotland where the age was raised to 12 in 2019 (McGuinness, 2016; Pierpoint, 2020; Billingham and Irwing-Rogers, 2022).

Thus, state responsibility for safeguarding and protecting young people up to the age of 18 has tended to involve different forms of interventions when parents, or young people, do not fulfil their designated responsibilities. Risk and harms to a child based on the (in)action of parents or carers have led to state intervention through child protection processes coordinated by social workers. In contrast, where young people's actions have placed them or others at risk of harm, interventions have primarily involved policing their behaviour through youth justice processes and agencies; these processes were often preceded or accompanied by other disciplinary measures, notably exclusion/expulsion from education settings or dispersal orders and civil injunctions from local council departments (Child Safeguarding Practice Review Panel, 2020).

In contexts of limited statutory responsibilities to safeguard young people from EFRH, young people themselves, and their families and communities, have been directly or indirectly responsibilised in relation to risks, harms and their wider contexts and consequences: this has ranged from framing contexts of harm as being created by young people's 'lifestyle choices', by parents' failures to 'control' them or by neighbourhoods categorised as 'zones' of criminality and anti-social behaviour (Bancroft, 2012). Where institutional responses to EFRH have existed, responsibility to deliver those responses has often fallen to different non-governmental and community agencies, without state oversight or funding support (Butler et al, 2017). Notably, this situation has not been unique to the UK; in some welfare contexts service provision by non-governmental organisation also constitutes the norm, with varying levels of state involvement (Firmin et al, 2022; Peace, 2023; Wroe et al, 2025).

Unease about the division of responsibility, and its implications for young people impacted by EFRH, has been growing in the UK since the early 2000s. In 2001, child sexual exploitation was first named a safeguarding issue in England, a position further reinforced via safeguarding guidance in 2009 (Department for Children, Schools and Families, 2009). Over time, all forms of EFRH, as they impact young people under 18, have come to be designated as child protection issues in statutory guidance – in England in 2018, and by 2021 in Wales and Scotland (HM Government, 2018; Welsh Government, 2021; Scottish Government, 2021) – gradually increasing social work responsibility for coordinating state responses to this form of harm. In the process, state agencies have become responsible for safeguarding young people under 18 from EFRH, via child protection processes, including in scenarios where such harm is not attributable to parents and carers and – in theory at least – young people are no longer responsibilised in the same way for harms they face. The situation for young people over 18, however, is very different, with much more limited statutory adult safeguarding interventions (discussed later), prompting calls for Transitional Safeguarding approaches (Holmes, 2022).

Our work on the Innovate Project was undertaken in the context of both these processes of change for young people under 18 and calls for change to better support young people into adulthood. It helped us understand that responsibilities were shifting on the surface but remained constrained by wider system influences outlined earlier in this chapter and throughout this book. We now detail the implications of these shifts and constraints for systems attempting to innovate responses to EFRH and for young people, families and communities who are affected.

Shifting responsibilities

We entered our six research sites at a time when national policies were asserting new responsibilities for safeguarding young people from EFRH. However, enacting these responsibilities, even using innovation, proved a complex task – resulting in unequal and limited access to protection and support. Complex and often contradictory understandings of consent, agency, culpability and vulnerability govern how responsibility for safeguarding continues to be constructed and apportioned based on age (over-and-under-18), processes of racialisation, exclusion and criminalisation, and the intersections of these. Furthermore, the reframing of state responsibility for safeguarding young people under 18 in relation to EFRH has also changed the roles of professionals and services in social care and related sectors, of parents and of communities – leading to new forms of responsibilisation. For young people over 18, critical consideration of responsibility and responsibilisation were key for sites that were trying to adopt Transitional Safeguarding approaches. Understanding the practical consequences of new policy and practice trajectories, what these have resolved and introduced, and what remains unaddressed is a key step towards reimagining safeguarding systems focused on well-being and flourishing.

In our research sites, practice and policy developments and innovations brought about some significant changes in how professionals and agencies in social care, youth justice, policing, education and beyond were responding to EFRH. A common starting position among professionals in welfare-based roles and services was that young people, at least up to 18, were usually not *explicitly* framed as responsible for the abuse they experienced in the context of such risks and harms. This position counted as progress from what had pertained pre-2000. In most sites this also applied to the majority of parents or carers (highlighted in Chapter 6). Responsibility for many of these young people, and for their welfare, shifted to statutory organisations, predominantly those led by social work. Two of the six research sites were also attempting a similar shift in beginning to reimagine moving from the status quo whereby young people over 18 remained individually responsibilised towards more inclusive, integrated and collectively held well-being-focused responsibility as part of Transitional Safeguarding approaches. Beyond shifting responsibilities for individuals, we also observed social workers assuming responsibility for assessing and supporting young people's friendship groups (in three sites – as will be explored further in Chapter 7) and for building safety in school and community contexts in two sites.

However, with shifts in responsibility also came shifts in the individualised, blaming and risk-orientated character of organisational cultures. This same way of thinking about the nature of responsibility – sitting with individuals and being responsible for risk – was transferred from young people and their families to professionals. Such a transfer has created a multitude of new issues in how safeguarding responsibilities for EFRH are enacted.

First, some social work organisations fulfilled their responsibilities to safeguard young people under-18 from EFRH primarily through the use of policing and surveillance techniques; for example, the sharing of '*intel*' (as opposed to information) at professionals' meetings, sharing vehicle registrations, the numbers of visitors to young people or the names of their friends on social media, or by taking actions to monitor their mobile phone usage. In these ways, social workers were responsibilised for *monitoring safeguarding concerns*, rather than for *meeting safeguarding needs*. On occasion, we observed that such practices placed potentially contradictory responsibilities on professionals and agencies to pursue divergent goals and outcomes that hampered effective safeguarding work, and on occasion privileged crime prevention over child welfare concerns. This is a tension that has increasingly been identified in safeguarding reviews (Gamble and McCallum, 2022) and research papers (Lloyd et al, 2023). In contexts characterised by surveillance or other policing techniques, increasing social work responsibilities for EFRH had negative impacts on young people's freedom, particularly in respect of privacy (explored in Chapter 5) and in ways perceived by young people as breaching trust and respect (see Chapter 3).

Second, the 'owning' of responsibility for young people's safety (both at practitioner and managerial levels) was experienced by some professionals as a 'burden' – one they expressed through forms of coercive 'care' that rendered young people as 'cases' and 'bodies' to be managed through surveillance and risk-rating, scaffolded by an over-reliance on quantitative 'data' reports:

> [Social worker] there's nothing for me to say. Child is number 1 in all of [the region] not just [the local area] for knife crime. [There are] outstanding mental health referrals but issues are more behavioural and not related to mental health. He's seen and known as a 'rational choice actor' – he knows what he does. (Researcher observation, multi-agency safeguarding panel)

Such coercive tendencies are not unique to EFRH. They are instead features of systems that discipline young people, families, communities and professionals by responsibilising them in punitive and blaming ways. The costs of professional 'failure' to prevent harm experienced by young people have been extensively documented in the UK, with prominent child safeguarding reviews prompting a series of reforms and initiatives to overhaul systems (Parton, 2014). There is no doubt that critically and collectively engaging with learning from situations of harm that could have been prevented has been a key driver of safeguarding developments over many decades (Brandon et al, 2012; Dickens et al, 2022; The Child Safeguarding Practice Review Panel, 2025). However, this has often involved blame searching for those 'responsible' for failures. The subsequent social shaming of individuals or groups of professionals, along with the mental pain associated with harm or death of children and young people (Rustin, 2005), has, however, also meant that anxieties about 'failing' have become deeply etched into the individual and collective psyches of those tasked with safeguarding, with often counter-productive consequences (Lefevre et al, 2024). Indeed, the scarring effects of large-scale devastating events and scandals, along with the ratings-based logics of inspection regimes in England for example, may lead to blame being extended to a whole community or local area, rendering them place-based representations of 'failure'.

In this manner, therefore, we see the third challenge, one in which shifting responsibility was also experienced as shifting 'blame'. Fearing individual and collective blame-based responsibilisation may lead to professionals and services passing responsibility (as a form of 'hot potato syndrome') on to *other* professionals, services or even sectors (for example, the police or children's social care). We observed this through practices in multiple professionals' meetings in which responsibility to respond to EFRH was enacted via 'referrals' of young people into other services, or 'offering interventions' that young people did not need or want. Through these processes responsibility was transferred back to a young person, or family, to take up the referral or intervention that had been offered. The reliance on 'interventions' as a response to issues like EFRH is termed by Stevens et al (2025, p 173) as 'interventionitis' – a cosmetic focus on individual behaviours or 'superficial symptoms of social problems [...] distracting attention from efforts to address the deeper societal drivers or wider social context of the problem'. As Stevens and colleagues identify, initiatives that contribute to interventionitis may indeed mask as innovations but actually harbour little potential for transformative change, as they remain grounded in the limits of existing paradigms – including selective and commodified perspectives on responsibility-as-blame.

Fourth, as responsibility for EFRH, for young people under 18, shifted to social workers and their statutory partners, new questions emerged about the responsibility of more informal, community, familial or peer partners in safeguarding. Applying neoliberal ideas of responsibility frames all these potential partners through questions of who is 'risky' to work with, and issues of both liability and accountability, as opposed to who is trusted, present, wanted and effective. In four sites, we saw a desire to involve more voluntary and community sector partners in safeguarding in public places, but all sites raised questions about how much information such organisations could be told by statutory partners and/or what 'levels of risk' they should be legally responsible for holding. This is despite working in contexts in which the potential and actual contributions of such organisations are often neglected (Owens et al, 2024). Such neglect can present as situations in which community organisations know more about the harms young people are facing than statutory organisations and have been responding via informal and relational mechanisms, but their contribution is not recognised by statutory partners (see Chapter 8). It can also manifest in situations where these organisations find themselves overburdened with responsibility beyond their means and capabilities (Butler et al, 2017), while being absorbed within competitive funding 'markets' that commodify safeguarding capabilities and responsibilities

(Billingham and Irwing-Rogers, 2022). Similarly, parents and carers, young people themselves, as well as local communities, may be subjected to selective modes of responsibilisation, or conversely excluded from key conversations altogether, particularly when protecting matters of 'intel' as noted earlier (Firmin et al, 2026). As we detail in Chapter 6, parents, particularly mothers, were also inadvertently screened out of processes altogether when responsibility for protection shifted from them to professionals. Conversely, for older young people, responsibility shifted – sometimes dramatically – back to young people themselves upon their 18th birthdays, while data protection concerns sometimes seemed to prevent professionals from considering how parents or families might continue to provide sources of support.

Fifth, and finally, despite broad moves away from responsibilising young people for their experiences of EFRH, variations were evident across our dataset, particularly across intersectional lines related to race, ethnicity, class, gender and (dis-)ability (among other factors), with age being a particularly pervasive barrier. The exclusive framings of statutory adult safeguarding responsibilities as applying to people with 'care and support needs' (Care Act 2014) mean that for many young people over-18 experiencing EFRH, statutory safeguarding interventions are the exception and not the norm. This can lead to a sudden drop-off in support, with statutory welfare organisations no longer positioned as responsible for supporting young people and a seeming 'invisibility' of young adults: for example, a social worker in one of our research sites described how intensive contact with a young woman several times a week reduced after she turned 18 to a six-weekly duty for her personal advisor to contact her. In another example, during an extensive discussion at an extra-familial risk panel about concerns regarding a mixed-age peer group, the one young person who was 18, despite being named on the meeting agenda, was not mentioned once by professionals. At the same time, adult safeguarding frameworks, notably Making Safeguarding Personal (Local Government Association, 2013) along with the key principles of Transitional Safeguarding (Holmes, 2022; Cocker et al, 2024) also provide many opportunities for reframing safeguarding beyond the narrow limits of statutory duties and responsibility, including by highlighting principles such as empowerment, prevention, proportionality, partnership, as well as accountability and transparency – some of which are arguably under-developed in children's safeguarding frameworks. However, chronic underfunding across sectors, as well as the long-term nature and complexity of boundary-spanning whole systems change all meant that in our sites, at the time of research, shifting towards safeguarding systems that involve inclusive, integrated and collectively held responsibility for young people under and over 18 remained an ongoing endeavour.

Questions about where responsibility (and resources) for safeguarding young people over 18 ought to lie featured prominently in our research. One senior leader in children's social care wondered whether a preventative 'broad approach thinking about need, risk and harm' might detract from a focus on 'young adults at the most acute risk of harm, i.e. death, rape, etc'. One council member described a 'sense of not-my-responsibility-ness' among adult social care services. Another senior leader expressed concerns and frustrations that 'the scope for us in the children's end just keeps getting extended, and actually these are adults … [and] Adults' [services] need to take responsibility for adults, Children's [services] need to take responsibility for children'. Fearing overburdening in the face of increasing complexity is a common feature both in safeguarding work (Rustin, 2005), and in systems change work (Huegler and Ruch, 2022; Huegler et al, 2024). Such fears are also indicative of how deeply embedded and pervasively our safeguarding systems (and other public sector work) rely on the logic of responsibility-as-burden – something that must be individually or corporately 'owned' so that risks, costs and blame can be appropriately 'dealt' out.

It is clear that to safeguard young people from EFRH, shifting responsibility from young people, families and communities to the state, or from criminal justice to welfare organisations, has been insufficient. We cannot shift responsibility; we need to reimagine it.

Reimagining responsibility

In reimagining responsibility for safeguarding young people from EFRH, therefore, the system we envisage needs to resolve a five-part system insufficiency (Figure 4.1).

Only transformative change can bring about better ways of safeguarding young people in ways that avoid reproducing existing and new forms of harm. However, this transformation is not something likely to be achieved through new sets of limited interventions that remain rooted within disciplining and often punitive cultures that responsibilise: young people for their behaviour, parents for how they 'control and manage' young people's behaviour, or how well they perform within intervention or wider system expectations of parenthood; individual professionals, services or sectors; or fast-paced (and short-term) initiatives which do not recognise or resolve structural issues that intersect with interpersonal and contextual harm.

As described previously, a universal *statutory* safeguarding 'duty' for all young people does not exist beyond the age of 18. With all the major gaps and limited abilities to respond to emerging need this entails, this absence of universally codified professional and service *duties* also highlights

Figure 4.1: Reimagined responsibilities

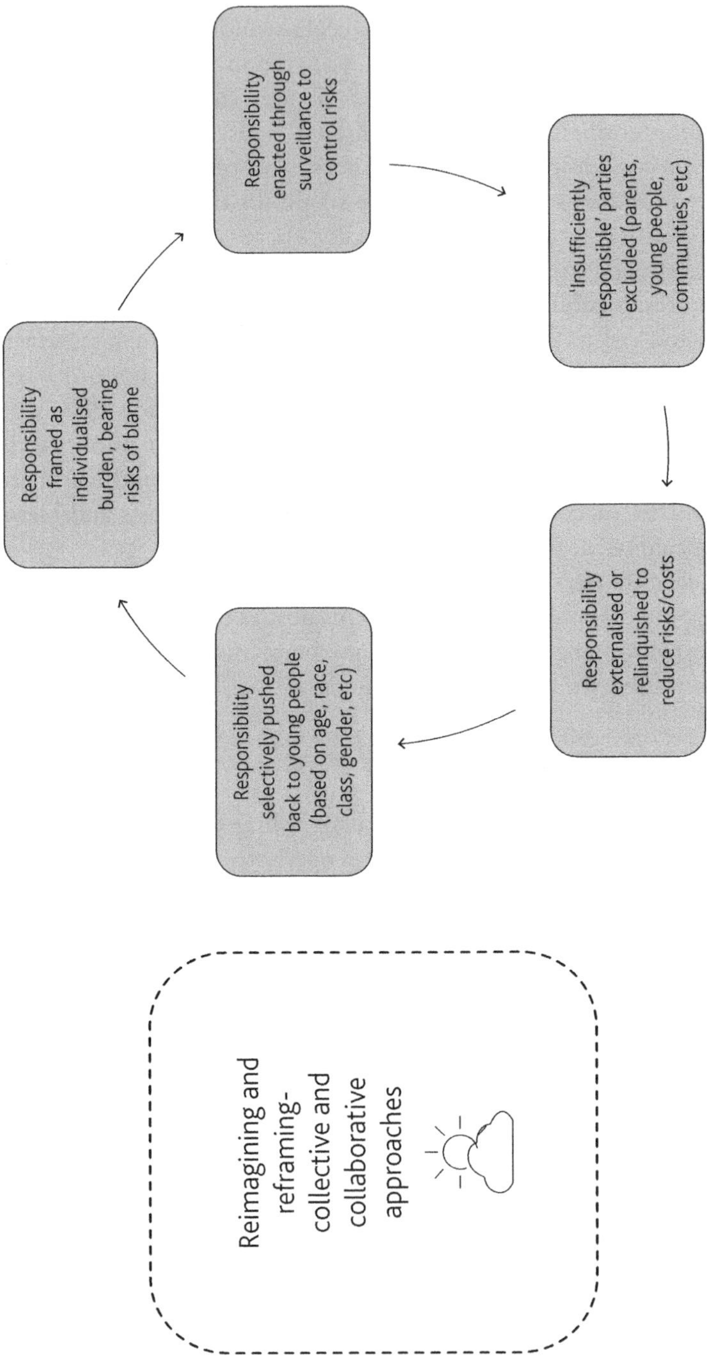

(perhaps paradoxically) the importance of reframing safeguarding through the lenses of partnership, collaboration and 'whole systems' responsibility. If we understand safeguarding as 'something to do with a person when their safety is undermined' (Holmes, 2022, p 8), this view shifts the focus away from individual or service-based responsibilisation. Instead, a collaborative framing of responsibility centres relationships and relationality, a capacity for 'boundary-spanning' work across services and sectors (Holmes, 2022), for systems leadership (Cairney and Toomey, 2025), as well as a focus on structural inequality and redistribution. If responsibility arises out of an ethics of care and relationality that we all hold for each other and our contexts (from neighbourhoods through to our planet), responsibility is not just individually (or corporately) 'owned', governed and commodified. Moreover, rather than casting or carrying burdens of risk, cost or blame, such an approach involves professionals, young people, families, and communities collectively 'holding' responsibility for the safety, well-being and flourishing of young people, families and communities.

Fundamental to the system(s) we propose in this book, therefore, is an understanding and enacting of 'responsibility' in which:

- services recognise that agency and vulnerability coexist, below and beyond a person's 18th birthday, and that vulnerability is contextual and situational – rather than as label;
- parents and carers are recognised for their capacity to be young people's unique advocates and supporters, contributing to conditions in which young people flourish, and to in turn be involved in the collective endeavours of safeguarding alongside professionals, potentially also – with a young person's consent – into adulthood;
- approaches taken by professionals and parents/carers to enacting these responsibilities reflect collaborative and relational principles, supported by capacity building, including for dissenting views and conflict resolution, focusing on creating the conditions that enable young people to be safer, have their needs met and to flourish.

Realising such a vision, however, requires more than adding new ideas – it also requires us to relinquish unhelpful practices and paradigms. Resting responsibility solely with individuals drives responses that extract young people from harmful contexts to control their individual behaviours and avoid individual professional blame if things go wrong. It also makes invisible the wider social and cultural barriers to recognising responsibilities to protect young people across intersectional lines – for example, assuming responsibility for safeguarding a White British 15-year-old young woman who is being sexually exploited but failing to respond in the same way to a Black British young man experiencing the same thing at the same age.

Instead, space needs to be created for risk and responsibility to be held more collectively, respecting and supporting adolescence as a life phase in which young people themselves develop their capacity to contribute to communities and societies, based on care rather than punishment (see Chapter 2). This will allow us to create the conditions in which young people can access safe relationships, rather than attempting to enact responsibilities to get young people to behave safely in persistently unsafe conditions.

To get us to this place we propose a rebalancing in how our systems are orientated; increasing orientation towards collective responsibility and decreasing orientation to individualised responsibility. We do not suggest there is no room for individual accountability in our systems, and would not propose an approach that ignores, or minimises, the importance of individual agency of those who interact with or make-up the system. Rather, in this rebalancing we propose systems that recognise individual agency and responsibility in relation to others, and the ways in which collectively holding responsibility creates contexts in which individuals can act with support. In Figure 4.2 we illustrate how such a system orientation would be characterised, in relation to what such a system measures as a marker of efficacy, the language it uses and how it views young people: working towards a goal that prioritises increasing the collective capability of young people, families, communities and professionals to support each other.

Systems orientated in this way would represent a reimagining of responsibility that is thick – in terms of the relational webs that bring it to life – and deep in terms of layers of harm, and protection from it, that influence young people's access to safety, belonging and conditions in which they flourish.

Figure 4.2: Features of safeguarding systems orientated to collective responsibility

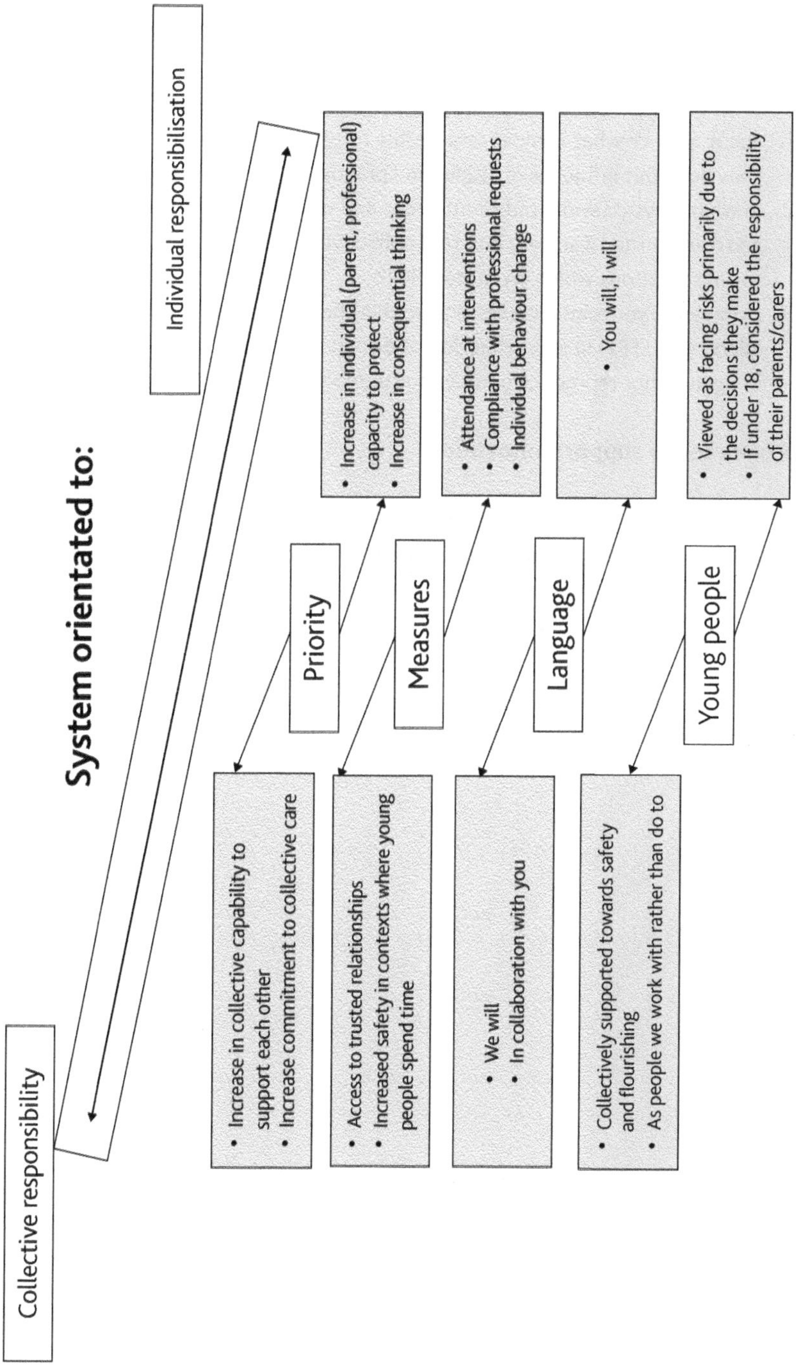

Box 4.1: Reflective questions for leaders and practitioners raised by Chapter 4

1. What messages does your organisation and profession give in its culture and guidance about who or what is most responsible for young people's involvement in EFRH? How does this influence attitudes and practices – your own and that of your staff?
2. In what ways do wider public attitudes and welfare policies need to be challenged and transformed if society is to take collective moral responsibility for changing the social conditions which promote EFRH?
3. How would you reimagine systems so that they frame and position responsibility for addressing EFRH in ways that do not disregard either young people's vulnerability or agency, nor reproduce punitive cultures of discipline and control?

Resources to support innovation

We suggest using the Four Quadrants tool, which was developed through the Innovate Project, as this can support you and your colleagues to uncover the wider system influences that shape culture and practice in an organisation. This tool and its guidance pack can be freely downloaded at: www.theinnovateproject.co.uk/practice-tools/.

5

Privacy

Article 8 of the UN Convention on Human Rights protects an individual's 'right to respect for their private life' as well as their family life. This is further enshrined in Article 16 of the UN Convention on the Rights of the Child, which makes it clear that the individual right to a private life is extended to children and young people, stating that: 'No child shall be subjected to arbitrary or unlawful interference with his or her privacy, family, home or correspondence.'

But why? What is important about privacy for young people's growth, development and flourishing?

The idea of privacy introduces a threshold in respect of 'interference' or intrusion. We see this reflected in child protection and safeguarding-related legislation for young people under 18 in terms of the 'no order principle' which enshrines in law the need for minimal state intrusion into young people's lives and those of their families – so that a court cannot make an order 'unless it considers that doing so would be better for the child than making no order at all' (Children Act 1989 1(5)).

Likewise, The Care Act, as it would apply to young people aged 18+ emphasises the need to respond proportionately to safeguarding concerns, and wherever possible to seek consent to both share information and act upon information shared. Legislative terms such as these introduce boundaries between the state and an individual's decisions and relationships, in recognition that not everything is up for scrutiny. It imparts a level of control and self-determination; this is something important to us all, but particularly so during the developmental period of adolescence, in which we have a growing desire to make decisions for ourselves and without the interference of others (Coleman, 2011; Hanson and Holmes, 2014; Blakemore, 2018).

In this chapter we consider how privacy is (and could be) protected, and worked with, to increase young people's access to safety. We also reflect on the ways in which privacy is obscured by discussions about 'confidentiality' and the extent to which it can be breached. Confidentiality is often positioned as a mechanism for *withholding* information, with the breaching of confidentiality being something done in the name of safeguarding (HM Government, 2023). In contrast, 'privacy' is something that may be protected and enabled in order to provide safety – particularly safety in relationships. Through this discussion we propose the development of systems that move beyond confidentiality to both engaging with privacy as a central cornerstone to keeping young people safe and creating conditions within which they can flourish.

Why is privacy important to young people?

Privacy is integral to psychosocial development in adolescence, shaping young people's sense of autonomy, identity and intimacy (Smetana, 2010; Peter and Valkenburg, 2011; Wisniewski et al, 2022; Vespoli et al, 2025). The need for privacy is expressed by a desire for choice and control over personal information – what we share, when we share it and who we share it with. Privacy offers us 'limited and protected communication' (Westin, 1967, cited in Peter and Valkenburg, 2011) creating 'boundaries that ensure the psychological distance necessary for the functioning of interpersonal relationships, regardless of whether they are formal or intimate' (Peter and Valkenburg, 2011, p 223). These agreed boundaries enable us to share intimate information with those we trust – and this trust relies on mutual understanding and expectations around privacy. Misalignments in privacy expectations and breaches of privacy can strain young people's relationships with their families and friends, with detrimental consequences for their well-being (Hernandez and Ebersole, 2022; Laird and Hawk, 2024). Likewise, privacy is central to developing trusting relationships with professionals in healthcare (Hardin et al, 2020; Agostino and Toulany, 2023), educational (Warnick, 2013) and children's social care settings (Stabler et al, 2023). Fear and/or experiences of intrusive practices and breaches of privacy from their loved ones and/or from professionals is a key common barrier to young people sharing concern, disclosing experiences of harm and seeking support (Mapes and Cavell, 2021; Augusti and Myhre, 2024).

Privacy and inequality

Despite the recognition of privacy as a universal right, and integral to young people's psychological development, children do not experience privacy violations in the same ways or to the same extent. Those from racially minoritised and socio-economically marginalised backgrounds, for example, are more likely to be subject to intensive surveillance by statutory services (Williams, 2018; Koch et al, 2024). Intrusive practices within child protection systems are also more readily experienced by young people in care (Stabler et al, 2023, Simpson, 2025) and those seeking asylum or with irregular immigration status (Chase, 2010; Campbell, 2022). Research further shows that young people with disabilities and additional learning needs are more likely to be subjected to assessments and increased information sharing across multi-agency partners without their consent (Morris, 2003; Stalker and McArthur, 2012; Jones et al, 2017). When privacy is no longer upheld as a universal right for all young people, it can function as a form of social privilege, defended for some young people but considered conditional or expendable for others.

For these reasons, privacy should be carefully considered when addressing extra-familial risks and harms (EFRH) in adolescence. Professional and system responses to EFRH often constitute severe breaches of privacy (alongside violating other young people's fundamental rights) and can considerably undermine young people's ability to form trusting relationships. Respecting their privacy should form an essential part of a protective response.

A problem shared: what are professionals talking about

Given the apparent importance of privacy for young people's development and flourishing, it is important to be clear on the ways that it is often not honoured, nor even considered in responses to ERFH. What private things are professionals taking about? During the Innovate Project, and in our wider collective work on system responses to EFRH, we identified five private topics that professionals often discussed.

Relationships

Professionals often talk about the vast array of relationships that young people have – family relationships, peer relationships, romantic relationships and community relationships, particularly when they think harm may be occurring, or could occur, in those relationships. They discuss who these people are, the nature of the relationships, where they spend their time together and the amount of contact they have with each other:

> [Social worker] She has assaulted a teacher. She has anger/rage issues and a fraught relationship with mum. There is a co-dependent relationship between mum and child. (Researcher observation notes, multi-agency panel meeting)
>
> [Social care meeting chair] says Child 2 has talked about a couple of friends and disclosed that they are dealing (implication that he is dealing with them).
>
> [Youth worker] he says these two are friends, but we don't know if they are exploiting him.
>
> [Social care meeting chair] asks if anyone knows the other names. (Researcher observation notes, multi-agency panel meeting)

> Discussion of relationship between Child 5 and girlfriend. It is a 'complex relationship' and concern expressed that it is emotional abuse (Researcher observation notes, multi-agency panel meeting)

In some situations, this involves professionals creating visual maps of those relationships, and in the process discussing an array of young people whom they may or may not know personally. On other occasions, it includes agreeing plans for these young people to spend time together, or to be separated, in a bid to keep them safe; this may involve social workers, police officers, school leaders and youth workers all playing a role in those plans (as outlined in Chapter 4 and further developed in Chapter 7).

Detailed experiences of harm, health and well-being

Professionals also share details about the harm young people have experienced and any consequential impacts on a young person's health and well-being. In meetings convened to consider the risks young people face, we observed professionals talking about injuries young people have sustained, assaults they have disclosed (or that other people have described on their behalf), the state of their mental health, including young people harming or injuring themselves and information about their sexual health:

> [Social Worker] [the young person] has lots of adverse childhood experiences. Mum's mental health and domestic violence. When worker saw her living at the YMCA it was firefighting. Most recently she was adamant she was pregnant, and I don't know what happened with that. She needs a therapeutic intervention, she's on a waiting list for Child and Adolescent Mental Health [services]. (Researcher observation notes, multi-agency panel meeting)

Access to, and contact with, services

Professionals routinely discuss and record young people's contact with a range of services, including how regularly they attend school/college, whether they attend mental health or sexual health appointments, if they go to any youth clubs locally, whether they have been stopped by the police and/or arrested, and whether they comply with any court orders to work with youth justice practitioners:

> [Social Worker] Child 5 was involved in a stabbing two years ago. Was permanently excluded. History of paternal domestic violence and concerns of involvement in County Lines in 2019. School had been dealing with 'aggressive behaviour' for a number of years. Referred

> to CAHMS [Child and Adolescent Mental Health Services] who said he was vulnerable to exploitation and could be referred to Youth Offending Service. (Researcher observation notes, multi-agency panel meeting)
>
> [Social Worker] Child 3 was found in possession of large amounts of Class As [drugs] that were plugged. Now with Youth Offending Service five days a week – making application to college and re-engaging with [worker]. Then [social worker] reads out long list of what child 3 is under investigation for includes drug offences, knife offences. Then [social worker] repeats bail conditions, includes strict curfew, exclusion zones, reporting into police station, YOS [Youth Offending Service], living at home.
>
> [Youth Offending Worker] says Child 3 has complied and is attending [service] every day. (Researcher observation notes, multi-agency panel meeting)

In this sense, young people's voluntary contact with services (such as youth clubs) may be shared in addition to their required contact with services (such as youth justice services). On some of these occasions the reason for the contact will also be shared; for example: 'they have been referred to mental health services as they told a pastoral worker at school that they had thoughts of suicide'; or 'they have been referred to the youth justice service for preventative work because they were stopped by the police and found to be carrying a "screwdriver"'.

Personal and family histories

In addition to sharing current reasons for referring young people into services, professionals will discuss young people's personal and family histories – often to provide context or 'background' for the current situation the young person is in. This may include situations where a young person's parent was in an abusive relationship previously, or where the young person or their parent had been charged with criminal offences in the past:

> [Police officer reading from a screen] Malicious comms (No Further Actioned), sexual assault (No Further Actioned), stalking, domestic with ex-partner. Partner listed for the sexual offence and stalking. Domestic with mum. Sexual activity, suspect ex-partner. Sexual activity with another older male. Indecent images of children being sent to her. Child Protection plan under neglect. Seeing friend get groomed. Domestic violence recorded between mum and partner. History of

> vulnerability because of her history of relationships with older males. (Researcher observation notes, multi-agency panel meeting)

Much of this information comes from children's social care records or police systems (both confirmed facts and that which is considered as 'intelligence'), and gives an account of the level of contact a young person or family has had with statutory services over their lives, rather than an account of the full family history, or elements of their history that the family and/or young person may consider most relevant to the current situation that they are facing.

Contexts where young people are spending time

Finally, professionals will also talk about the places and spaces where young people are spending time: public spaces like libraries and parks, hospitality and retail settings, social media platforms and particular streets, may all be discussed. Professionals may share this information between statutory agencies – for example informing the police or youth workers where young people are spending their time, in a bid to increase the presence of these professionals in those spaces. Alternatively, they may also share this information with non-statutory services, and more informal organisations/individuals, such as people who run libraries, community hubs, transport hubs and so on, where young people have been harmed. In some scenarios this might include providing these people with photos of young people they are worried about, or photos of young people who have been banned from these spaces.

> [Social worker] The family has been moved to [town] and placed in temporary accommodation. Family are now in a caravan after leaving other accommodation in the place they were moved to. Child 3 has had multiple missing episodes. He was also found in a [city] train station with a 13-year-old girl but there are no details from the police about who this girl was. (Researcher observation notes, multi-agency panel meeting)

> Meeting Chair then moved on to another action on the plan, this one about a community hall – two sources of 'community intelligence' suggest behaviour that may be linked to drug supply. (Researcher observation notes, multi-agency panel meeting)

> [Social worker] Child 10 met a friend [name] and ended up at an overnight party at an adult male's house. (Researcher observation notes, multi-agency panel meeting)

All of the above matters are, to varying degrees, private. We, ourselves, would normally wish to decide who we will inform about who our friends are, where we were on Friday night, our sexual health histories, what our parents' relationships had been like and so on. Our decisions on this would normally include factors such as telling people we know and trust about intimate details, rather than people not personally known to us. And we would usually have our own reasons for how much information to share, or deciding what to hold back from certain people and when. Finally, we would usually be basing these decisions on the interpersonal nature of relationships, not state-based relationships. The extent to which we would share this type of information with governments, or individuals working for government agencies, is often informed by whether we need some form of additional help.

A note on policy: confidentiality trumped

Before we consider the practical rationale for, and implications of, professionals talking about such personal matters, it is important to note the wider policy context in which the above practices occur. Various public inquiries and processes of 'case review' in the UK have concluded that professionals missed opportunities to safeguard young people because they failed to share information with each other (McAllister, 2022; Action for Children, 2024); the implication of such criticisms is that if information had been shared, those in authority would have better understood the situation a young person was in and would have been able to respond accordingly. As a result of these conclusions, various public statements and practice guidance have focused on encouraging information sharing, particularly as it pertains to young people under 18, with statements such as 'sharing information for safeguarding purposes can be justified solely based on preventing harm to a child' or that 'it is only through sharing information that agencies or organisations and practitioners build a richer picture of the day-to-day life of the child and family they are working with' (Department for Education, 2024, p 15).

It is unsurprising, therefore, that in this policy context professionals share an array of information with each other about young people, their lives, relationships and experiences, often unquestioningly: they are told that they won't know how valuable their information might be for safeguarding young people until they have shared it with others and its place in the whole picture can be appraised.

This policy landscape has created the conditions in which the nature of confidentiality and information-sharing are debated far more than the idea of privacy. Such conditions are ones in which professionals have 'over-shared' – and where surveillance of young people, particularly those who are racially minoritised is a daily reality (Williams, 2018; Firmin et al, 2024; Koch et al, 2024; Pantazis et al, 2025). In some scenarios, the volume and nature of data sharing has been criticised, including by the courts. In 2022 the Metropolitan police were found to have unlawfully collected and held information about young people on a 'gangs' matrix', with a significantly low threshold for their inclusion (see Williams, 2018). Such scrutiny of this practice was only achieved due to advocacy of organisation, rather than through internal critical reflection within the police or other statutory agencies, many of whom argued that the matrix should be maintained. These concerns reflect broader, emergent scholarship on the ethical challenges of multi-agency responses to EFRH. These challenges include the potential of increased surveillance of young people impacted by EFRH (Wroe and Lloyd, 2020), particularly of racially minoritised young people (Lammy, 2017; Williams, 2018; Koch et al, 2024), without any increased protections, and the corresponding expansion of that surveillance into peer groups, schools and public places where EFRH occurs. Such practices have come under particular scrutiny when they occur in the context of multi-agency arrangements that are geared more towards policing young people and preventing crime, than protecting young people and meeting their needs (Lloyd et al, 2023; Firmin, 2024).

Ignoring privacy: practical implications of that context

In Innovate Project sites we witnessed the practical implications of such a policy context: extensive professional consideration of how important it was to share information and little consideration of privacy.

First, we observed an urgency to share information among professionals, particularly in meetings where young people's plans were reviewed: 'The young person declined consent for [an assessment to be conducted] but the Youth Offending Team has been advised they can still collect info without his consent' (Researcher observation notes, multi-agency meeting to discuss peer group).

The level of urgency created little space for privacy to be discussed. The real anxiety that, if information was not shared something awful would happen, drove practice, leaving little space for reflection on whether sharing that information had made any difference to young people's safety. It also created situations in which social workers and youth workers experienced pressure from external agencies to share information with them, particularly from police and schools. However, some practitioners did push back on this, in recognition of the harm that a decision-to-share might cause, as highlighted by the following two extracts:

> So those tensions are difficult because we want the young people to trust us, but also, we do need to … kind of pass on that information. But also, we're not going to be telling … we're not going to be going straight to the police with information around say, oh those young people smoke weed, or those young people do this. (Youth worker)

> they'll just use the relationship [with young people] you know. So you know a young person will have a [charity worker] and they'll have a really good relationship because … because we're not statutory, and then you know social care might kind of try and use that relationship [to obtain information]. (Voluntary sector worker)

Such challenges from practitioners appeared to occur despite wider policy landscapes and were justified by them on the grounds that information-sharing would undermine trust, and the relationships upon which such trust had been built, rather than them expressly promoting privacy as something worth protecting.

Such push backs from some social workers and youth workers were unsurprising given that much information-sharing occurred within the context of 'monitoring' situations rather than 'responding' to them. For example, as illustrated by many of the extracts earlier in this chapter, many professionals engaged in oversight panels that were designed to provide a space for practitioners to update senior leaders on situations of most concern to them and, in doing so, to share the responsibility for young people they were most concerned about. In some cases, such information-sharing was used to jointly determine further actions to be taken by organisations. In other situations, it meant professionals agreed to keep young people's names on lists that they monitored at weekly or monthly meetings, or to remove them from such lists if risk appeared to have sufficiently decreased.

Some of the challenges around knowing when to share information, when to withhold it and when to share partial information, were due to a lack of clarity about *why* information was being shared in the first place – for what purpose? The complexity that we comment on throughout this book, that comes with responses to EFRH straddling both criminal justice and child and social welfare frameworks, cultures and practices, is relevant here. Are professionals sharing information to assist in the criminal investigation of crimes against young people? Are they sharing information to identify young people's unmet needs and agree actions to meet them? Are they trying to do both? What happens if by sharing information to pursue the former, the latter is undermined? Or, indeed, the reverse?

Moreover, when analysing our data we often wondered, 'who does the act of sharing information protect?'. Some of the extracts provided earlier in this chapter outlined scenarios in which practitioners shared information because they believed that doing so would help them, and others, to protect young people. In other situations, there appeared to be little evidence that a young person was directly benefiting from an act of information-sharing; rather, the practitioner involved was released from the burden of care and anxiety by sharing concerns – and were additionally protecting themselves in the process. In a number of examples we observed, we wondered whether the drive to breach a young person's privacy was more about protecting the service – in other words, ensuring an organisation was viewed as compliant with the wider policy conditions in which safeguarding trumped all legal safeguards associated with confidentiality. If something happened to the young person, they would be able to evidence that everything that they knew had been handed over to other people; the buck would not stop with them.

The imperative to share information, and the fear about the impact of not doing so, was also expressed by practitioners' frustration at young people's unwillingness to share; this unwillingness was often framed as 'non-engagement' with services, as illustrated in the following excerpt from observation notes of a multi-agency meeting that discussed children who went missing:

> [Police Officer says] Child 1 will not disclose details of the boyfriend. 'She is just not being very forthcoming', she says with a frustrated sigh that is very audible.
> [Police Officer] is irritated. Her interpretation is that Child is being stubborn or bloody minded about this, rather than there's something else going on that might be stopping her from giving this information. Perhaps she doesn't trust the police or think they can help her? This might be her experience.
>
> ...
>
> How can a system make people do things they don't want to? How is non-compliance or resistance understood by professionals? (Researcher observation notes, multi-agency panel meeting)

At no time in the ethnography did we hear non-engagement described as young people being reluctant to share private information with people they did not know or did not trust. Instead, their unwillingness to 'engage' with professionals was framed as something that made young people unsafe, and/or prevented professionals from being able to safeguard them – rather than possibly being something young people did to protect their privacy and themselves. Given the importance of privacy for all, but particularly during the period of adolescent development, we suggest that young people's unwillingness to share information with various people, who are in their lives temporarily and who sometimes use that information to control, sanction or intervene with them, could be described as rational and in line with developmental norms. Moreover, recognising non-engagement as a possible effort to preserve privacy can help professionals reframe responses, shifting the focus from overcoming resistance to understanding the conditions under which young people feel safe to share personal information.

Could proactive engagement with the idea of privacy, therefore, afford professionals new ways to think about, and respond to, 'non-engagement', as well as to critically reflect on their own desire to share information and/or receive it?

Foregrounding privacy: a way forward

It is clearly important that professionals are able to access information that is central to supporting and protecting young people impacted by EFRH. It is equally important that this information is accurate, and that sharing it does not undermine the exact goal for which sharing it was intended. To accommodate both matters we propose a safeguarding system underpinned by a 'Triple P test of Privacy', namely:

1. Purpose: What is the purpose of breaching a young person's privacy (rather than sharing information)? What is the purpose of seeking to protect young people's privacy (rather than withholding information)? What is the objective of each action and who is expected to benefit from it? What is risked, and is this risk justified to achieve the identified purpose and benefit? How might assumptions about race, disability, class or culture shape what is defined as a risk?
2. Proportionality: What aspects of a young person's privacy must be breached or protected to fulfil that purpose? Is the breach of privacy, or effort to protect it, proportionate? If this information was/wasn't shared with specific people, what difference would it make to the support the young person receives and the likely outcomes of this? Would this breach of privacy be considered proportionate for a child from a more privileged and/or different ethnic background?
3. Participation: Has the young person been involved in the decision to share personal, private information about them or to sense-check its accuracy with them? Have they agreed that this information is shared with specific people? Or has information been generated about them in systems without their knowledge and been shared without their permission? If they have not been involved in this process, what are the reasons and are they justifiable? How are power, communication or other special needs, language, or previous experiences of services affecting a child's ability to participate meaningfully?

This Triple P test moves us away from the idea that the General Data Protection Regulation (GDPR) is something with need to 'work around' or 'trump' in order to protect young people, and move us towards practices that provide safety by respecting young people's dignity and relationships. Research into EFRH is saturated with evidence that young people benefit from relationships with people that they trust. The Triple P test honours this evidence base and outlines the considerations that are needed for 'information-sharing' to be an enabler of privacy, rather than a means of breaching it. It is not that we believe information about young people should not be shared between professionals to keep young people safe. It is rather that greater thought is needed to both the 'what' and 'how' of that process if a young person's safety is to remain the driving goal.

Figure 5.1 illustrates how orientating safeguarding systems towards privacy, in which information sharing is subsumed, opens up new ways to describe impact, view young people and agree measures of efficacy. As Figure 5.1 illustrates, information will continue to be shared to safeguard young people within systems that afford equal consideration of privacy. In reaching these conclusions, we promote systems in which young people are held, supported and valued above all else.

Orientating safeguarding systems towards privacy offers a means of alleviating the ethical and relational tensions visible in youth work and social work practice within interagency partnerships (Knijn and Van Nijnatten, 2011; Meysen and Kelly, 2018; Segal, 2023; Harju et al, 2024; Rannala et al, 2024). Practitioners from various countries have reported pressure to hand over information about young people to the police, information that they are privy to through trusted relationships, and not through 'information-gathering' or 'intelligence-gathering' processes. Asking the Triple P questions in times of pressure and framing the pressure they experience in relation to privacy, rather than in relation to information-sharing and confidentiality brings an element of clarity to the debate. It introduces a rights framework into safeguarding practices, seeing children's and human rights as an enabler of protection/safety rather than a barrier to it. Moreover, it moves us towards a place of respectful practice – a place upon which the previous chapter was focused.

Figure 5.1: Features of safeguarding systems orientated to the protection of privacy

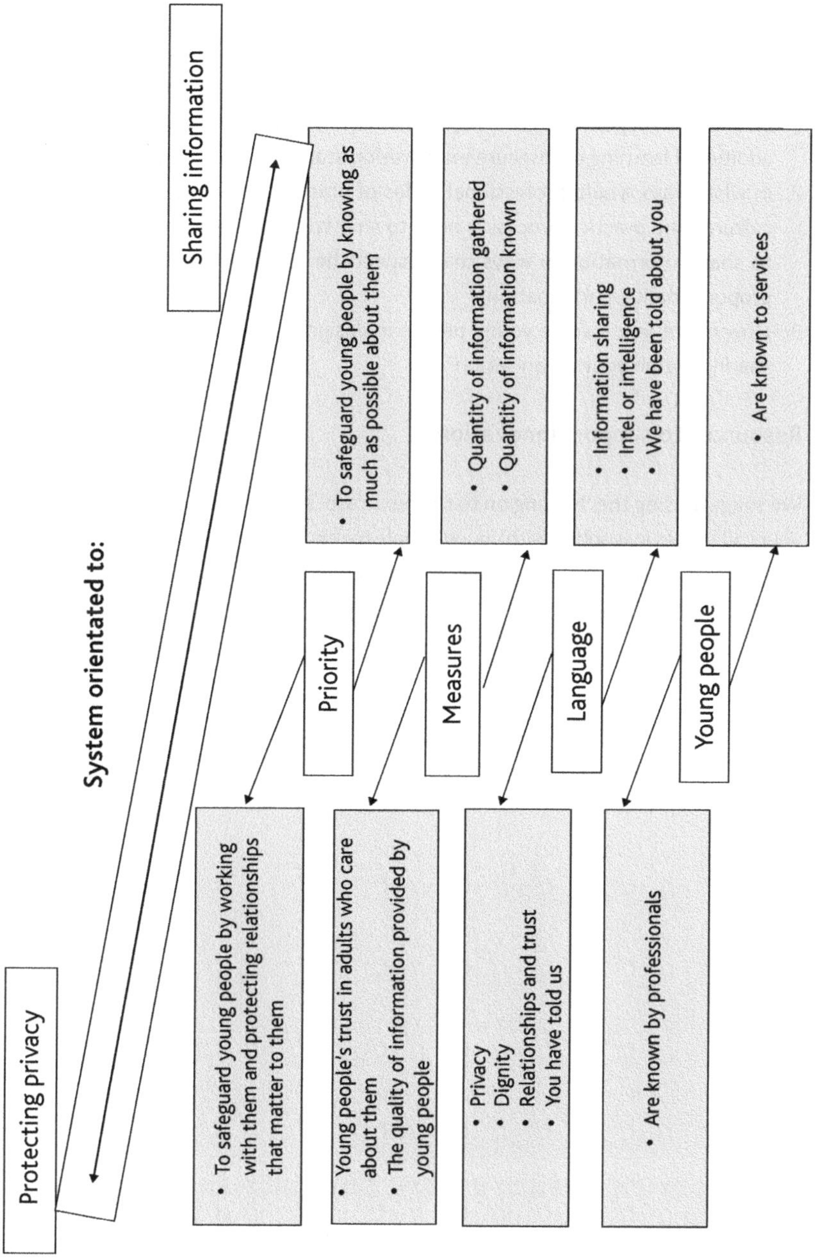

Box 5.1: Reflective questions for leaders and practitioners raised by Chapter 5

1. When applying the 'Triple P test of Privacy', are you considering the privacy of some children more negotiable than others (such as those in care, from racially minoritised or underprivileged backgrounds, those who are neurodivergent, with disabilities, additional learning or insecure immigration status)?
2. In what ways would professional codes of practice, organisational or interagency cultures and practice processes need to shift to ensure that workers are prompted to share information in ways that respect the 'Triple P test of Privacy' (purpose, proportionality, participation)?
3. How might you involve young people in designing new guidance on information-sharing within your organisation?

Resources to support innovation

We suggest using the 'Moving on to the next case' set of resources, to support you and your colleagues in working with young people to reimagine and co-produce new guidance on information-sharing. The resources, which were developed through the Innovate Project, can be freely downloaded at: www.theinnovateproject.co.uk/practice-tools/.

PART II

System relationships

6

Parents and families

Introduction

As understanding of extra-familial risks and harms (EFRH) has grown, among service leaders, practitioners and researchers alike so, too, has recognition of the shifting and complex roles played by the parents, carers and wider families of the young people who are impacted. Two key matters have come to the fore. First, EFRH largely impacts young people during a period of adolescent development and, as such, it happens at a time where young people's relationships with parents and wider family gradually shift as they grow in independence. Second, EFRH occurs in physical and relational contexts that are often beyond parental control/oversight and can impact young people who are living in relatively safe and protective family homes. For both these reasons, Western neoliberal models of child protection that associate and situate risk and protection with parental (in)action, and fail to consider young people's families at all in adult safeguarding systems, are likely to fall short in both assessing the nature of EFRH and developing mechanisms of protection.

This is not to say there is no role for parents/carers or wider family networks in responding to EFRH; far from it. Instead, we assert that our systems need to better reflect the shifting position of families during the period of adolescent development and, in the contexts of EFRH, to harness the protective power of familial relationships. We draw attention, too, to how the absence of an intersectional gaze compounds the dominance within child welfare and child protection systems of deficit-based assessment frameworks that obscure how systemic barriers actively constrain parenting capacity while intensifying statutory intervention of parents/carers of young people under 18 (Pimm-Smith, 2026).

In this chapter, utilising evidence from the Innovate Project, we reflect on where family relationships have featured in system responses to EFRH, and where service redesign has taken us to date, before proposing a way forward. Drawing on ethnographic fieldnotes from our observations of multi-agency risk management panels in particular, we outline ways in which parents and carers were positioned or described by professionals, where opportunities for collaboration were lost and found, and the implications of each for approaches to safety planning and support. We go on to propose a collaborative care ecology (Bowlby and McKie, 2019) for safeguarding and supporting young people both under-and-over-18, which weaves the 'parental caringscape' (Nagy and Horkai, 2021) into a wider contextualised tapestry alongside the formal carescapes provided by services and the 'informal caringscapes' of young people's wider families, friends and local communities (McKie et al, 2002). In so doing, we offer a vision in which systems understand and value young people's family relationships, and create conditions in which families can provide love, take responsibility, protect privacy and offer recognition respectfully to the young people in their care and/or for whom they care. We end the chapter by concluding that the positive contributions of families will only be scaffolded and extended where attitudes begin to shift from blame to support and where there is a respectful positioning of families as potential allies.

The positioning of 'parents' and 'families' in safeguarding systems

The care and safety provided by young people's families has a significant impact on their development and well-being (Johnson, 2013). During adolescence, this impact has been conceptualised in the context of a liminal period where young people, on the one hand, challenge parental regulation and reach out to new horizons but, on the other, need and seek out (albeit sometimes sporadically) an ongoing connectedness to family relationships and habitus during this period of instability and change (Noller and Atkin, 2014). It is essential to note in this that 'adolescence' is a particularly Westernised concept, and its norming of increasing individuation does not hold true in many Global Majority cultures (Greenfield et al, 2003). What can perhaps be more relied upon is the recognition that the 'parent-child bond persists through the life course and likely continues to inform and shape behavior beyond adolescence' (Johnson et al, 2013, p 786).

In Western, particularly neoliberal, policy contexts this evidence has been applied with a narrow focus on the role of parents – as opposed to wider family networks and kin – in keeping young people safe and specifically on the concept of 'parental responsibility' (Featherstone et al, 2018). Part of this emphasis is explained by evidence of children's high dependency needs and nurture requirements in the earlier years of childhood, and the deleterious effects of intra-familial abuse and neglect which can impact through the life cycle (D'Andrea et al, 2012; Gregorowski and Seedat, 2013). However, in societies such as the UK, this parenting-focused paradigm has fostered a pervasive perception that if a young person comes to harm, and/or their behaviour poses risks to others, and they are under 18, then the primary responsibility for this rests with parents and guardians. This responsibilisation persists, even when poverty and intersecting forms of marginalisation, including racism and asylum status (Davis and Marsh, 2020; Pimm-Smith, 2026), have seriously undermined family well-being and parenting capacity

(Bywaters et al, 2020). Within safeguarding assessments, racialised narratives shape how risk, responsibility and parental credibility are interpreted (Davis and Marsh, 2020), while the effects of criminalisation, neighbourhood exclusion and wider structural violence on parental authority remain largely unacknowledged (Billingham and Irwin-Rogers, 2022). As a result, the structural constraints shaping parents' capacity to protect are frequently rendered invisible within child protection decision-making.

The relative availability of family support services, too, seems rarely to be taken into account by professionals (Gupta et al, 2018). A narrow lens of parental responsibility (as a source of protection and harm) has been maintained even in cases of EFRH (Thornhill, 2023). Such practices have commonly failed to acknowledge how young people's increasing agency and desire for autonomy during the years of adolescence takes them into places and relationships beyond parental awareness or oversight – spaces where peer social structures and cultures are at least as influential as family relationships and practices (Pike et al, 2019).

Given the often narrow and negative framing of parents, and the lack of consideration of wider families in much of the research, it is unsurprising that parents and carers are often positioned as the subjects of child protection systems rather than as partners in safety planning for their children; and then latterly excluded from adult safeguarding systems from which young people over 18 struggle to accept support. The Children Act 1989 has called for more participatory and relational work to be done with parents and carers of young people under 18 in the child protection system in England, Wales and Northern Ireland (Smithson and Gibson, 2017). However, this call has not been fully realised and parents' concerns about lack of inclusion are not without foundation. Parents continue to report feeling humiliated, misunderstood, intimidated, blamed and threatened by the power that workers in statutory services have over them (Gupta et al, 2018). Conversely, once over 18, young people's consent for involving parents and families in supportive ways may not be considered or sought by professionals.

Professionals' positioning of parents in situations of EFRH

Mirroring the individualised and risk-orientated focus of neoliberal child protection systems, a substantial international body of research has examined how parental behaviour, parenting styles and family dynamics may hinder or support child development and well-being, and influence the degree of vulnerability in adolescence to victimisation, exploitation and involvement in behaviours framed as 'anti-social' or 'criminal'. Across diverse contexts, studies have identified broadly consistent patterns: warm, nurturing parenting has been associated with higher social competence and lower rates of depression, while parenting described as manipulative or guilt-inducing has been linked to increased depression and anti-social behaviour (Barber et al, 2005). Related research highlights the importance of the quality and predictability of parent–child relationships, and of young people's sense of belonging and mattering within the family, in fostering well-being, confidence and internal security (Carr and Springer, 2010; Golombok and Tasker, 2015; King et al, 2018).

Reflecting this lens, particularly prior to 2010, many studies focused on the parental and family backgrounds of young people impacted by EFRH or involved in harm or interpersonal violence. The extent and type of parental control and boundary-setting was the focus of a substantial body of work, with associations identified between 'coercive' parenting styles and young people's 'risk-taking' or 'anti-social behaviour' (Heimer and DeCoster, 1999); between too-lenient parental boundaries and problematic under-age drinking (Repetti et al, 2002); and between 'authoritative' parenting and lowered rates of depression, educational difficulty and offending (Simons and Conger, 2007; McKinney and Renk, 2008). Other work suggested that fathers experienced as 'anxious' and 'untrustworthy' could undermine their sons' internal sense of safety, increasing the likelihood of them seeking protection and a sense of belonging outside the home, including within 'gangs' and groups associated with criminality (Heaven et al, 2004). Later studies, including in the Netherlands (van Dijk et al, 2022) and the US (Augustyn et al, 2017) focused on the increased likelihood of young people's involvement in criminality or gang-related activities if their own families were involved in organised crime.

However, a 2014 review of the literature by Young et al cautioned against simplistic formulas that tie together 'troubled families' and 'criminalities', observing that other environmental factors, such as poverty, are equally influential. This caution has since been reiterated by a range of studies which have noted the ways in which parenting-focused responses to EFRH have been informed and reinforced by a research landscape focused on parental and family dynamics of young people impacted by EFRH – often without equal consideration of peer, school, neighbourhood or structural drivers of harm (Adams et al, 2022; de Vries et al, 2025).

Despite these cautions, a dominant and decontextualised focus on parental responsibility and influence in research has been well aligned with practice models focused on the extent to which parents are, or may be, responsible for problems with their child's behaviour and/or their child's experiences of exploitation, abuse or criminality (Hunter et al, 2020). This 'ruling relation' (Smith, 2005) of parental responsibilisation by professionals commonly lacks attention to the contextual and structural aspects shaping not only normative adolescent development and well-being, and young people's likely involvement with EFRH, but also the emotions, choices and relationships of the parents and other family members (Featherstone et al,

2018). An intersectional perspective highlights how these ruling relations operate unevenly, with racially minoritised and economically marginalised parents, particularly mothers, subject to intensified surveillance and moral judgement. In such contexts, the likelihood of a negative experience of intervention is increased for parents with prior or ongoing experiences of trauma, abuse, inequalities and oppression (Berelowitz et al, 2013; Shuker and Ackerley, 2017; Featherstone et al, 2018).

Professional cultures and attitudes play a central role in parents' experiences. Some practitioners appear to believe that more collaborative forms of working are not suitable for all families, are concerned that participatory approaches might undermine their status or authority in a contested situation, and fear that working relationally with parents might deflect their focus from the harm experienced by the young people (Pike et al, 2019). Even when a reasonable degree of co-operation has been reached, professionals often do not fully trust parents (Langhoff et al, 2024) and assume they may be seeking to obscure the extent to which they are responsible for harm coming to their young person (Leigh, 2020).

As a result, practice in the field of EFRH has been found to be less likely to acknowledge the constructive actions already taken by parents in seeking to nurture, support and protect their child in the aftermath of or prior to abuse, or scaffold such actions as a foundation for future safety, but rather to target intervention towards tackling (actual or perceived) parental inadequacies (Hallett, 2017). While parental involvement is commonly noted as a protective factor, there appears to be limited understanding of how best to promote constructive work between professionals and parents towards the goals of safety and support for young people caught up in risky relationships/situations or criminality (Pike et al, 2019). The positive aspects of parents' roles and relationships with their young people seem often marginalised by the common strategy of removing a young person entirely from their home and locality, often to some geographical distance, to provide immediate protection from the sources of EFRH (Wroe et al, 2023). Indeed, this glosses over, too, the importance of young people's other relationships and ties within families (such as with siblings, grandparents, uncles and aunts) and wider social networks, and the ways these play out in their lives.

Parents, carers and EFRH in systems under re-design

During the Innovate Project, we witnessed the less collaborative attitudes identified previously among efforts made to innovate towards more constructive, trauma-informed and relational ways of working alongside parents and carers. We go on now to use these contrasting observations to highlight practice challenges and to illustrate how shifts in professional attitudes and behaviour at the individual (micro-)level might be overcome if there are concomitant shifts at organisational and wider system levels (meso- and macro-levels). We draw here specifically on our observations of monthly online multi-agency meetings in our research sites that were held to review plans for children considered at high risk of EFRH in that local authority area (the methodology for which we outlined in the introductory chapter). For this chapter we undertook a secondary analysis of the researcher's contemporaneous fieldnotes and subsequent reflective record produced in relation to each of the multi-agency meetings observed in the two sites that were implementing trauma-informed approaches.

Neither parents nor young people were included in person in these meetings; in essence the meetings were *by* professionals and *for* professionals and comprised talking *about* young people not *with* them. Perhaps the most striking feature of our re-reading of all the meeting observation fieldnotes for this chapter was how little parents, and families more widely, were even mentioned in discussion, let alone the extent to which their perspectives and contributions were considered alongside those of professionals. The impression received by our observing researchers was that many parents or carers were little known as people and often seemed to matter hardly at all as key actors within safety planning or assessment activity. This impression was reinforced by the tendency to refer to parents and other family carers by role rather than by name – 'mum', 'dad', 'the grandmother'; this produced a sense of them being seen as objects rather than active partners in the support and protection of young people – something noted in other safeguarding-related studies (Smithson and Gibson, 2017; Wilkins and Whittaker, 2018). To this extent, a growing recognition that parents/carers rarely instigate exploitation or other forms of EFRH may have inadvertently screened them out of protective processes altogether – with professionals focused on building relationships with young people impacted by the harm and less with their families (Owens and Firmin, 2022); a matter that only became even more pronounced as young people aged-out of otherwise parent-focused child protection systems and into either individual adult-focused safeguarding, mental health and/or probation systems.

Moreover, we observed a further 'ruling relation' of safeguarding practice in sites, namely that the only parent that statutory services commonly focus on in the context of safeguarding is the mother (Thornhill, 2023). Fathers had little or no attention paid to them in these meetings. They were most often dismissed as 'not on the scene' and the professional gaze usually only turned towards fathers where they were viewed as offering a potential risk of harm. The construction of mothers was more varied. In contrast with fathers, they were recognised as being an important source of information about their young person's history, family context, peer group(s) and local community relationships; these were often significant gaps in professionals' knowledge about the young people. However, the knowledge mothers held and sometime shared was not always seen as trustworthy by professionals: 'We need to be careful of interaction with mum, because of disguised compliance. Mum has a history of not wanting to engage with services. If she's saying child is at home and not going out, then we need to be sceptical about that' (Social worker).

Here, the social worker was referencing a pervasive professional construct to explain parents' assumed motivations that has almost become a diagnostic label (Hart, 2017). An accusation of 'disguised compliance' seems to place parents in a no-win scenario: if parents do not go along with professionals' expectations, then they are categorised as risky, hostile or feckless; if they do comply, then they are suspected of superficial engagement and compliance with professionals' objectives to hide their (supposedly) subversive resistance to the systems' regulatory procedures and disguise the extent to which they are exposing their children to harm (Leigh et al, 2020, p 282). Parents and other family members/carers were often blamed in panel discussions for failing to keep young people safe in situations where they were thought not to have sufficiently surveilled the young person's relationships and activities outside of the home nor controlled their behaviour. We witnessed how common service practices that we critiqued in Chapter 5, such as breaching young people's privacy, and working with young people on basis of surveillance and control rather than trust and collaboration (Wroe and Lloyd, 2020), were pushed onto parents to enact, with little attempt to recognise the harm that such expectations could have on enduring family relationships.

This is not to dismiss situations where a parent, carer or family member could or should have taken protective actions. One grandmother, for example, was reported to the interagency meeting to have said 'that she doesn't see an issue with the crack, she said if it's once a week it's OK' (Social worker). In this scenario, the professionals were concerned that the child's guardian was neglecting to take account of where the young person was getting the money from and of the risks associated with the drug itself. However, we use our observations to draw attention here to the pervasive dynamic of responsibilisation that we detailed in Chapter 4 being played out in interagency meetings. In these meetings any parents and carers who were not actively abusive were placed in a double-bind: those who were seen as irresponsible or ineffectual tended (in our observations) to be marginalised or blamed; those whose capabilities were recognised and appreciated were often 'rewarded' by being left alone to manage risk and keep young people safe without the support of services.

Our perception was that mothers stood the best chance of receiving support when their vulnerability was recognised by the key professionals involved; this could act as a gateway to services. Although vulnerability was usually discussed in relation to parents' capacity (or not) to support their young person, we witnessed many examples of an empathetic and trauma-informed tone which provoked professionals' compassion for parents' own struggles and consideration of what supports the parents themselves might need if they were to adequately support their adolescent child. In such circumstances, professionals were able to recognise and acknowledge the effort parents had made to overcome their own psychosocial struggles and improve their parenting capacity: 'Protective factors [are that] mum is in a better place. Reports for addiction services is that she's doing the best she ever has done. Treatment programme and doing extra activities' (Social worker).

This more strengths-based perspective was consonant with other examples where professionals validated certain actions and initiatives made by parents and carers in support of their young person's well-being and protection. In these latter examples, professionals foregrounded what parents and carers *were* doing for young people as opposed to what they were *not* doing and enacted their professional responsibility to create the conditions in which such actions could be sustained or enhanced. In some instances, parents were noted to have taken quite substantial risks themselves in striving to protect young people from EFRH. One young person's social worker shared that, 'mum did [pay off a drug debt] and dad is supposed to have called the gang and told them to leave his son alone'.

Our ethnography also observed many examples where professionals in these meetings seemed to understand parents as collaborators in the safeguarding endeavour. At the most basic level, this involved recognition in the meeting of where parents' relationships with practitioners had improved: 'now it seems that Samuel's mum has a good relationship with Support Worker' (fieldnotes). At a higher level, it was possible to see positive recognition of instances when parents had taken a central role in significantly moving forward the young person's safeguarding plan. The more collaborative approach tended to be apparent when practitioners in these multi-agency meetings were able to describe parents and carers in more nuanced ways, describing not only their characteristics but also the mechanisms of their everyday lives and the barriers that impeded a young person's safeguarding trajectory. This is the kind of knowledge that indicated a professional's attention to parents' lived experience and an (ongoing) relationship with them; we have previously termed this as being 'known by' the professionals as people, rather than just 'known to services' as an object of intervention (Firmin et al, 2024). Positioning parents as potential collaborators was not restricted to situations where parents were believed to have formerly managed everything perfectly nor did it necessarily imply full agreement between parents and professionals on how risks had emerged or how they were to be dealt with. Rather it reflected a stance of openness, respect and inclusion which centred parental voice and expertise in such a way that, while professionals' and parents' opinions might differ, there could and should be respectful dialogue which could move things forward. This moved practice towards the respect-via-recognition approach presented in Chapter 3.

Building a collaborative care ecology with parents, carers and wider families

In Chapter 2 we introduced the idea of formal 'carescapes' (Bowlby and McKie, 2019) to interrogate the social and structural role that institutions such as public policy, societal norms, organisational systems and cultures, and professional practices play in families' experiences of care services. We drew attention at the end of that chapter to the limitations of what could be achieved by services alone and the importance of professionals working collaboratively with the informal 'caringscapes' offered by young people's families, friends and local communities (McKie et al, 2002; Nagy and Horkai, 2021). The insights from the ethnography that we report in the current chapter chime with a key finding from our 2022 review of practice interventions in the field of EFRH which identified that parents, carers and families can make an important contribution to the support and protection of their young people but that their strengths as active partners in safety planning require facilitation by the practice field (Firmin et al, 2022). We go on now to summarise some key considerations for professionals in weaving a more productive and supportive 'care ecology' with and for families, based on what we have surfaced and discussed in this chapter.

First, we propose that, regardless of the specific form of EFRH, all practice with parents, carers and families should be trauma-informed and relationship-based. A young person's experiences of EFRH are likely to have evoked complex and powerful emotions for the whole family, such as anger, fear, distress, grief and helplessness, all of which take a substantial toll on emotional well-being and capacity to think 'under fire'. Whatever limitations there might currently or previously have been with parenting capacity or where familial interpersonal relationships are conflictual, all involved family members may well be also feeling shame, guilt and humiliation; perhaps they feel that they should have seen or done more, understood better, whether or not that was the case in reality. This may have wider, harsher consequences in families that already deal with social marginality due to their ethnicity, poverty or other social positions. These feelings cannot be readily resolved when dangerous scenarios and conflictual relationships continue, so the impacts of the trauma at an individual and family system level need to be validated and responded to by professionals. Building physical, psychological and emotional safety with family members is a key priority (Hopper and Bassuk, 2010), but this is best done relationally; it cannot be done in the absence of trust or if parents, carers and families, do not feel cared for by practitioners (see Chapter 2). Practitioners will be most successful in building relationship with parents and other family members through their own 'use of self', including warmth, genuineness, empathy and openness (Lefevre et al, 2008).

Second, constructive collaboration by professionals with informal caringscapes, to build and sustain their positive contribution, will only be achieved where the underpinning narrative in practice guidance and professional cultures begin to shift from blame to support. Parents and carers need to be re-positioned as potential allies and protective partners, not passive observers or guilty parties, in forming plans to create a safer and more beneficial family life for all family members. Practitioners do need to challenge their own attitudinal biases in this shift, but culture change needs to be led at a service and sector level; it is draining and often traumatising for practitioners to try to hold onto a supportive stance among a hostile inter-professional network, and pervasive (inter-)organisational 'ruling relations' may subtly and invisibly influence individuals' perceptions and actions, often without their awareness. Moreover, the absence of workload time and support provision must be addressed directly by the service as over-stretched and under-resourced practitioners cannot compensate for service inadequacies.

Third, if the strengths of parents, wider family and close community are to be maximised, the informal caringscape needs to be educated, empowered and included in safeguarding plans, rather than being sidelined due to stigma or assumptions that, as a young person ages towards, or even into, adulthood, their families play no role in their protection. Professionals would not expect to know how best to safeguard and support young people without learning about the subtle complexities of how young people may be drawn into exploitation, peer-abuse, crime and violence, and what strategies might help young people find safety, joy and flourishing beyond the risky relationships, scenarios and situations they are currently in. So, parents should not be blamed for lacking such expertise, or appearing distant from it, but, rather, helped to understand the signs, tactics and impacts of exploitation, grooming, coercion and online risks in accessible language, and brought closer to young people in the process. This can be particularly empowering in peer groups alongside other parents in similar situations, where they can share experiences, coping mechanisms and strategies to keep their young people safe, and build resilience together. (Pike et al, 2019). Parents will have little emotional bandwidth to support their young people where they are dealing with multiple challenges, so practitioners can help by signposting and brokering their access to mental health services, housing support and financial aid where needed, for example.

Finally, family-focused work must be included in young people's plans – including when they age-out of child protection systems and into adult-orientated ones; as well as young people who remain excluded from protective systems altogether and are situated within youth justice or adult probation services. It is parents and wider family members who hold together precious elements of a young person's history and who will often remain involved to some degree in their lives long after professionals have receded. The young person's experience of EFRH will have shifted relationships, routines, expectations and dynamics between family members, and often not for the better. A solely youth-centred approach, which focuses primarily on the young person's trauma and agency, and the consequential choices/behaviour they display, will not nurture the informal caringscape of siblings, parents and extended family that provides a wider scaffolding of support and safety for young people into – and often through – adulthood. As well as helping parents rebuild safe and secure relationships with their young people both 'in the eye of the storm' and its aftermath, the whole family will benefit from support in rebuilding routines, boundaries and trust; and ultimately a stable place in which to belong.

A final thought. We do wish to emphasise that our research observations were necessarily partial; occurring as they did at a particular moment in time and place, they cannot be presumed to represent the diversity of practice in the UK. They also capture far more about how systems do, or do not, include families of young people under 18, when responses to EFRH are convened by child and family social work; and hold far fewer insights into how adult safeguarding, probation, mental health or youth justice responses to EFRH frame and collaborate with families. However, we do believe that the common structuring of the meetings we observed, around fast-paced risk-assessment of a number of young people does (a) reflect structures in other systems that coordinate responses to EFRH and (b) undermine the potential for reflective and compassionate discussion of the lived experience, views and potential of the parents, carers and families in these scenarios. Where opportunities for in-depth critical reflection among a professional group is limited, such as in these multi-agency panels, we would suggest that underlying attitudes and professional discourses relating to risk, power, strength, vulnerability, worth and responsibility are more likely to hold sway.

Figure 6.1 illustrates how young people's relationships with families may be responded to in safeguarding systems orientated to the system foundations detailed in Part I of the book: in short, in systems weighted towards radical love, collective responsibility, recognition–respect and the protection of privacy.

Such a system would view and support families and kin of young people in ways that seeks conversation with, rather than control over young people, and would pay attention to the contexts in which families are responding to EFRH. In the process, professionals would be well positioned to see, and further build, love within and between families, and play a role in unlocking resources and services through which such care can flourish.

Figure 6.1: Family relationships in a reorientated safeguarding system

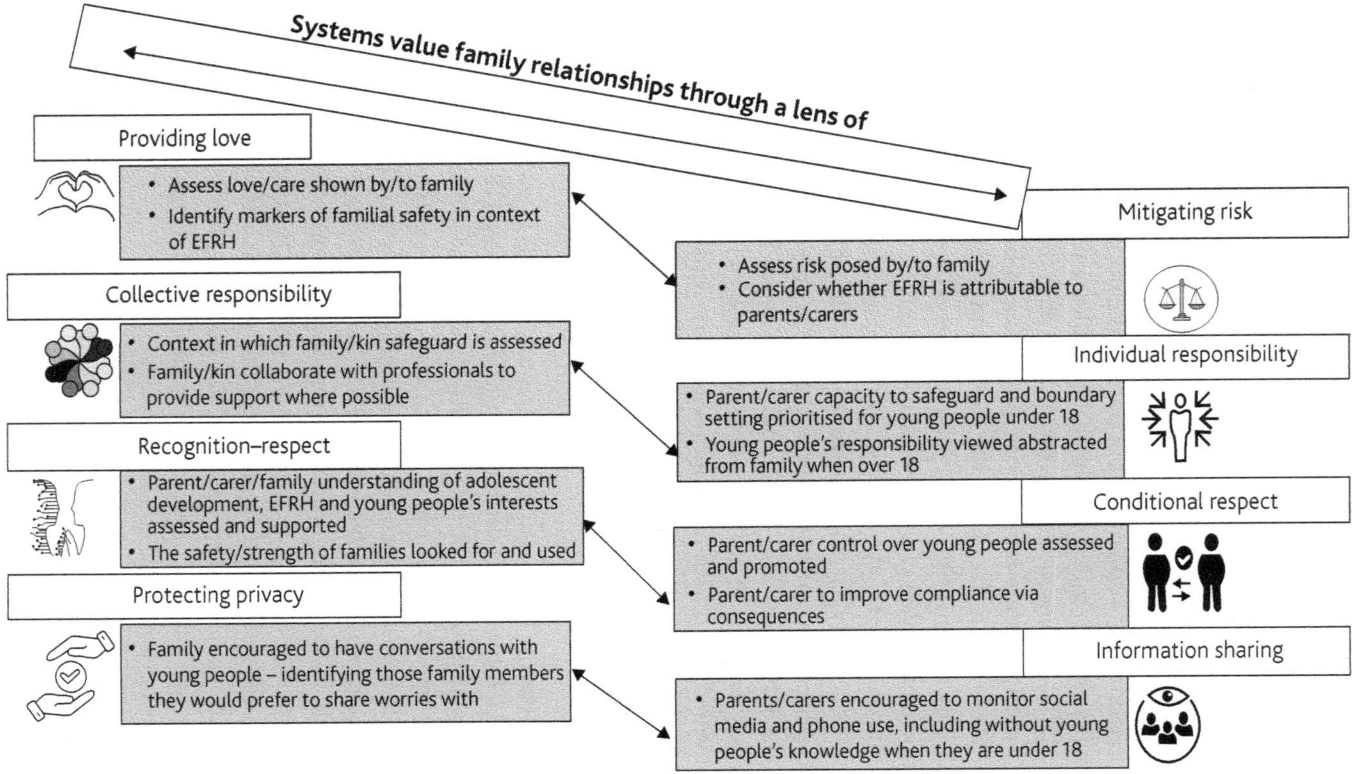

Box 6.1: Reflective questions for leaders and practitioners raised by Chapter 6

1. Think of an example where you/your staff have been open to collaborating with parents and carers as equal partners in supporting and protecting a young person affected by EFRH, and another where this has felt less possible. What cultural norms, personal values and emotions have played a part the degree of trust and openness to parents as allies in each scenario?
2. What would need to change so that your organisation or system would consistently support power-sharing and the reflective and compassionate consideration of the lived experience, views and potential of the parents in situations of EFRH?
3. What would be the first steps for involving parents and carers in designing more collaborative approaches to safeguarding in situations of EFRH?

Resources to support innovation

We suggest reflecting with your colleagues on the 'Next level facilitators' in the resource pack on 'Creating system conditions for ethical and effective innovation', particularly as regards what is needed to mobilise co-production with parents and carers. This set of resources, which were developed through the Innovate Project, can be freely downloaded at: www.theinnovateproject.co.uk/practice-tools/.

7

Friendship, partners and community

One way that we start to realise our increasing desire for autonomy during adolescence is to choose who we spend time with. Our friends are no longer the by-product of playdates our parents, grandparents and other relatives were willing to endure, sipping coffee at soft plays and parks with other adults they could relate to. Instead, our friends are those *we* can relate to or want to relate to; relationships through which we express, and in many respects build, a sense of identity away from adult supervision. We can belong to social structures that we were not born into, and to which we can opt-in and opt-out of accordingly. It is thus unsurprising that extra-familial relationships, including friendships, romantic relationships and wider (informal) community relationships, are viewed as central to young people's sense of safety and well-being.

Having said this, it is important to note that the extent of peer influence during the developmental period of adolescence varies globally and has been highlighted particularly in Anglophone countries (Warr, 2002; Adams et al, 2022). Research in these countries has documented the increasing influence of peer and community relationships on decision-making during adolescence (Cossar et al, 2013; Foshee et al, 2014; Blakemore, 2018; Roesch-March and Edmonds, 2021). Yet such knowledge has not been central to the design of systems used to safeguard young people. Not only have such systems continued to prioritise safety in caregiver–child relationships for young people under 18 (adopting an often narrow and Western view of 'family'), but they often overlook peer and community relationships as an alternative route to safety/protection or source of safety/harm (Rogowski, 2012; Gorin and Jobe, 2013; Johnson, 2013; Latimer et al, 2020; Firmin and Owens, 2022).

In this chapter we explore the ways in which professionals observed within the Innovate Project ethnography attempted, struggled, or neglected, to consider extra-familial relationships in their safeguarding practices. Reflecting on this data in the context of our wider work on extra-familial risks and harms (EFRH) we illustrate:

- how professionals make sense of young people's relationships and what these relationships mean for their safety and well-being;
- what can happen when friendships aren't prioritised as an essential element of safety when young people are being supported by social workers;

- the ways professionals are challenged by wider systems that work against, rather than with, young people's friends, partners and community contacts, and the barriers that this creates to building safety.

In exploring these three challenges we articulate what is missing in our data and reimagine the roles of professionals in creating conditions in which young people can access supportive, extra-familial, relationships that outlive service intervention.

Extra-familial relationships and young people's safety

Friendship is crucial to well-being (Ewell Foster et al, 2017; Rees, 2017), particularly during the period of adolescent development when the significance of our peer and wider community relationships can intensify (Coleman, 2011; Blakemore, 2018). Our friends influence our behaviour, and for young people this shows itself in various ways. Young people can share, reinforce or challenge each other's beliefs via processes of socialisation (Coleman, 2011). They can also influence each other as a desire to belong and cohere to a shared identity (distinct from their families) increases (Barr, 2017). Young people are more likely to accept risks to their health and safety to avoid social risks, for example, to save face in front of their peers (Blakemore, 2018). Whether through socialisation, influence, pressure or a desire to conform, during adolescence we often act in ways that bring us closer to the social norms of our peers (and sometimes distance us from our families), through a desire to belong and achieve social status (in education, when entering the workforce, in communities or in sports clubs, for example) (Henry, 2008; Adams et al, 2022).

Wider social networks – such as with older people in schools and communities – are also critical to young people's development and mental health (Barber and Schluterman, 2008; Oberle et al, 2024). Most young people encounter people who are older than them in the spaces where they spend time daily, and often rely on these people for access to various services – such as bus drivers, shop vendors, park wardens, sports coaches or youth workers. From informal chitchat to personal relationships, there are many opportunities for young people to form a sense of connectedness with people around them, who are not the same age as them nor are they related to them. This is important because it can help young people feel that they 'matter' in their community. The concept of 'mattering' (referenced in other chapters) is also useful in helping us make sense of young people's social relationships. 'Mattering' is experienced both through the development of meaningful relationships – 'a sense of being connected to other people' (Flett, 2018, p 63) – and through feeling that our actions make a 'difference in the lives of others' (Elliot et al, 2005, p 223).

The importance of young people's peer and wider community relationships to their development and well-being, and the proximity of these relationships to the (often unsupervised) spaces where they spend their time, means they can be both a source of protection and potential harm.

For all young people, but especially those living in challenging family circumstances, positive peer relationships offer pathways to form both positive attachments with others and a new sense of self (Coleman, 2011). Friendships and romantic relationships can provide opportunities for pro-social activities and skill-building (Ramey et al, 2022; Veenstra and Laninga-Wijnen, 2023). Friends can influence each other around pro-social behaviours and attitudes – such as healthy living, equality and anti-discrimination, and ambition (Foshee et al, 2014; Laursen, 2018; Banyard et al, 2021; Veenstra and Laninga-Wijnen, 2023). Young people will also often disclose experiences or concerns about abuse to their peers, before seeking advice from their parents or other adults (Allnock and Atkinson, 2019; Brennan and McElvaney, 2020; Russell and Higgins, 2023). Because of these factors, friends and partners can be a young person's safety net.

Yet young people's extra-familial relationships can also be a source of harm or can exacerbate or accelerate young people's exposure to harm. Peer-victimisation is a global problem (UNICEF, 2019). In March 2018 the crime survey for England and Wales estimated that 4.4 per cent of children aged 10 to 15 years (423,000) were a victim of violent crime in the previous 12 months (Office for National Statistics, 2018). Some 92 per cent of these children knew who had instigated violence against them; 86 per cent had attended school with the person/people who harmed them; 13 per cent identified the instigator as a friend (including boyfriend or girlfriend). Concern about peer-instigated sexual harassment, bullying and assault in school and college settings in the UK (BBC, 2015; McGuinness, 2016; EVAW, 2017) resulted in an investigation by the schools' inspectorate in 2021 (Ofsted, 2021) and the publication of specialist advice for schools from the UK Government in 2022. Research into intimate partner violence during adolescence has found that such abuse can be a 'collective' endeavour, with young men's peers, specifically, encouraging them to control their partners (Connolly et al, 2000; Barter et al, 2009; Fox et al, 2014; Gibbs et al, 2015). A recent child maltreatment study in Australia (Mathews et al, 2023) found that the majority of survey respondents nationally who disclosed abuse in childhood said they had been abused by a peer and not an adult.

Young people can also come to harm in wider community relationships. The grooming of young people into exploitative relationships for sexual or other criminal purposes has been documented in the UK and internationally (Pullmann et al, 2020; Wroe, 2021; Benavente et al, 2022; Action for Children, 2024). Young people who lack supportive relationships with adults that they trust and/or don't feel that they belong in their communities can be more vulnerable to these exploitative relationships. Many young people in modern societies experience a 'crisis of mattering' and this interconnects with their experiences of harm (Billingham and Irwin-Rogers, 2020). Young people have reported being increasingly marginalised within their communities, lacking inclusive and safe spaces to spend their time, and being viewed as displaying 'anti-social behaviour' in public spaces (Malone, 2002; Egan et al, 2013; Billingham, 2018; Barron, 2022; Deakin et al, 2022). Austerity measures, combined with the deliberate exclusion of young people from public design and policies, have gone a long way to eliminate safe community spaces for young people in the UK and beyond (Owens, 2002; Davies, 2018), creating contexts that are often hostile to young people – which are often contexts that are ripe for abuse.

Young people's extra-familial relationships, therefore, are instrumental for their well-being, safety and protection. However, until relatively recently, these relationships have been absent from the design of safeguarding systems and practice interventions (Latimer et al, 2020; Firmin et al, 2024). Reviews of service responses to EFRH as it impacts young people under 18 have identified the insufficiency of social care and youth justice approaches to discrete planning around the individual families of young people who only come to harm when they spend time together in peer groups (Rogowski, 2012; Johnson, 2013; Firmin, 2018). Young people themselves have asked for peer and community relationships to be held more in mind when professionals are building plans to keep them safe. For example, a study into young people's experiences of living in domestic abuse refuges with a parent found that young people's peer relationships were often important to them and their well-being but under-recognised by the professionals around them who were largely focused on their familial safety (Bracewell, 2020).

The case for including extra-familial relationships into safeguarding systems seems to be made; how then might this happen or be happening already? And what do these efforts or challenges suggest about what it would look like for our safeguarding systems to recognise and utilise the value of young people's peer and community relationships?

How professionals make sense of young people's friendships and community relationships

In the Innovate Project, professionals saw the value of engaging with young people's friends and drawing on support networks provided by friendships in safety planning.

> [children] listen to their peers. So, let's acknowledge that some of those networks are hugely supportive, and so actually trying to solve the problem of the child outside of those networks doesn't make sense to

> me, whether they're positive or negative networks kids are going to be in them, so we have to deal with that. (Social worker)

In recognition of this, professionals in participating organisations sought to consider young people's friendships and community relationships in various ways. Some updated their referral, assessment and case recording systems to prompt the recording of information about young people's peer and community relationships. On some occasions they then collaborated with young people to generate information that could be documented in these systems, for example, by 'safety mapping' with young people. Safety mapping included working with young people to explore: specific spaces where they felt safe or unsafe; how to identify people who were older than them in those spaces that they trusted and could approach if they were worried; identifying alternative routes for their travel to school, college or work; and connecting them with a youth-facing organisations in the identified locations. We also saw examples of practitioners supporting young people to rebuild friendships. Such work appeared most effective when it was a feature of wider relational approaches, in which practitioners prioritised collaborating and building trust with young people, and in the process learnt about, or spent time, in the places and with the peers that mattered to them (see Lloyd et al, 2023). On occasions, working in this way created opportunities for working with peer groups – for example, to address harmful attitudes and behaviours they collectively shared:

> if the peer group is the place where you know there's unhelpful norms around you know how we treat each other or kind of what's acceptable behaviour, if we can get someone in the room with that peer group that can kind of challenge that thinking, kind of support them to think critically … and that could help that whole peer group. (Social worker)

This also involved recognising the ways in which young people's peers or partners offered them safety and/or stability, for example during a panel meeting which discussed a young man who was working in a garage owned by the father of his girlfriend and professionals considered what might happen if that relationship were to end.

There were also attempts to integrate young people's peer and community relationships within the plans developed by multi-agency safeguarding partnerships. New meetings were established in the research sites that were modelled on child protection conferences but whose purpose was to assess and develop support plans for peer groups or locations impacted by EFRH. This was new and challenging territory, not devoid of ethical and practice challenges, as will be explored later. Yet within them we saw examples of professionals challenging the framing of peer groups as 'disruptive' and 'creating risk' for the community. One of these meetings focused on a group of young people who had been reported by residents as displaying 'anti-social behaviour' in a park. Youth workers spent time with young people in the park and reported back to the partnership that these young people wanted to access activities in the community. In response, the partnership facilitated a 'youth club taster' day in the park where young people met a range of local organisations. This youth work organisation was able to shift the focus of the meeting away from dispersing this group of young people onto the importance of addressing their needs. This approach increased young people's sense of connectedness with other adults and organisations in the community.

In another meeting the friendship between two young men were seen by a police officer as problematic due to concerns around them carrying weapons and being involved in serious violence. While a police officer was keen to separate them, social workers understood that this was unlikely to be successful and instead suggested working with the two friends together. They noted the young men's shared interests as a means of engaging them, as shown in this extract from observation notes taken in this meeting:

> [Early help worker]: I'd be really interested to find out what they are interested in. Maybe we can find an alternative from climbing out the window at midnight. I'm sure we could provide a pot of money for activities.
>
> [Social worker]: they like football. Let's see what we can offer them apart from just the one-to-one work. (Researcher observation notes, multi-agency panel meeting)

What happens when extra-familial relationships are not prioritised in safeguarding systems

While they recognised the value of drawing on young people's friendships or fostering supportive relationships with adults in the community, practitioners did not always feel they had the expertise nor organisational processes in place to do this. Missed opportunities to build safety emerged when professionals did not (or were not able to) meaningfully consider young people's extra-familial relationships. This was reflected in safety plans focused entirely on changing a young person's behaviour despite recorded concerns of EFRH and in written records where professionals often struggled, even when prompted by forms, to identify strengths within young people's friendships or wider community relationships.

Approaches to working with peer groups developed in some organisations were not always welfare-led. In meetings that sought to assess the safety of peer groups, we observed an overreliance on intelligence from the police as a proxy for information about friends. Professionals with direct knowledge of these young people (such as youth workers) were either absent from these discussions or were given fewer opportunities to speak. In these situations, professionals often maintained an overarching focus on risk and criminality within young people's relationships, and were less likely to ask questions about strength or safety, such as: how do young people in the group look out for one another; what are their relationships with other young people and adults; where do they feel safe and unsafe; do they have access to community facilities and resources? Even when information about loyalty and protective factors within friendships was shared, as in this extract from a written assessment of a peer group (also discussed in Chapter 3), this was seldom identified as an area of strength to be built upon: 'the group is very loyal to each other i.e. if one of the group has an altercation or is owed money, the whole group will come together to support the aggrieved' (Written assessment).

Professionals struggled to see how they could build safety for peer groups when the wider system they operated within did not support this. The lack of systems in place to recognise extra-familial relationships, a lack of capacity on the part of practitioners, and their limited expertise in conducting in-depth assessments with groups of young people, were all key challenges. One professional related their frustration with safeguarding meetings where information about groups of young people is shared but no plan is formed: 'We go into those meetings and nobody really knows how to fix it ... that feels quite self-defeating. ... let's have a peer group conference and talk about young people ... at least we've spoken about them, but I've not really come away with a plan' (Social worker).

Even when tangible efforts were made to engage with young people's friendships, these could still be overshadowed by concerns about criminality. One multi-agency safeguarding partnership, for example, sought to address concerns about a group of young people who were at risk of being criminally exploited. The safeguarding partnership, which included professionals from the young people's schools, had built a good understanding of these young people in their community context and youth workers had formed relationships with them as a group. However, 'intelligence' shared about weapon carrying, drug use and concerns about the group forming a 'gang' led the police to deploy civil injunctions to break up the group. A professional who attended this meeting reflected on how this approach had failed to build safety for these young people:

> Those young people don't hang out anymore and offences in the local area have really calmed down ... it tackled the offending, but it didn't tackle the exploitation ... one of the main young people of concern, who happened to be my young person he's still at risk of being exploited, just in another area. (Youth offending worker)

Professionals from the voluntary and community sector were often best placed to draw on their group work expertise and knowledge of communities to engage with young people's friendships. However, they, too, faced important challenges due to the absence of sustained funding and lack of capacity. One youth worker explained how the withdrawal of funding could undermine work with peer groups:

> If you stop working with a group, and you're in a good place where you're starting to build that relationship with them, or you're working on certain things and you get pulled off, they're much less likely to engage with another group of youth workers because they'd be like, well what's the point because they just left, you know. (Youth worker)

Challenges of systems that work against, rather than with, extra-familial relationships

The issues outlined previously are not inevitable consequences of trying to engage with extra-familial relationships. The extent to which social workers and youth workers struggle to work with, and to prioritise and sustain support for, young people's peer and community relationships reflects the systems within which they work. Child protection systems in the UK and in former British colonies are shaped by Western child welfare paradigms that privilege a nuclear family model of care and neoliberal individual risk frameworks over community-led knowledge and care (Featherstone et al, 2018; Mabuvira, 2020; Oates and Malthouse, 2021; Nyamu and Wamahiu, 2022). Social care organisations, and the wider safeguarding partnerships of which they are a part, operate within these paradigms, feature conceptual, legal and practical barriers that produce the challenges outlined thus far. Risk saturates social work responses to young people and, in respect of peer and community relationships, this saturation is multi-faceted.

First, child and family social work in the UK is orientated to risk monitoring and management (Featherstone et al, 2018). Professionals extend this framing to extra-familial relationships, which is reinforced by an evidence base that frames peer relationships, particularly for young people under 25, in relation to deviance (criminology) or fails to consider them at all (child and family social work). Where harm/violence during adolescence has been studied, it often demonstrates that association with peers who are 'violent' or 'deviant' escalates young people's trajectory towards harm. The same level of consideration has not been given to protection from peers. The starting point for increasing social work consideration of peers has been in respect of risk, such that social workers develop this element of their work only when peers are associated with risk, rather than *always* considering young people's extra-familial relationships; it is much less likely that social workers will consider whether and how friends or partners may be a protective factor when young people are living in challenging family circumstances and can only access safety through contexts outside of the home and family. This dominant narrative is reinforced further through the framing within community safety policies (and associated systems) of young people's friendship groups as 'gangs' or 'anti-social' groupings. This is particularly true for young people who are racially minoritised or marginalised in other ways, for young men, and as young people get older (Hallsworth and Young, 2008; Smithson et al, 2013; Williams, 2018). This has led the way for the disruption and dispersal of groups of young people, or decades of discouraging young people from associating or congregating in public spaces, for fear of what 'might' happen, rather than what has occurred. Framings of risk management also pervade how young women's friendships and romantic relationships are perceived by professionals, albeit in different ways. Romantic or intimate relationships are frequently sexualised and moralised, positioning young women simultaneously as vulnerable and responsible for the harm they experience (because of their own failure to 'manage risk'), particularly in relation to sexual harm (Pearce, 2013; Ringrose, 2016; Beckett, 2019; Lloyd, 2022). This trend is particularly pronounced for Black girls, who are disproportionately adultified across child protection and youth justice systems and in schools (Davis, 2022; Hood, 2023; Ikomi, 2023).

Broadening the lens of safeguarding systems to see peer and community relationships also brings connections between young people under 18 and those over 18 into the spotlight. Given the well-founded concerns about the criminalisation of young people aged 18–25 who would have been recognised as exploited up until their 18th birthday (Holmes, 2022), there is a real risk that recognition of community relationships in safeguarding systems may create even further opportunity to sanction young people who remain vulnerable but have aged-out of systems capable of viewing them in that manner (Koch et al, 2024).

Hence, we suggest that the systems we encountered in our study conceptualised extra-familial relationships through a fourfold lens of risk (noting that this lens is unevenly applied to different groups of young people) (Figure 7.1).

The problematisation of peer and community relationships in social work, and wider statutory systems, paves the way for legal challenges. When professionals share information with each other about young people they are required to balance young people's right to protection, to association and to privacy (see Chapter 5). In a risk-averse system we see professionals 'over-sharing', that is, sharing information to pre-empt a 'risky' situation escalating, in the name of prioritising protection. This can include sharing information about young people's peer relationships, including those that are

Figure 7.1: Risk-orientated approaches to peer relationships

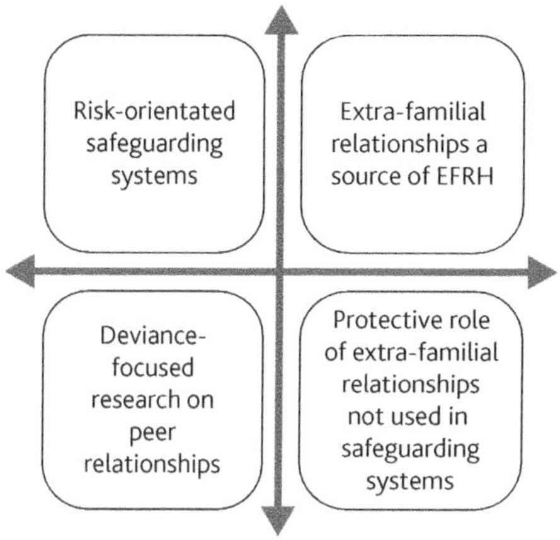

based on hearsay or loose associations, without young people's knowledge or consent. Some professionals may even cite risk as a reason for not discussing this information with young people; 'if they know we are talking about their friends it may make the situation worse'.

Policy frameworks are yet to provide clarity on how to balance privacy and protection when considering peer and community relationships in safeguarding systems. A small number of local authorities have sought their own legal advice to fill the gap (Lloyd et al, 2019; Firmin and Knowles, 2020). However, in this gap legal tensions have emerged as summarised in Chapter 5. Researchers and activists have noted similar tensions in the practice of social workers mapping young people's peer relationships, as detailed earlier in this chapter. Such tensions appear more likely in systems that frame young people's relationships in relation to risk, rather than through safety and care (see Chapter 2). Moreover, when the information used to map peer relationships comes through agency data, such as 'police intelligence', as opposed to from relationships with young people, information on young people's relationships will reflect the bias of those systems: in short, they will disproportionately feature racialised young people who are more subject to police surveillance.

At a practical level (and as noted in various places in this book), individualism still characterises safeguarding systems. The assessment frameworks promoted by statutory child protection guidance in the four UK nations focus on individual young people under 18, and the capacity of their parents and carers to meet their needs; the assessment frameworks for young people over 18 focus on their individual capacity to meet their own needs. Interventions commissioned by these systems are built on case-work models; from youth work through to mental health support and social work intervention, the work of practitioners is organised around the provision of services to individual young people and at best their families (parents/carers and siblings). As such, even if practitioners were able to recognise peer relationships, conceptualise them as valuable/protective and ethically gather or share information about those relationships with young people, a casework-orientated system could quite easily reduce these efforts into practice interventions with individuals who collectively make up a group of friends, rather than *with* that group and their dynamics. Moreover, the tendency in casework models to 'do-to' people, intervene with them and subject them to processes, as opposed to work alongside, collaborate and 'do-with' people, further leans into the legal tensions noted previously. If young people become partners in the design/delivery of planning/support, the issues outlined previously are not challenges any more; in many respects they could become opportunities. Integrating consideration of young people's friendships and other community relationships into safeguarding responses could offer insights previously unseen, including alternative avenues to safety and support. These are system problems, and they can be reimagined.

How systems (and professionals within them) can create the conditions to value the social support provided by extra-familial relationships

There are five ways that systems can create conditions that value, and work with, extra-familial relationships, and overcome the challenges outlined in this chapter.

First, social workers, youth workers and other care-orientated professionals must form relationships with individuals and organisations considered to be informal, non-traditional or non-statutory partners. Efforts to form these relationships cannot be reactive or occur in response to a crisis alone. If these relationships are only formed in a crisis, questions will immediately be raised about procedures, what such partners can and cannot know about EFRH, whether it is safe to involve them, whether it is ethical and so on. Instead, these relationships should be nurtured as part of daily safeguarding practices. Who are the individuals and organisations in any area that young people value, trust and like? Asking young people directly, and/or listening to what they already say through where they go and who they talk about, is the place to start. In some countries, particularly those that have maintained and resourced detached youth work, such relationships are already in place. In other scenarios, particularly those where casework models of practice dominate not only social work but youth work as well, moving response models beyond individual workers being 'targeted' to support individual young people is a bigger and yet essential ask.

In order to foster relationships with non-statutory safeguarding partners in extra-familial settings, social workers need the flexibility to practise differently. The casework model that shapes children services in the UK can restrict professionals' ability to form such relationships. For example, a practitioner might want to support a young person by meeting them alongside their friends. Within the current casework model in the UK, they would need to establish whether these friends were 'open' to the service. If not, the practitioner would need to make the case for them being 'open' to services, but this would require for these friends to be at risk of harm; and if some were over 18 and some were under 18 the situation would become more complicated still. Similarly, if a practitioner wanted to collaborate with a security manager in a shopping centre, or the manager of a bus terminal, the casework model requires for those individuals to be formally associated to a specific young person 'open' to the service – with a corresponding file in the case management system. Under these constraints, practitioners are prevented from engaging with these individuals as non-traditional safeguarding partners who can support all young people they encounter in their professional settings – whether these young people have been referred to statutory services or not.

The justice-orientated logic of casework models – rooted in individuality, certainty and decontextualisation – cannot accommodate the relational, fluid and multi-layered nature of extra-familial safeguarding partnerships. Yet it is precisely these characteristics that constitute their greatest strengths.

Identifying the right extra-familial partners and doing so in a way that honours the system foundations set out in Part I of this book requires collaboration between professionals and young people. When systems recognise extra-familial relationships currently, all too often this occurs in ways that disregard privacy, fails to recognise love or care in those relationships, does little to respect those relationships and struggles to understand the extent and limits of professional responsibility. Adopting a collaborative approach would mean that young people felt able to tell professionals about the relationships they trusted and valued. Such an approach would in turn require professionals to recognise that the relationships young people value may not always be the ones that professionals view as safe or beneficial; and it would mean professionals had to recognise that both love/care and risk might co-exist within the same relationships at the same time. Consent-based connections between safeguarding systems and the extra-familial relationships that matter to young people are essential to the system-reimagining we propose.

Finally, such collaboration becomes possible when extra-familial relationships are framed in relation to safety and strengths first, rather than risks and challenges. In what ways might these relationships be helping to keep young people safe? How can young people's loyalty to each other be harnessed for good? If they want to spend time in the local fast-food restaurant – a place that is familiar, well lit, regularly staffed and used by a range of customers – how can that be leveraged as a source of protection?

While in many ways these four features are the opposite of how our current systems are designed, our research shows that they are feasible. In one research site we saw green shoots that reflected this vision. We witnessed collaboration with young people to identify the friends that mattered to them and the activities that they could do together to build safety – without 'opening' all those friends as 'cases' within statutory services. We observed efforts to involve local businesses and transport providers in safety planning prior to critical incidents. The difference was that this work happened despite, rather than due to, system expectations. It is essential to recognise that such innovative work is near impossible to sustain without wider system buy-in.

From afterthought to a first thought

When it comes to extra-familial relationships and safeguarding, the process of reimagining must be systemic. How we conceptualise, legislate for and practice with young people's relationships all needs to be rethought. This rethinking sits not with individual practitioners but instead with the systems in which they operate. The absence of extra-familial relationships from existing safeguarding systems is not an oversight. Current systems were not designed with them in mind, and much of the research that safeguarding systems draw upon for guidance also either centres parent/child relationships or frames extra-familial relationships in relation to peer-deviance. If services and professionals are to move in their thinking and action to respect the value of extra-familial relationships, take responsibility for nurturing them, and protect their privacy, then this will require a more radical system re-design. Part of this radical rethinking needs to challenge how power and inequalities can shape professional perceptions of extra-familial relationships – and the extent to which they are framed as risky or supportive – in line with international calls for the decolonisation of social welfare to move beyond Eurocentric, bureaucratic practices (Rankopo and Osei-Hwedie, 2011; Pease et al, 2017; Schmid, 2021; Lines et al, 2025).

Simply attempting to integrate peer or community relationships as appendages or afterthoughts to a system that will always struggle to accommodate them is likely to surface the challenges we outline in this chapter. Figure 7.2 illustrates how peer and community relationships would be viewed in safeguarding systems orientated to the system foundations outlined in Part I of this book. If safeguarding systems were transformed in this way they would be capable of recognising, respecting and resourcing the love and care in young people's extra-familial relationships – importantly in collaboration with young people and the people who matter to them.

As such, we recommend that, rather than start by trying to include extra-familial relationships within existing safeguarding procedures and processes, those committed to improving responses to EFRH should focus instead on creating system conditions that can appropriately value and support those relationships, enabling them to flourish.

Figure 7.2: Peer and community relationships in a reorientated safeguarding system

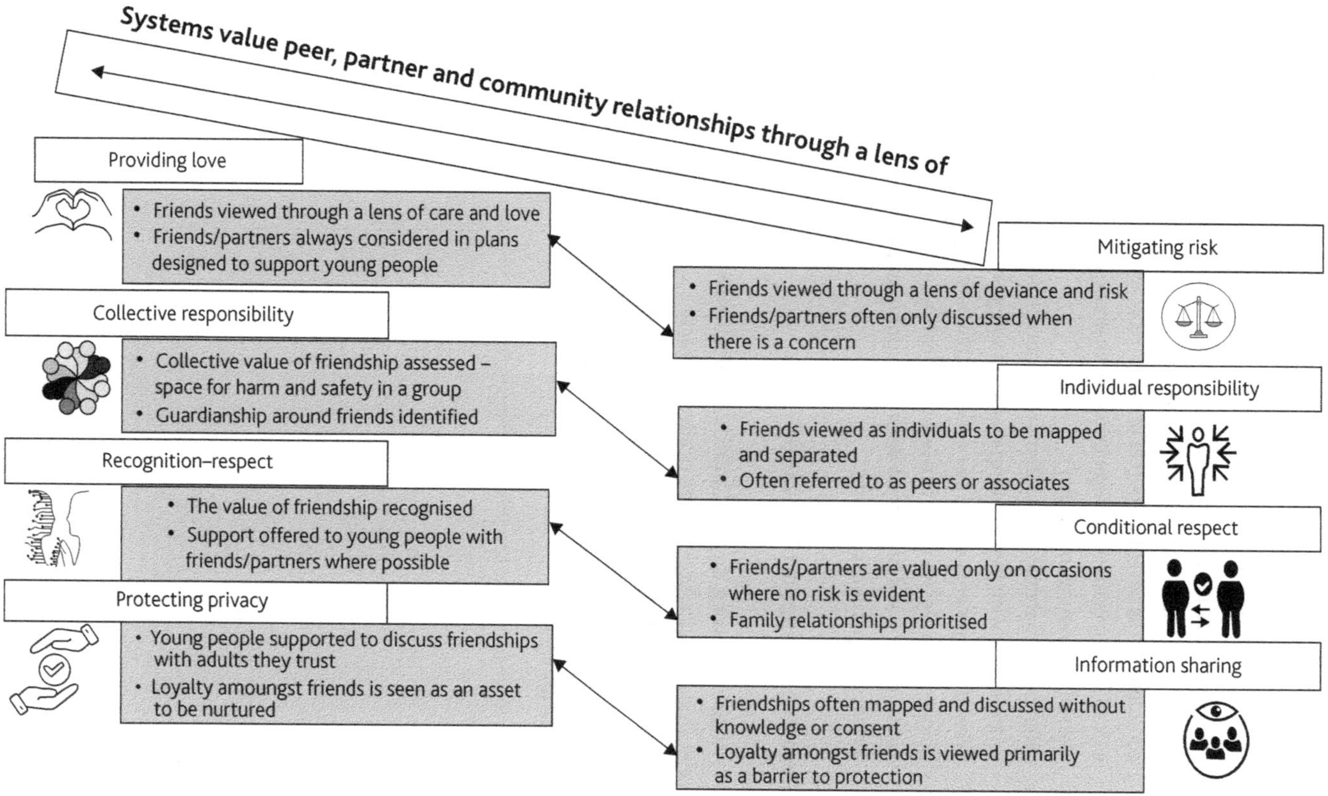

Box 7.1: Reflective questions for leaders and practitioners raised by Chapter 7

1. Do professionals in your service routinely consider whether and how a young person's friends, partners and local communities might play a role in supporting and safeguarding them? Or do these peer and community relationships only come under consideration as potential sources of harm? How are professionals' interpretations of extra-familial relationships influenced (even unconsciously) by gendered, racialised, classed or other assumptions?
2. What needs to shift in your systems to support professionals in forming and nurturing relationships with these potential allies in safeguarding?
3. What developments would be needed within national policy frameworks and local guidance if professionals are to feel confident in balancing concerns about consent, rights, privacy and protection when incorporating peer and community supports within safeguarding systems?

Resources to support innovation

We suggest drawing on the Contextual Safeguarding 'Scale-up Toolkit' to consider what kinds of changes might be needed in practice systems and methods if peer and community relationships are to be fully integrated into safeguarding work with young people. This set of resources, which were developed by the Contextual Safeguarding Team, can be freely downloaded at: https://www.contextualsafeguarding.org.uk/toolkits/scale-up-toolkit/.

8

Professionals

As detailed in Chapter 4 of this book, who is responsible for responding to, and preventing, extra-familial risks and harms (EFRH), and what they are responsible for, has undergone significant change since the early 2000s. In short, social workers, and other professionals with whom they work, have been increasingly responsibilised for responding to EFRH (when it impacts young people under 18). In theory, they are sharing the weight of expectation placed on young people and their parents/carers to be 'responsible' for their safety. More recently, in addition to this mounting accountability for protecting the individuals affected when they are under 18, there has been growing recognition of need to afford appropriate safeguards to young people over 18 (Holmes, 2022; Alliance for Youth Justice, 2025) and of the potential for social workers, youth workers, the police, health professionals, educationalists and others to directly address the contexts within which EFRH occurs and the impact of system/structural harms on those contexts (Action for Children, 2024; Firmin, 2024). Within this book, we are additionally conceptualising professional responsibilities as encompassing an obligation to realise young people's safety by meeting their needs, and not solely by disrupting the (actual or perceived) risks they face. We make this assertion while also acknowledging that in the UK, and in many other systems with a neoliberal orientation, this aspiration is a long way from being made a reality. It is against this backdrop of these obligations and objectives that we go on now to consider existing relationships between young people impacted by EFRH and their relationships with professionals who play a role in supporting them, to paint a picture of what these relationships could be like in the future.

This perspective is relatively black and white, and it is important that we introduce a few shades of grey. First, while generally there is now recognition (within UK safeguarding systems and even in wider society) that young people have been made too responsible for their safety in the past; the balance of this has shifted to a lesser degree for young people who commit offences, or are physically violent to others, in the context of their own abuse, as well as for young people over the age of 18 (see Chapter 4). For these young people, other legal boundaries – of 'criminal responsibility' and 'adulthood' – further complicate the balance of responsibility between young people and the professionals charged with keeping them safe (Action for Children, 2024; Alliance for Youth Justice, 2025). Second, in a bid to recognise the victimisation of young people impacted by EFRH, some professional approaches deny young people's agency completely, directing responsibility solely towards professionals to keep young people safe, despite knowing there will be many situations in which a young person's (often constrained) decisions will be a key contributing factor to ongoing risk (Warrington, 2013; Lefevre et al, 2019). We contend that the relationships that young people have with professionals need to exist in a grey zone where their agency is not denied, and control is not a prerequisite for their protection, but where they can also look to professionals for support and guidance and expect professionals to play their role. To achieve this, we suggest this role needs to move from (1) being responsible for knowing exactly what is going on and how to define or label a type of harm, or (2) changing the behaviour of young people and/or their parents/carers, to actively contributing to conditions in which an alternative way of being can become a reality for young people. In this chapter we ask what types of relationships with professionals might help achieve that reality?

To encourage policy makers, systems and professionals to begin shifting in that direction, we reflect on the 'paradox' that may be encountered in the field of EFRH and why this paradox creates barriers to reimagining the professional role. We explore two related challenges, observed both within Innovate Project data and our wider research over many years, that hinder professionals' collective capacity to facilitate safety, and that affect how practice is organised, how problems are assessed and named, and how professionals feel about themselves, within the context of this work. In addressing each challenge, we suggest how professional relationships might be reimagined as a role that creates the conditions for young people (and the people who matter to them) to thrive.

The paradox

Working with EFRH in any professional role means we encounter the paradox of adolescence – a life stage that requires simultaneously working to achieve independence (and being seen as independent by others) while still being dependent upon the same people you are trying to pull away from (Benjamin, 1988). As with any paradox, the dilemma and the way forward requires accepting, tolerating, respecting the contradictions – and not seeking to resolve them or surrendering to their insolvability (Winnicott, 1971). Holding this tension – avoiding either trying to prematurely resolve or surrender – gives the paradox 'potential space' (Carmeli, 2022, p 97), and in this space there is room for the hypothetical, the possible. According to Winnicott, failure to see a paradoxical reality is a defensive operation of the ego. In the context of EFRH, professionals might encounter both personal and institutional defences against accepting the paradox.

Throughout the Innovate Project, we spent time observing professionals struggle with their own discomfort (that is, of not knowing) and experience collective anxiety when no one in a group of professionals really knew the young people that they had been tasked with keeping safe. Professionals lacked enough information to assess young people's safety or struggled to measure 'progress' for young people who remained uninterested in the interventions that professionals had created or offered. The pull to resolve the paradox here – to avoid the discomfort of not knowing – must have been incredibly strong for these professionals. However, when an individual cannot stay with the paradox, it becomes harder for them to see either the cracks in the system or how, when the system as a collective entity cannot tolerate the discomfort, it pressures those within it to resolve the paradox too early – before anyone actually knows what is going on. It is also more difficult for individuals to bear what might feel like confusing or frightening behaviour by young people; if a professional doesn't come to understand a young person as fast as the system is pressuring them to do so, they can lose confidence – and that is when the paradox becomes intolerable. This pressure, evident within the UK-based Innovate Project data, is seen elsewhere. In Denmark, changes in the youth justice system intended to increase the speed of system responses to young people who have committed offences has resulted in a more punitive and complex system overall (Henriksen et al, 2024). In Sweden, efforts to create new labels for 'sexual risk-taking' (often among girls) have further dichotomised 'good' and 'bad' sexual behaviour, removing the complexity of subjective experience (Wall and Johnsdotter, 2024).

While the pull to resolve the paradox is strong, it is not inevitable. To live with the paradox is to live within the spaces of possibility – to become sceptical of currently available measures of 'success', to understand that so much of the work to keep young people safe is to get it both right *and* wrong, simultaneously, and to retain a radical curiosity as all stakeholders forge a path forward together. In this space, young people's resistance to self-identifying with risk categories or professional intervention can be experienced as hopeful and generative; they are rejecting how things currently are, and leading us subtly towards something more complex, realistic and changeable (Warrington et al, 2024).

If change is needed, to enable new and more functional relationships between professionals and young people experiencing EFRH, we suggest looking at two key issues upholding the status quo: one-to-one casework models of practice and narrowly defined 'ways of knowing' about young people and the harms they face.

Casework-orientated relationships

Individually focussed, one-to-one casework models of service delivery remain pervasive across all disciplines in the field. A young person may have a social worker, a youth worker, a substance misuse worker, a youth justice or probation officer, or any number of professionals involved in their life through health and education. Each professional is tasked with reaching out, organising meetings, developing or delivering targeted interventions (to varying degrees) or providing services to that young person, and reporting back to other professionals the progress they have made within specified timeframes. In order for this to work, young people must agree to meet and engage with professionals and as the risk of harm increases, the list of potential professionals involved with their lives, holding meetings with and about them, often grows (Marsh, 2024). This is, practically speaking, unmanageable. Where it might be considered normative adolescent behaviour for a relatively 'safe' 15-year-old to hide away in his room, ignoring even his parent's bids for conversation or connection, the teens we are most concerned about are often required to meet with ever-lengthening lists of adults who do not have time to slowly build connection and relationships – but just need to focus on their problems. Each of these adults might have a different form to fill out, a different requirement for the regularity of meetings and different timeframes for work. At a point when young people may feel in the least control of their lives (a key feature of exploitation, intimate parter abuse and most other forms of EFRH), professionals are asked to schedule these individual meetings with them during working hours. We believe this casework model contributes to the action plans we observed in the data that focussed on changing the young person's mindset and 'lifestyle' (Phillips, 2025), even when referrals noted significant risk of harm related to the contexts surrounding the young person; or when organisations made efforts to focus on peer groups by mapping who-knew-who and which professionals were connected to each group member. If professionals remain stuck within this casework model, they are all the more likely to focus on (1) changing the young person's behaviour rather than the context, and (2) turning robust contextual conversations about the nature of young people's peer groups, schools or public places where they socialise, into recommendations for individualised interventions. In doing so, they continue foreclosing other possibilities for the kind of relationship they might have with young people.

If we step momentarily outside of this casework model – imagining what it might be like if this was not the standard/normative way of relating to a young person – we might enable professionals to see themselves as part of a community, with the young person, their family/support network and other professionals. As each member of the community holds some responsibility (see Chapter 4), they also hold some information, never a full picture, acknowledging that a full picture is perhaps not possible when EFRH is inherently a moving, changeable risk landscape to navigate. As a member of a community working to collectively safeguard young people, the focus of the work might shift in the direction of creating space for safety (see our further discussion on this, Lloyd et al, 2024) rather than ensuring their individual work with the young person is progressing in accordance with the targets set by their organisation. It may also enable a more culturally responsive and agile approach to creating safety for young people. In an Innovate Project interview, one participant began imagining what this space might feel like, saying: 'I suppose … it's about involving everyone in the discussions as well, giving everyone a voice, both the parents, the children, the community … involving GPs more'.

While the call to work in partnership is not new (see HM Government, 2023), we are suggesting here that a more radical reimagining to partnership working is possible. Innovate Project ethnographic observations of each substantive innovation being implemented all support the argument for rethinking the one-to-one casework approach: for recognising safety as both an embodied, individual experience *and* a context that can be created within peer groups (Contextual Safeguarding); understanding safety through the lens of what feels safe to a young person and what relationship(s) already contain a foundation of trust that can be built upon (Trauma-Informed Practice); and through creating structural change that enables safe continuity as young people age-through and transcend child/adult system binaries (Transitional Safeguarding). While casework models are deeply entrenched, they can be reimagined as a cultural norm, rather than the singular vehicle for intervention and service delivery. Casework approaches can be unpicked and dismantled to make way for more expansive, dynamic approaches to supporting safety from EFRH, just as we saw within Innovate Project observations, as social workers decided to work jointly with young people and their families and challenge system rules to allow continuity of trusted relationships that fell outside of 1:1 commissioning arrangements.

In order to effectively uproot the established one-to-one casework model, enabling professionals to develop new kinds of safe, protective relationships with young people, issues related to identifying, defining and assessing 'risk' – as a proxy for knowing and understanding a young person – must also come under the microscope.

Knowledge-orientated relationships

When child sexual exploitation was identified as a serious concern in the UK following several high-profile incidents of harm (and subsequent insufficient attempts at protection) (for example, Jay, 2014), significant multi-disciplinary efforts were made to define the term (Beckett and Walker, 2017), identify effective approaches to intervene, disrupt those who were exploiting young people and help those they harmed. This work resulted in an advancement of both knowledge and skill in working to support, safeguard and advocate for young people impacted by sexual exploitation (for example, Wroe et al, 2025). However, when the numbers of young people identified as being *criminally* exploited began to surpass those identified as *sexually* exploited (HM Government, 2023), under-resourced local authorities were forced to make even harder choices (Children's Commissioner, 2022) about how and where to direct help. This siloing of different forms of EFRH can be required by funders (that is, when charities are asked to articulate the target population for their service) and professional disciplines such as police and social work, when making their own assessments of risk or harm. Yet it is hard to rank forms of EFRH in order of severity or immediacy, without a wider historical and contextual understanding of each young person who is being, or is at risk of being, harmed. It is also hard to meaningfully categorise or label young people as impacted by a single form of EFRH when many will experience multiple and intersecting forms of harm (Firmin, 2020; Langhoff et al, 2024). Moreover, most young people do not often understand the terms professionals use, nor would they use them, to describe their own experiences of victimisation (Warrington, 2013; Warrington et al,2024). Migrant youth, and those leading transnational lives, might experience additional barriers to understanding terminology that has been developed in such a distinctly British context, along with the 'hyper securitised discourse' (Mansouri, Beaman and Hussain, 2025, p 1) that often surrounds these harm types; and while Black young people's experience of violence may be labelled gang-associated, the same may not apply to a group of their white peers, despite the only visible difference between the two groups being their skin tone (Alexander, 2008).

Yet this focus on obtaining knowledge for the primary purpose of accurately identifying and assessing risk, or ranking harm type and severity, characterised the majority of professionals meetings that we observed during the Innovate Project. When support was organised along the lines of siloed harm-types and/or in accordance with relatively static ratings of severity, we observed this being at the expense of getting to know and help young people through the lens of who they were, in all of their complexity and contradictions, as knowledge – often via 'intelligence gathering' and information systems – was the goal. This level of prioritisation was expressed in written as well as verbal forms. In one site a template to record assessments and plans included a question 'what more do we need know', without a corresponding question of 'what more do we need to do'. We would argue that, sometimes, the efforts professionals make to get these things right are inhibited by the fact that they often just do not know (and cannot know) what is going on. In fieldnotes taken by one Innovate Project researcher observing a multi-agency meeting, she noted how a young person who had been reported as missing from home was discussed by attending professionals:

> He took no money, clothes or other belongings, and there has been no real 'sighting' of him – possibly he was seen by one friend, making his situation 'very underground'. This is not his first 'missing episode' but his longest so far. In fact, professionals had previously been under the impression that he was settling down and making plans. (Researcher observation notes, multi-agency panel meeting)

In this example, no one was in contact with this young person, no one knew how to reach him or why he was missing and, prior to this 'missing episode', professionals had thought he was doing relatively well. In fieldnotes taken by another project researcher during a similarly structured multi-agency meeting, she noted: 'When asked during his LAC [Looked After Child] review what his plans for the future were, he had said "nothing" and that he didn't need any help.' This young person was frequently 'missing', potentially at risk of criminal exploitation and had only recently stopped going to school after a period of stability, during which time he would talk of college applications and a future. In this meeting, the adults in the room once again did not know what was going on, did not know how to improve their engagement with him and so they did not know how to help.

When professionals' roles are structured around evidencing knowledge of a young person, through written or verbal accounts of an identifiable risk category ('is he being criminally exploited?') and evidence of potential harm ('is the likelihood of harm closer to "red" "amber" or "green"?'), the spaces where curiosity, creativity and collaboration might exist are squeezed out because labelling and rating is inherently transactional and definitive. Boxes cannot be half ticked; there is no colour that accurately captures being rated 'green'/safe on Monday, 'red'/high risk on Wednesday, and perhaps – if there is a falling out among friends and a re-ignited interest in school or sport – back to 'green' again by Friday.

This issue of thresholds – and risk ratings – is perhaps commonplace across safeguarding work – not unique to EFRH. However, it is made all the more complex by how little the professionals who are making decisions about a young person's life actually know about who a young person is and what they need or want. In the absence of a real, contextual and relational understanding, professionals might feel compelled to focus their time on piecing together what they do 'know', based on what is held in their systems or 'known by' other services. Yet research indicates that, in the context of EFRH, an overreliance on risk assessment tools comes at the expense of professional judgement (Franklin et al, 2018) and leads to an inconsistent understanding of how interpersonal, contextual and structural risk factors intersect to create vulnerability to exploitation (Mason-Jones and Loggie, 2019). This can create situations in which the adults who know young people best are overlooked. For example, we observed the voices of youth workers (who appeared to have the closest and most in-depth 'soft' knowledge of young people) frequently sidelined or have the information that they shared with others de-prioritised in favour of acting on the 'intel' provided by police. In other situations, the practice of information-gathering in and of itself was viewed as a route to safety, while minimising active consideration of foundational issues such as privacy (Chapter 5), what it means for this to be breached and how the ways in which professionals act on the information gathered is what most influences safety for a child. In the absence of this we wondered at times whether a key function of information gathering is to provide some sense of safety for the professional; particularly given the wider operating context of scrutiny and blame in which they operated (see Chapters 2 and 4).

Over the years, local services in the UK have adapted. Multi-agency panels are now commonplace across local authorities, filling a void created by the lack of detail from central governments about how to organise local services in order to fulfil ever-increasing expectations to safeguard young people from EFRH. These panels often aim to bring all relevant professionals together, in order to improve communication, information sharing and decision-making across organisations. However, a recent 18-month study found that, among children with 'child exploitation flags', only 9 per cent of 'repeat victims' (that is, children who have more than once incidence of exploitation recorded) were discussed in multi-agency panels (Wilson and Mueller-Johnson, 2024). When comparing those who were – and were not – brought to these panels, researchers found no significant differences regarding the harm they sustained. A study in 2026 further questions the purpose of information sharing in panel forums, stating that they primarily appeared to offer multi-agency 'containment' over 'coordination' (Firmin and King, 2026). While it may not be functional to simply get rid of definitions, assessment tools or meeting structures for identifying risk of EFRH, we would argue that it is equally dysfunctional to allow these evidentiary tools and the meeting structures they inform, to replace relational, human and welfare-focussed understanding of a whole child.

Throughout the Innovate Project, we observed professionals trying out new ways of working with, and 'knowing about', young people that foregrounded their collective commitment to young people's safety (for example, as described in Firmin et al, 2024); these gave professionals permission to *not* know, to change plans, and to work flexibly and responsively as they got to know more about the young people they were tasked with making decisions for and about. So, we end this chapter by identifying what needs to shift in order for these new ways of working to shape a new cultural norm within EFRH practice, and for professionals to be able to reimagine their role, within the unique skillset and values of their discipline.

Care-orientated relationships

It is almost a universally accepted mantra, that young people impacted by EFRH benefit from 'trusted relationships' with adults who are invested in their safety (Pearce, 2009; Hallett, 2016; Lefevre et al, 2019). Yet in this chapter we have outlined that, when those relationships are constrained by casework models of support and/or utilised to meet a primary goal of information gathering, they can fall short of what young people need; worse still, they can create conditions which dehumanise, limit and pressurise young people in need of support. This should worry us all, but in our project, we were particularly worried about the implications of this for social workers and youth workers. Whether it was a comment made in a multi-agency panel that a young person would be okay after their social worker left as a local police officer knew him so he still had someone to go to, or situations in which the value of youth work provision was measured via the 'numbers of young people engaged in support' or the fact that they knew young people so could share a lot of information about them in meetings, the value of relationships and their role in providing care for young people was all too easily missed. The worth of a relationship cannot be judged by the extent to which information can be extracted from it; its value must be from the safety it can leverage (both in itself and in connection to others).

To achieve such enriched and enriching relationships, professionals need permission to see themselves as part of a community, to admit what they do not know, to accept a partial or incomplete understanding of a dynamic and changing risk landscape, and to be able to sit together, in support and solidarity, within that grey zone – the discomfort of the unknowable. We saw emergent evidence of this in organisations that were breaking away from the conventions outlined in this chapter. In one research site, during a forum for practitioners, a social worker shared, about another worker: 'I think she thinks that she's doing something wrong, but she's been walking alongside them in the woods and is getting a better understanding of what life is like for them. I'll invite her in to share.'

In the same site we heard meetings in which professionals acknowledged that plans were 'interim' due to limited understandings of what young people needed, and agreed actions that were focused on working with the people, and relationships, that already mattered most to young people. In the process, professionals seemed able to give up some space to hear from the voices of people who often knew young people the best but were less powerful or influential within the system.

In these newly refocussed professional spaces, the work is no longer primarily about assessing risk but about creating conditions where young people can be knowable and where professionals feel safe enough to say the hard or risky things to them. Such conditions involve both relational and practical resourcing: ringfenced budgets for trips to cafes; realistic expectations when paperwork deadlines outpace what a young person who is being exploited might be able to engage with. These changes are structural and may be difficult to gain higher-level agreement for, but we observed many occasions where team leaders and managers were able to just forge ahead in some respects: opening multi-agency meetings by foregrounding information that humanised the young people 'at risk'; leading by example via admissions of uncertainty or worry; and being deeply pragmatic about how to engage with impossible timescales. In doing so, they began creating conditions for the state, through professionals, to reflect love, respect, collective responsibility, a commitment to privacy and respect for rights in their relationships with young people – as we illustrate in Figure 8.1.

In such a reorientated system, we create space for young people's relationships with professionals to be valued due to the care they show, provide and leverage, as opposed to the knowledge they unlock or the casework outcomes they evidence.

Figure 8.1: Professional relationships in a reorientated safeguarding system

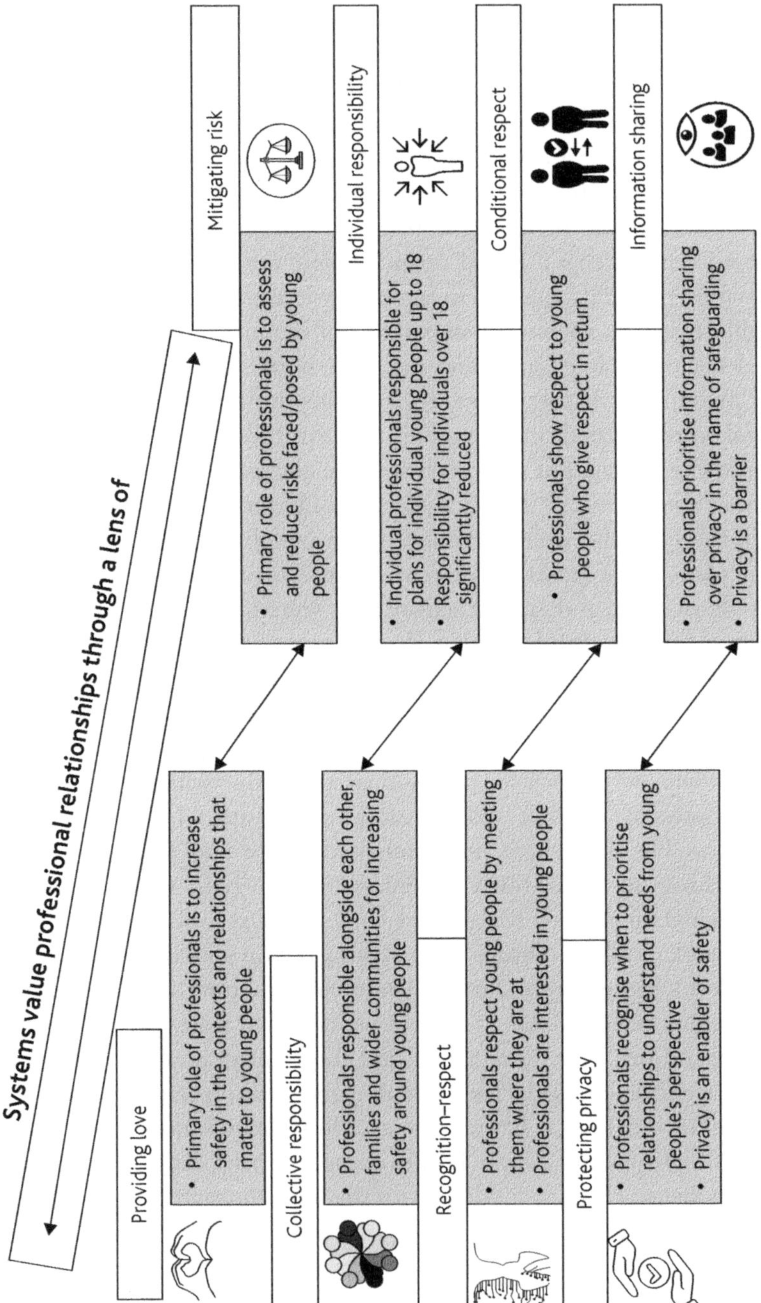

Box 8.1: Reflective questions for leaders and practitioners raised by Chapter 8

1. What signs are there in your organisation or interagency network of professionals being able to sit with anxiety and maintain curiosity in the face of a dynamic and changing risk landscape – or is the reverse apparent?
2. To what extent do care-orientated relationships predominate over information-orientated ways of working by professionals in your system?
3. In what ways do cultures and structures need to shift in your organisation or interagency network to bring about more human-centred ways of getting to know, understand and value young people as the unique individuals they are?

Resources to support innovation

We suggest drawing on the visual of 'Creating a conducive zone for innovation' which is figure 1 in Lefevre et al (2025). This diagram, created through Innovate Project research, will enable you and your colleagues to consider the extent to which your organisational culture and climate is conducive to the innovation that would be necessary to bring about the previously recommended changes.

PART III

System goals

9

Safety and justice

With the foundations of love/care, respect, responsibility and privacy underpinning a system, and young people's relationships with family, friends, community and professionals reimagined within it, what goal then should such a system pursue?

To begin to answer this question, in this chapter we return to where this book started – the goal of safety. We outline how we might design systems with the primary purpose of increasing young people's access to safety, as an antidote to the goals of risk reduction/mitigation that often dominate our existing cultures and structures. We present safety as multi-dimensional, complex and defined by young people. As we have noted throughout this book, young people's experiences of safety, the extent to which their voices are heard, their rights are respected and the types of interventions they receive are far from homogenous. In exploring safety as nuanced and multifaced, we also describe ways in which justice may contribute to safety, moving beyond criminal justice outcomes as a route to safety to also include (and at times prioritise) social and epistemic forms of justice as a means of providing safety. As such, we identify ways in which justice can contribute to safety, as well as ways in which a pursuit of justice could undermine safety; thus, we move beyond care/justice ethical binaries and towards carescapes in which both can co-exist but with justice subsumed within the primary goal of safety.

Approaching safety holistically

This book proposes new ways of conceiving and designing systems that enable young people to live fuller and safer lives. We believe safety is something to be built with young people – not managed on their behalf. To create safety *with* and *around* young people, we need systems that understand and engage with their varied experiences of safety: physical, relational and psychological (Shuker, 2013). These would be systems that love, care and respect young people, do not responsibilise them for the harm they experience, that protect their right to privacy and centre collaborative relationships between young people and professionals, their families, their peers and communities. Such systems can build an ecological understanding of how young people experience physical, relational and psychological safety beyond their front doors. What makes them feel safe or unsafe with their peers, at school/college/work, in public places and online? What would make them feel safer? And who has the capacity to increase safety in these spaces? We cannot know this unless we ask young people. When professionals asked these questions during the Innovate Project, they were able to come up with creative responses tailored to young people's needs in contexts. For example, when mapping safe or unsafe places in the community with young people; or acknowledging peer relationships as young people's safety nets and therefore working with friendship groups to harness safety (and challenging calls to disrupt these relationships); or connecting groups of young people with youth services as a collective effort to safeguard them together (see Chapter 7).

Taking a holistic approach to safety can help professionals understand the impact of the support they are providing young people and amend plans accordingly. For example, a team of researchers led by Lauren Wroe used Shuker's multi-dimensional model of safety to understand young people's experiences of relocations, when they were moved out of their local area due to extra-familial risks and harms (EFRH). The team's work highlighted a sense of ambivalence among young people who had been moved away from their families, friends and local communities. This was communicated by young people through vague responses and physical shrugs. Young people suggested, not without some uncertainty, that relocations often achieved physical safety at the expense of their emotional and relational safety when used in ineffective conditions (Wroe et al, 2023). The study also showed how professionals manage risk through relocating young people without always considering their needs/preferences or exploring alternative ways of keeping young people safe in their communities. In the absence of sufficient safety planning, young people were relocated to manage their physical risk, while at the same time being exposed to various relational and emotional harms, and other forms of physical risks through increased missing episodes, limited professional relationships, isolation from family, peer and community networks, disrupted education and/or poor mental health support (Wroe et al, 2023). Similar concerns have been raised about the volume of young people subject to Deprivation of Liberty Orders in the UK, in a bid to protect them from experiences of EFRH (Nuffield Family Justice Observatory, 2025). In the absence of alternative policy and practice frameworks to address EFRH, other countries in Europe, the US, Canada and Australia among others are also using out-of-home care, including residential children's homes that are a significant distance from young people's home communities and secure settings that deprive young people of their liberty, for their own protection (OSCE, 2019; Aussems et al, 2020; Pullmann et al, 2020).

Young people's experiences of safety are thus integral to safety plans. This might seem obvious, yet we encountered few examples of professionals discussing young people's *feelings* of safety during the Innovate Project. When we did, it was a stark contrast with the way we saw young people described elsewhere – as illustrated in the following extract taken from observation notes of a practitioners' meeting that discussed a young woman who had just returned from secure care:

> She was returned back to the community and there was a lot of anxiety around that. What would her care plan look like? … Got agreement that we could build a bespoke care plan that would meet her needs. … Relationships with this young girl made her feel safe and when she didn't feel safe all of the risk factors came to the fore. She's feeling so safe, so regulated, she's travelling independently, taking herself to doctors and dentist appointments, completed a week's intro to college. She was self-harming every day and suicidal ideation but now hasn't scratched herself for six weeks. She's had significant triggers – death of an aunt, relationship issues with her mum, breakdown of a friendships. We've been blown out of the water by her progress. She called me and thanked me because she feels like we're listening to her. Staff are coming on shift and saying I know you want to do this. We don't hear enough of the positive stuff, but we've had a period of six weeks where she's been so settled. I wanted to highlight the really positive relationships. Knowing people had her back and that we're fighting her corner and the feeling of safety she has paid massive dividends. (Researcher observation notes, practice development session)

In this extract the practitioner discussing this young person referred to her feeling of safety four times, foregrounding this young person's relational and psychological safety and demonstrating a caring and strength-based approach. Relationships are centred as key to the young person's feeling of safety. Indeed, the solid relationships between professionals and this young person are evident and reflect the types of relationships we propose in Chapter 8: consistent, trusting, collaborative and respectful of their autonomy and agency (Gilligan, 2014; Ellis, 2018; Aussems et al, 2020).

Across the sites, we saw stark contrasts between responses to young people who were 'known to services' and situations in which young people were truly 'known by professionals' (Firmin et al, 2024, p 1). In sites where young people were 'known to services', professionals' decisions were driven by risk-management, based on information obtained from services/systems without involving young people. Whereas in sites that foregrounded relationship-based practices, professionals made decisions that were informed by a relationally driven understanding of young people's needs before young people felt safe enough to share their concerns (Firmin et al, 2024) and were better equipped to understand and create safety in the places and peer relationships that were meaningful to young people (Lloyd et al, 2023).

Often, professionals we engaged with really did value relationships with young people; but these relationships were overshadowed by wider system features:

> as a social worker you're working in a system that is just … very challenging because you might personally want to you know be person-centred and strengths based, but actually because resources are so limited and you only have a certain amount of time and you don't have the time to build up that relationship and you're probably starting your assessment from a perspective of you know where's the harm and who's responsible for it, rather than, how can I help you? What can I do to help you? (Social worker, interview)

Whereas when processes were amended and reimagined to centre young people's voices, practitioners were able to build safety plans with them, as in this quote referring to a new type of child protection meeting that was developed in one of the research sites to address risks to young people outside of their home in which young people were invited to participate:

> I think it's really enabled professionals as well to treat the young person in a different way. So instead of it being that the child's sort of separate and we put these expectations on parents, the way I've done it is that the young person attended the meeting, we've made a safety plan with her. So, the professionals are then all part of that, her voice is heard … she knows what's expected of everyone else, and it's really … it's like a really restorative way of working with her, by saying what can we do to support you with this? (Social worker, interview)

At times, when relationships between young people and professionals are new and do not feature the level of trust needed to facilitate joint safety planning, practitioners can engage with and attempt to create safety in contexts around that young person, such as through providing support to their families or engaging with their peer groups, as illustrated in this extract:

> if we've received a referral for a young person and we've met them and … we're unable to engage them at that point but we're still concerned and think that some support would be helpful we won't sort of pressure the young person to work with us … so maybe we'd offer support to the parents instead to help them support their child in a different way. And then we might then expand that to think about you know if we get information from mum and dad, you know, that what they're

> really concerned about is their child's friendship group, then that might give us an opportunity to speak to the school, that would then help us think a little bit differently about how we offer an intervention. (Social worker, interview)

Why pursue safety? The issue of de-centring risk management

Professionals operate in systems that seldom enable them to explore and build safety with young people. National reviews of England's response to EFRH specifically (Action for Children, 2024) and its social care system generally (McAllister, 2022) have highlighted ways that child protection systems in particular, as originally designed, fail to create safety for young people at risk beyond their homes. Beyond failing to provide safety, such systems have also been found to do further harm when their ability to provide safety is not interrogated, and such harm disproportionally impacts young people who are racially minoritised, older or marginalised in other ways (Davis and Marsh, 2020; Wroe, 2022). We have illustrated this matter in every chapter of this book. Our proposed reimagining of current ways of working is counterposed to systems that centre risk and in doing so fail to show young people love and offer them care (Chapter 2); disrespect young people's views when they are considered risky or at-odds with how professionals view risky situations (Chapter 3); responsibilise young people for making 'risky' choices (Chapter 4); breach young people's privacy due to perceived risks of not doing so (Chapter 5); frame collaboration with young people's families as 'risky' (Chapter 6); view young people's friends through a lens of risk alone (Chapter 7); and constrain the capacity of professionals' to do what young people may need, when to do so would be contrary to how risk-averse systems operate (Chapter 8).

Using data from the Innovate Project we can evidence the ways that risk-orientated systems shape the nature of safety plans. First, we observed meetings and analysed case files in which 'safety plans' were organised around reductions in risk. These plans were used to support young people to navigate or stay away from risky contexts, rather than increase safety in the contexts within which they came to harm. Actions included raising young people's awareness of specific issues/risks or supporting them to engage in positive activities away from their usual contexts, as illustrated by these extracts from research observations:

> [Researchers' notes]: from the intervention plan it seems the onus is largely on the young person to 'keep away' from risky associations and engage in positive alternative activities (such as joining the gym and finding a job). (Researcher observation notes, multi-agency panel meeting)

> [Researchers' notes]: This young person appears to have experienced a lot of trauma. It seems that he is still at risk in his community though the degree to which this is the case is unclear – the case file primarily focuses on the young person's desire to break away from 'gang associations' [as described in the case file] and action plan places the onus entirely on young person to essentially come up with a plan for his life. (Researcher observation notes, multi-agency panel meeting)

When these plans were developed in meetings, or documented in case files, young people were tasked to 'keep themselves safe' and avoid 'putting themselves' at risk, as illustrated by the following extracts:

> [Young person] is aware of areas in which he is unsafe and states he is making wiser decisions, when outside, to ensure he prevents himself from getting into bad situations [Social work case files]

> [Researchers' notes]: Risks around child sexual exploitation appears to be addressed primarily through the lens of individual behaviour change, once again using language that frames the exploitation as the result of a personal choice: [extract lifted from assessment] 'Work to be done around child sexual exploitation and encouraging [young woman] to make positive choices around her own safety' [Social work case files]

Research shows how blaming narratives of risk in safeguarding, such as those illustrated in these examples, tend to align with racialised or gendered assumptions (Smithson et al, 2013; Davis, 2022).

Second, when plans looked beyond individual young people and instead intended to target contextual drivers of harm, they were often also risk-orientated. Such plans largely relied on policing and community safety techniques to disperse or disrupt risk in extra-familial contexts – without considering whether such approaches increased young people's access to safety. These techniques were evident even when sites were attempting innovative responses to peer groups and public spaces. While professionals clearly had a desire to create safety holistically with and around young people, they often relied on policing or surveillance methods to achieve this, and these methods were not designed with safety in mind. The following extract from observations notes of a meeting which aimed to create safety around peer groups illustrates this conflicted approach. In this meeting, professionals agreed on the use of civil orders to 'disperse' a group of young people from an estate where they were spending time together following complaints from residents:

> [Researcher's observation notes]: [The chair] suggested as an action that Housing should be part of this discussion and that the group could look at disruption activities that might deter having young people come to the estate. He did note that he anticipated this may end up moving the problem elsewhere but that it might resolve some issues at this address.
>
> [Youth Offending practitioner] will organise an urgent meeting with the safeguarding officer to look at the best way to move forward using civil orders and acknowledge the need to work collaboratively. (Researcher observation notes, multi-agency peer group meeting)

It is not surprising that the desire to manage risk is so prevalent across our systems. Risk management has been at the centre of Western bureaucratic and managerial cultures that have pervaded social work in the UK, ex-British colonies and other Western countries, driven by New Public Management reforms keen to remould the public sector according to private sector criteria of performance and efficiency (Lapsley, 2009; Munro, 2011; Parton, 2011). The impact of this culture on the UK's response to EFRH was made clear in March 2015, when the then UK Prime Minister David Cameron gave a public response to an independent inquiry report into child sexual exploitation (CSE) in Rotherham: 'Today, I am sending an unequivocal message that professionals who fail to protect children will be held properly accountable and council bosses who preside over such catastrophic failure will not see rewards for that failure' (Prime Minister's Office, 2015).

Cameron's speech famously announced a set of new measures to increase the accountability of professionals, making social workers and local officials across the country liable to five years of imprisonment were they to be found guilty of 'wilful neglect' in cases of child abuse (Prime Minister's Office, 2015). Such a position failed 'to acknowledge the wider context of contemporary child welfare issues' that impede social work practice (Crossley and Leigh, 2017, p 24) – issues we outline in this book – and reinforced a position that safeguarding systems work from a position of threat, risk and fear – rather than safety, care and hope.

Not only are professionals safeguarding young people from EFRH working within a system under incredible pressure, but their work is by nature anxiety-inducing as it involves potential serious harm to young people. This anxiety is compounded by the fact that responding to EFRH is an emerging area of work for social workers, often necessitating a significant shift in organisational cultures and practices; while at the same time navigating great uncertainty, social care reforms and shrinking resources (HM Government, 2023; Murphy, 2023; Firmin, 2024; Firmin et al, 2024). Risk-orientation therefore shapes, and impedes, systems from various angles: risks young people face and pose; risks practitioners face when responses are ineffective; and risks organisations face when practitioners struggle.

In some ways, we can see mirroring in how blame is placed on individual practitioners (like it is on individual young people) rather than recognising how organisational processes and cultures (shaped by wider policy frameworks and discourse) can influence and/or constrain their choices and actions. Just like individuals, organisations that are not emotionally contained can act in ways that defend themselves from the anxiety and pain that the work generates (Rush, 2011; Lefevre et al, 2024). This was suggested across research sites by language used in safeguarding or child protection meetings that translated an anxiety to protect organisational reputation by evidencing that the right processes had been followed, that things were being done in the right way. It was manifested through an urgency to 'track' levels of risk on matrices, update information records and demonstrate the disruption of risk.

Holistic approaches to creating safety for young people can uphold young people's rights to protection from harm in these spaces, and, at the same time, help professionals ensure that interventions that seek to protect young people centre their welfare and best interests. This caused us to wonder, are such actions taken because it is believed they are the best way of helping a particular young person – or more to protect an individual or service from the danger of being perceived as not doing enough should things subsequently go wrong (Munro, 2019)? When seeking to answer these questions we suggest it is imperative to not only consider what is *safe* for young people but also ask what would be *just*.

Safety as a route to justice

Our ability to move beyond risk-focused systems and towards safety-orientated systems will be informed by how we approach the concept of 'justice'. In different ways in this book, we have called for justice to be de-centred. A call to ground systems in an ethics of love and care (Chapter 2) could be interpreted as a move away from a justice ethic (Tronto, 2005), particularly when the proposed ethic is relational and contextual, as opposed to rational and individual (Gilligan, 1982; 2023). Arguing that young people's relationships with the police (Chapter 8) should be significantly reduced in systems orientated around well-being, flourishing and decriminalisation again reduces the role of justice agencies. In some respects, it would be right to conclude that we are calling for a reduced focus on justice. However, in this book we propose that justice is reimagined within, rather than removed from, safeguarding systems. This entails reducing the dominance of criminal justice frameworks, and increasing consideration of epistemic and social justice, in systems charged with keeping young people safe. It is through these broader conceptualisations of justice that we believe we can create conditions conducive to young people's multidimensional safety (as outlined previously).

Proponents of a 'care ethic' (Tronto, 2005; Steckley and Smith, 2011) position it at odds with a 'justice ethic', on the basis that the former values context, relationships and interdependence and the latter values rational thought and individualism. This framing of a justice ethic is familiar to criminal justice interpretations of justice. One pursues justice through the identification and punishment of individuals that have done wrong; context is for the most part screened out of the process. Lloyd et al (2023) articulated this well when they conceptualised what a welfare-orientated response to EFRH would entail. They argued that services created the conditions for welfare-orientated practice when they centred young people's needs, led with a caring tone and intention, and built knowledge relationally (all akin to a care-ethic), whereas services that centred risk-mitigation (instead of meeting need), led with a fact-based and intelligence tone, and gathered information through agency systems (rather than relationships) did not facilitate practices reflective of welfare-orientation. In this book we have built on the framework offered by Lloyd and colleagues to articulate the foundations (Part I), and the relationships (Part II), through which such welfare-orientated conditions can be sustained.

This is not to say that there is no place for criminal justice practices within the systems we envision. However, the dominance of this aspect of justice would be greatly reduced if criminal justice interventions were to play a small role within wider welfare-orientated systems. In our reimagined system, criminal justice goals are not goals in and of their own right but practices to be drawn upon to realise goals of safety, or to meet needs, as outlined earlier in this chapter and throughout this book. In doing so, there is a place for the criminal justice system to intervene when children and young people have been harmed, particularly when such intervention will bring about safety for young people. However, such an intervention, without consideration of safety, is not of value – and, we suggest, all too often safety is an afterthought at best, or at worst disregarded, when in pursuit of criminal justice goals (Wroe, 2021; Marshall, 2023).

But this is not the end of the justice story. Our book has signalled that other forms of justice not only have a place in, but may serve to enable, welfare- and care-orientated safeguarding systems.

Epistemic and relational forms of justice are pivotal to systems we propose. Epistemic justice is often defined in relation to Fricker's (2007) conception of 'epistemic injustice', described as being when individuals' experiences are discredited, their views silenced, and they are disregarded as holders of knowledge. The concept sheds light on power imbalances between diverse epistemologies and belief systems shaping the production of knowledge. Children and young people whose voices are excluded are prevented from influencing social work interventions and policies that directly affect them (Dore, 2019; Dillon, 2021). Giving young people a voice in research, enabling them to exert choice, agency and control in practice and in decision-making about their life, is central to their experiences of physical, emotional and relational safety – and can form part of a trauma-informed response (Hamilton et al, 2019; Warrington and Larkins, 2019; Hickle, 2020). Yet, in the UK and internationally, children and young people's voices remain largely absent from safeguarding meetings and processes (Van Bijleveld et al, 2015; Dillon, 2021; Abela et al, 2024; Firmin and King, 2026). Decolonial perspectives offer us a route into epistemic justice by critiquing the devaluation of non-Western culture and indigenous knowledge at play in child protection systems (Leckey et al, 2022; Nyamu and Wamahiu, 2022).

Relational justice is closely connected to epistemic justice. Drawing on Lynch et al's (2016) conceptualisation of relational justice, Hanlon describes it as foregrounding 'the centrality of affective relations in equality' and 'of love, care, and solidarity to all social life and human wellbeing' (Hanlon, 2022, p 578). Epistemic justice in social work is crucial to relationship-building (Bostock and Koprowska, 2022) and, in turn, relational practices can facilitate epistemic justice. Hanlon highlights relational justice as central to social care, intersecting with other injustices, and requiring 'a political rather than a purely individualist ethic of care in practice' (2022, p 580). Thinking about safety holistically means thinking about justice holistically – and situating individuals, and the harm they experience, within the wider socio-economic and politic contexts that shape their experiences of harm and safety. This brings us to the final form of justice we would like to highlight in this chapter: social justice.

Relational and epistemic justice can bring attention to, and contribute to redressing, social injustice. Systemic inequalities are increasingly recognised as safeguarding issues (Wroe et al, 2023; National Safeguarding Panel and Davies, 2025), disproportionately affecting certain groups of young people, including those who are racially minoritised or have insecure immigration status (Horgan and Ní Raghallaigh, 2019; Davis and Marsh, 2020). These same groups of young people, along with those experiencing EFRH more broadly, are also those disproportionately harmed by criminal justice systems.

Asking young people holistically about safety, and recognising the impact of social conditions facilitative of abuse and harm, can help reveal the broader systemic issues at play that contribute to harm (Beckett, 2011; Melrose and Pearce 2013; Featherstone et al, 2018) and undermine young people's economic, social and cultural rights (such as their right to recreational spaces, job opportunities and so on), in turn restricting their ability to live safe and fulfilling lives. When creating safety with and for young people, we – researchers, practitioners, system leaders, policy makers – should therefore consider how interventions uphold these rights. Our research, however, found that when responding to EFRH through approaches that prioritised risk-reduction (as described previously), systems operated in ways that were often epistemically unjust. And when assessments did acknowledge a wider systemic issue (such as family poverty or housing conditions) safety plans rarely addressed them. Instead, as outlined in this book, plans focused overwhelmingly on the individual behaviours of young people and/or their parents/carers. We argue that this undermines principles of social justice.

Creating systems that prioritise young people's safety

When agreeing responses to EFRH, therefore, we suggest that one question should be under continual consideration: whose safety is foregrounded by the approach taken? The safety of young people or the safety of organisations who play a role in protecting young people?

If young people's safety and well-being is to remain centred, then the way they see the world needs to be fully understood. Owens et al's concept of 'relational epistemic safety', acknowledging the interweaving nature of epistemic and relational justice, offers a way to guide us through this: 'for a relational orientation to be achieved, professionals need to be guided by how young people know the world. We argue that this requires professionals to undergo a process of "undoing": giving up privileged ways of knowing and making decisions' (Owens et al, 2024, p 1).

Owens et al consulted with 66 young people who were existing or potential users of safeguarding services in relation to experiences of EFRH about what they needed in relationships from professionals tasked with creating safety. Young people wanted: professionals that cared about them and with whom they could share a social connection; equality in relationships, particularly around decisions about safety; for professionals to hold accurate, nuanced and developmentally appropriate perspectives about them, grounded in understanding of their lived realities; and for the support that was offered to align with these perspectives. Drawing on these findings, the authors developed a 'Young People's Relationship Framework' to help practitioners prioritise these factors in their relationships with young people (Owens et al, 2024).

Understanding young people's experiences and needs is the first step in prioritising their safety. Alongside this, as discussed in Chapters 2, 7 and 8, professionals need to consider who, beyond young people's parents/carers, has the capacity to safeguard them in the places where they spend time, and where they experience EFRH. These people can be anyone – other professionals, volunteers in community organisations, business owners or residents – who are present in the spaces where harm happens and who can not only look out for young people by reporting concerns, but who can also create safety by offering young people safe relationships and safe places where they can spend time. For example, detached youth workers getting to know young people in a park; the local sports provision organising football games on a Friday night, when young people have nowhere else to go; or public libraries providing teenage-friendly spaces. Again, we emphasise the importance of asking young people themselves whether there are people who are older than them, and who they already know and trust, in these spaces.

Finally, and just as importantly, safety assessments and plans need to account for the wider environmental factors that can influence the safety of a peer group or a location such as: physical features; community resources (activities available to young people); recent or recurring issues that might affect young people (including systemic ones, like racism, poverty and inequality); safeguarding policies; and cultural norms and socio-political narratives that can influence how young people are portrayed and perceived by the public. This involves considering how safety is defined and experienced differently by young people based on intersecting identities. Professionals and systems' understanding and definitions of safety might not reflect the lived realities of young people.

When all three key aspects of safety are triangulated – young people's experiences and needs, the presence of people they trust and the nature of the environments they spend time in – and when this is done guided by caring and equal relationships with young people, we would suggest that the resulting plans and responses are more likely to deliver both safety and justice.

Figure 9.1 illustrates the ways in which the reorientated foundations, and associated relationships, that we propose in this book could get us to this goal of safety and justice for young people impacted by EFRH.

Collectively these foundations and relationships create systems in which the things, people and feelings that matter to young people can be recognised and respected; with the hope that even in this process itself we begin to tell a different story about the roles of safeguarding systems in the lives of young people impacted by EFRH.

Figure 9.1: Goal of safety and justice in a transformed safeguarding system

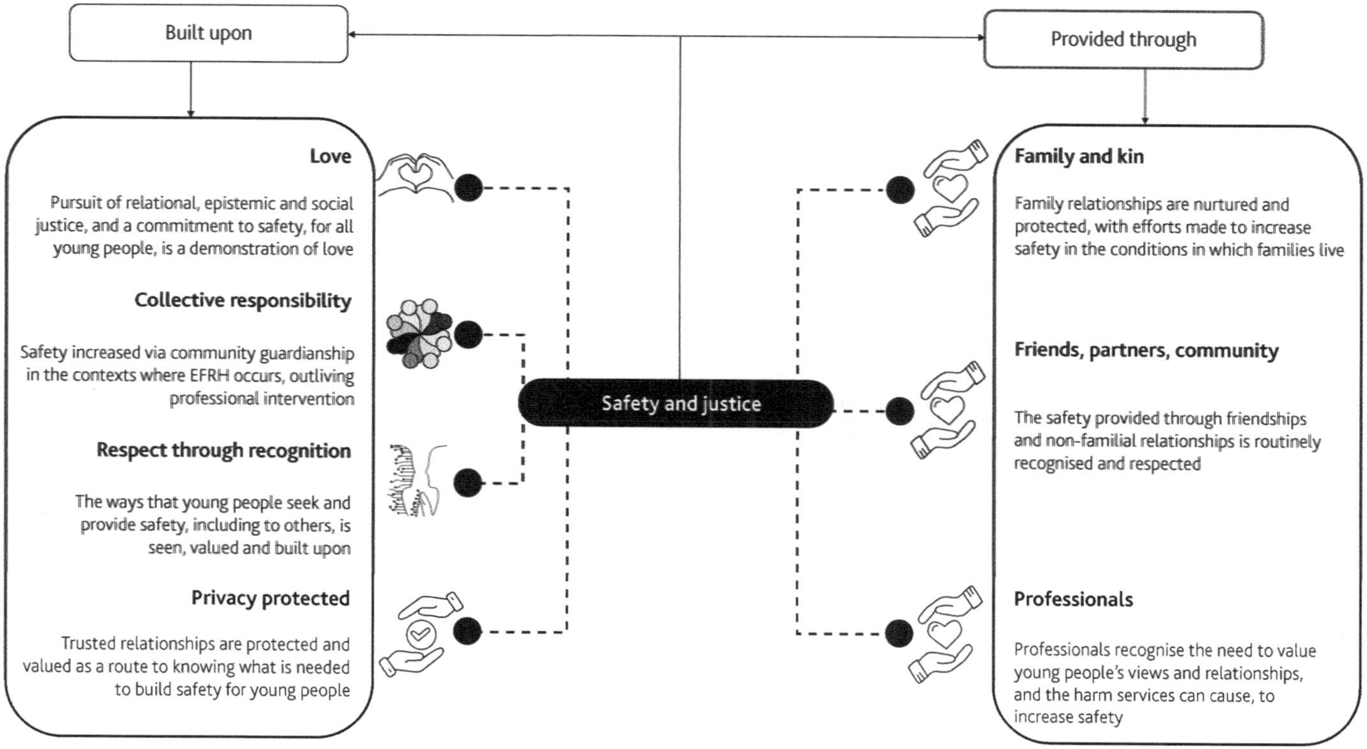

Box 9.1: Reflective questions for leaders and practitioners raised by Chapter 9

1. To what extent do your (inter-)agency systems ensure that a young person's views, their safety and principles of social justice are consistently centred in assessment and intervention, rather than professional self-protection in conditions of uncertainty?
2. In what ways might local guidance, organisational cultures, distribution of resources or practice methods need to be challenged and reshaped to ensure a more justice- and welfare-orientated route to safety for all young people?
3. Who would need to be persuaded that such change is necessary and what might the first steps towards change look like?

Resources to support innovation

We suggest using the 'Stages of Innovation Framework' to help you reflect on how to mobilise innovation through envisaging new possibilities and getting stakeholder buy-in. This tool, which was developed through the Innovate Project, can be freely downloaded at: www.theinnovateproject.co.uk/practice-tools/.

10

Needs and flourishing

One of the injustices that characterises the current status quo is the tendency of systems to respond to extra-familial risks and harms (EFRH) using the services that are available, and the practice frameworks that drive them, rather than the support or interventions that young people need and want (Firmin et al, 2021; Action for Children, 2024; Wroe et al, 2025). But, to realise the ambitions set out in Chapter 9 and deliver services and interventions that build safety and seek justice for young people affected by EFRH, systems need to be able to meet young people's needs and create the conditions they require to flourish. In theory, a commitment to meeting young people's needs is a cornerstone of many child protection and/or safeguarding systems (Merkel-Holguin et al, 2019). In practice, the system shortfalls presented in this book evidence the ways in which that commitment is hard for services to honour. When professional responses to EFRH orient around behaviour and situations which pose risk and incur harm (the knife, the grooming, the drug use), then young people's wider needs such as education, friendship, housing and access to digital technologies may be obscured. When responses to EFRH are organised around what services or practitioners need to feel comfortable and confident, or driven by negative social and political discourses about dangerous youth (see Chapter 2), rather than by what young people require, then risk-mitigation, control, containment, case-closure and information-gathering become key goals of the system. These mismatches between young people's needs and system-orientated priorities are exacerbated by persisting structural inequalities, such as racism, poverty, ableism and sexism, which further hinder young people's access to appropriate services, support and relationships.

In this chapter, we pause to consider what the objectives would be of a system where young people's needs, and their opportunities to flourish, were prioritised from the outset. We reflect on what the evidence shared in this book suggests about how close UK services are to setting and meeting such objectives, and what fundamental features of existing systems in the UK and beyond would require transformation to realise those objectives.

What do young people need?

Despite demographic, geographic and structural differences between the six sites that participated in the Innovate Project, there was much similarity in the needs of the young people they were all supporting.

Young people impacted by EFRH required support with their mental health and overall emotional well-being. In some sites this was evident in documented concerns about young people's use of both illegal substances and alcohol, and the association between this and wider experiences of interpersonal harm. These experiences included sexual exploitation in exchange for substances, use of substances in the aftermath of sexual assaults, physical violence as a consequence of debts accrued through the use of substances and exploitation via drug trafficking and transportation in exchange for substances. Early childhood experiences of violence and abuse, and wider experiences of social isolation, were also associated with young people's experiences of trauma and its impacts which included self-injury and risks of suicide. Young people's need for space to process and understand their experiences, and recover from or cope with them, was therefore a point of conversation in young people's assessments/plans as well as in some interagency meetings.

> [The young person] is positive about the placement, however we are likely to see some variations in [the young person's] behaviour until she settles in the placement. Some of this distress may cause [the young person's] behaviour to seem challenging or unmanageable by adults. However, it is anticipated that [the young person] will settle with support and consistency. (Social work assessment, case file)

Relationally, young people impacted by EFRH needed access to safe, consistent and supportive people – some who were older than them and some who were peers. Many parents and carers who featured in our data also needed support to understand the nature of EFRH, the impacts on their children, and the role they could play in planning for and creating safety (Chapter 6). However, to fulfil such a role they also often needed wider support to address systemic or structural issues such as unsafe or overcrowded housing, discriminatory practices in education or policing services that were negatively impacting their young people (particularly young people who were racially minoritised, had learning needs or were neurodivergent, those who were older – or existed at the intersections of these), and the impact of hostile immigration processes (and preceding impacts of war, famine or torture):

> Mum fled during the [redacted] war and has not returned to the country since … the family currently live in an overcrowded flat. The initial referral came into [redacted] service due to family breakdown. [The young person] had left the family home and his whereabouts were unknown. Conflict was due to his involvement in the community; he is under police investigation for criminal offences including [lists offences] … [the mother] has a history of mental health difficulties.

> During the initial visit she had a significant mental health episode. This was felt to be triggered by [the young person's] risky behaviour and the impact of younger siblings. At this point her partner does not have indefinite leave to remain and she is heavily pregnant. (Social work assessment, case file)

Other parents were also impacted by precarious employment, which pulled them away from their families – working multiple jobs to stay afloat – and did not afford the flexibility required to accommodate daytime meetings with professionals to discuss their child.

Young people also needed time with friends where they could have fun, socialise and form non-familial bonds. Many young people impacted by EFRH were faced with the loss of friends, sometimes because of interpersonal violence, and on other occasions due to professional interventions which included secure placements, school exclusions, 'managed moves' between schools, and bail conditions or civil orders that banned contact with each other (Chapter 7). They needed safe spaces where they could socialise with their friends, and support each other, including without parental supervision. In those relationships, they needed to experience loyalty and trust, love and care, respect, emotional support and laughter. As part of this they also needed ways to explore and develop romantic/intimate relationships as they developed into adulthood; they would seek and explore such connections both online and in-person.

In terms of relationships with professionals, young people needed space and time in which to trust, and be open, with a person who was supporting them and/or offering access to wider support and care (Chapter 8). We witnessed requests from both young people and their families for minimal and consistent professional relationships – this included lowering the numbers of professionals that young people had to meet with and ensuring those that they did spend time with were able to stick around. Such relationships required that professionals had the capacity for care, compassion, patience and advocacy, and an ability to be responsive and agile enough to cater to the dynamic nature of EFRH and its corresponding impacts on young people.

More contextually and structurally, young people needed access to key services including education, employment, housing and leisure activities. Yet in much of our data, such services were limited, withheld or unavailable either as a result of, or despite, EFRH. For example, in every multi-agency meeting observed during the project, professionals discussed young people who had either been excluded from mainstream education, were unsafe in their educational establishment (so had been asked not to attend) or who were on significantly reduced academic timetables. The rationale in many of these situations was that young people either posed a risk to other students or were emotionally unable to cope in school due to the wider harms they were experiencing; similar rationales were given for lack of, or limited, access to leisure activities, such as young people being asked not to use local amenities or being banned from them. Wider experiences of poverty and discrimination, and the impacts of austerity measures, also meant that some young people were living in overcrowded, temporary or insecure housing; this pushed them into public spaces, or the homes of others, where they were exposed to further harm. A growing concern across all sites during the research period was the numbers of young people identified as impacted by EFRH who had diagnosed, or suspected but undiagnosed, learning needs and/or neurodivergence. The need in this respect was timely diagnosis and associated support plans in relation to speech and language help and access to education.

> In summer [the young person] reported being a victim of an alleged sexual assault by another young person. Since he has returned to school he is noted to have increased distressed behaviour including physical aggression, sexualised behaviour and language … Two CAMHS (Child and Adolescent Mental Health Services) reports note that [the young person] has learning difficulties and is much younger than his chronological age. (Social work assessment, case files)

Finally, young people needed access to safety in extra-familial as well as familial contexts, in ways outlined in Chapter 9. In this sense they needed to be in situations where safety could be co-constructed around/with them, rather than being moved out of unsafe circumstances in a manner that disrupted other (often safe) aspects of their lives. Young people needed to be able to access safety in otherwise risky contexts, rather than be in conditions of sterile safety where all risk was removed. Engagement with risk, in and of itself, was often sought by young people who featured in our data, very much in keeping with the developmental needs of this life-stage. An associated need was that of growing independence and autonomy. Young people needed the space to make decisions, influence decisions made about their lives and to decline or accept support. Space to choose, and assert some control, is important for us all – but is particularly important for young people who are in otherwise largely constrained, coerced or limited situations over which they have little control or influence.

What do our systems need?

As illustrated in earlier chapters of this book, the systems charged with safeguarding young people are commonly orientated around the needs of professionals and the organisations for whom they work and driven by policy (often political) objectives; as a result, their process and outcome goals are often at odds with what young people actually want and need.

Safeguarding and welfare systems run on information, both to monitor risk and assess need. As discussed in Chapter 8, practitioners within those systems need information in order to reach decisions about the most appropriate actions to take. Information also meets a wider professional need; in the midst of the emotional anxiety that safeguarding work inevitably generates, concrete 'evidence' about a young person's actions or relationships can help professionals feel secure that their assessments are based on a degree of certainty or predictability – whether or not that is the case in actuality (Franklin et al, 2018; Lloyd et al, 2023; Firmin et al, 2024).

An effectively functioning safeguarding system is expected to include a range of appropriate interventions (HM Government, 2023) – time-orientated, targeted responses, the cost of which is known in advance, that can be drawn upon to fix specific identified problems that young people face/pose (Chapter 4). Structured or mandated interventions meet a wider professional need for containment in situations that can feel expansive and unsettling, and for which a resolution feels complex and hard to reach. Rather than a more holistic engagement with a young person's lived experience in the context of EFRH, an intervention-based system might intercede with individual elements connected to the EFRH, such as going missing from home or education, emotional instability or distress, substance use or interpersonal violence – each being treated as isolated behaviours in need of reduction or modification.

In order to generate public confidence in professional responses to EFRH, and justify the public investment incurred, safeguarding systems require measurable outcomes to be set; monitored by key indicators, these support the building of an evidence base on varied approaches to decision-making and intervention. These impact measures are generally set by professionals rather than being co-constructed with young people and their families, so the extent to which they have meaningful relevance for young people is debatable (Holmes and Lefevre, 2024). Being often framed as absolutes, they tend to imply a permanent change is being looked for if work is to be judged as 'successful'; for example, a reduction in offending, an increase in school attendance, a reduction in missing episodes. This approach, rooted in an 'over-reliance on rigid, quantifiable and monetisable data' (Holmes and Lefevre, 2024, p 455), aligns with a justice-ethic of rationality, individualism and abstraction from context.

Responses to EFRH, including the system innovations we witnessed during our research project, were often implemented in ways that reflected these system requirements for outcome measurements. Many structures were introduced that enabled professionals to share information with each other, and record that information in templates, on IT systems and in ways that could be analysed by others to reach conclusions about the likelihood and level of risk. Services available to young people within participating sites were often framed as interventions, including to address substance misuse or to provide education on healthy relationships, consequential thinking, weapon-carrying/weapon-awareness and the nature of exploitation. Such interventions were then measured in respect of their impact on young people's behaviour (as opposed to their impact on young people's relationships, feelings of and/or access to safety). In these instances, changes of behaviour (or lack thereof) were taken as a sign of system (in)effectiveness.

The system features we outlined previously reflect the foundational limitations we drew attention to in Part I of this book and sought to reimagine, that is, systems that: (1) prioritise risk management over love and care; (2) seek to get around principles of privacy rather than respecting it by sharing information with consent or consideration; (3) hold individuals (young people, parents, professionals) responsible for identifying, preventing and responding to EFRH; and (4) give respect conditionally. Such flawed systems are orientated around meeting the demands (needs) of those who govern, uphold and deliver many existing services, rather than the needs or preferences of young people impacted by EFRH. Moreover, in such systems, decisions are led by what has been mandated and resourced by and for services, rather than what young people and families require or prefer.

From resource-led to needs-led

While systems that respond to young people in the UK impacted by EFRH are ostensibly created solely for their protection, we argue that system structures and processes are equally, if not more, designed to shelter professionals – both from the overwhelming anxiety and distress provoked by working with traumatised young people in conditions of uncertainty, and from being accused of 'getting it wrong' when a young person is harmed or harms others. Hence, information is shared widely to distribute responsibility for decisions; interventions are circumscribed to agreed models rather than responsive practice; risk matrices and checklists predominate to evidence compliance with procedures.

The mismatch is clear. Professional-orientated systems are not conducive with meeting the holistic needs of young people impacted by EFRH, including their need for access to key services (that is, education, housing, mental health, leisure and community services) or support for their relationships – with family, friends, wider communities and a consistent, small number of professionals. In respect of both services and relationships, young people require safety and access to social and epistemic justice (Chapter 9). When we observed this mismatch in the Innovate Project, we witnessed practices in which young people needed something – such as access to education – but instead were offered something else – such as a weapon-awareness intervention or a referral to a mentoring service. This decision-making reflected situations in which systems were responding to EFRH based on what was available (resource-led) as opposed to what young people needed (youth-centred). Moreover, what was available reflected or reinforced system processes and cost-effectiveness constraints. In building a system that is largely committed to meeting professional needs, governance requirements and service efficiencies, the gulf between what young people need and system-led processes continues to expand, despite a proliferation of 'innovative' incremental improvements (Lefevre et al, 2024). Ultimately, if the gap to close is between how services are structured and resourced and what young people need and prefer, then the foundational structures and principles of these systems must shift.

If we – professionals, researchers, policy makers, young people, families – were to start again, what would human-centred, welfare-orientated safeguarding systems look like? We suggest that they be constructed with young people and the period of adolescent development in mind and rooted in a contextual and structural understanding of EFRH. Such systems would be geared towards creating the conditions for young people's individual and relational needs to be met. This would move us *away* from 'interventions' that address isolated and contained behaviours or risks and *towards* 'professional and community responses and services' that meet core needs such as education, housing, youth work, health and well-being. By resourcing services more broadly, professionals would be far better equipped to be responsive and agile to what young people need at any given time, and to be relationally supportive in a proportionate and consistent manner, in concert with wider communities who will likely remain in young people's lives long after professional involvement has ceased. The new systems would move away from 'measuring' impacts abstracted from relationships and contexts, instead recognising and documenting those relationships and contexts for their relevance to young people's access to safety.

These reimagined systems would be equipped to:

- support families, and recognise (and address) the contexts in which they are trying to raise and care for their young people;
- support young people in the context of their friendships and relationships;
- be responsive to emergent needs or concerns in respect of young people's mental health and well-being;

- recognise and address system shortfalls, should they become apparent (that is, gaps in service provision related to education, housing and employment).

System responses to EFRH would therefore, over time, become less about the harm itself and more about the full and important lives of the young people impacted by it. In this respect 'meeting need' may not go far enough; in order to fully rewire existing system paradigms, the conditions must be created in which there is a move from meeting individual needs and towards the collective flourishing of all young people, their families and communities.

From meeting individual need to creating conditions for collective flourishing

Moving in the direction of meeting needs and facilitating young humans to flourish is a tall order for the systems currently in place, as it requires the balance of power to be rethought, and for the urgency and immediacy that governs so much of professional practice in EFRH to be confronted. However, we suggest that this does not entail forging an entirely new path; there is a long history of understanding urgency as a tool of oppression and control (for example, Walter Benjamin's work in the 1940s, Beiner, 1984), of seeing power legitimised through this urgency (Agamben, 1998; Enns, 2004) and recognising that resistance – the counterforce to power – is always present (Foucault, 1982). When trapped within this dynamic power struggle (that is, trying to get young people and their families to adapt to system requirements and frameworks, rather than the systems being tailored to their needs), the aspiration seems no more than for young people to live a 'bare life' (Agamben, 1998): to biologically exist; to accommodate to expectations of intersectional oppressions, rather than protest or resist; to accept the scarcity of resources available for their needs; and to progress into adulthood. With such a modest objective, then safeguarding systems need to provide only enough to keep a young person alive and physically safe enough so that they do not fall below a risk threshold. Yet that is much less than what we all might hope for ourselves and our own children. Agamben (1998) contrasted this idea of the 'bare life' with a 'full life' – one in which a young person is recognised as full of potential, and has the capacity to fulfil that potential, on their own terms. The latter is one that creates, and perhaps demands, space for flourishing.

The concept of flourishing is multi-faceted (Vittersø, 2004), encompassing a range of features associated with positive well-being, such as emotional stability, feeling competent and purposeful, being meaningfully engaged in social life and having positive relationships, self-esteem and a sense of vitality (Huppert and So, 2013). In a recent systematic review of the (limited) research on adolescent flourishing, researchers Witten, Savahl and Adams (2019) found that flourishing – for teenagers – is often about focusing on how they thrive and the otherwise positive aspects of their well-being. Young people who flourish have positive relationships, positive beliefs about themselves, and feel able to put in the effort (that is, 'diligence and initiative') to achieve things for themselves. In this research, as in the findings from a large-scale study by Schotanus-Kijkstra et al (2016), flourishing is particularly associated with experiencing positive life events – and these positive life events contribute more to increased flourishing than the experience of negative life events might detract from it.

When we seek full lives, rather than bare lives, for young people, we are pushed again to think beyond the individual. Full lives cannot be pursued via case management systems and time-limited interventions; that would mean millions of interventions, vast amounts of paperwork and short-bursts of input that extend beyond 'need-met' or 'risk-reduced' – and neoliberal systems were not designed to accommodate such expansiveness. Rather, it is possible to move closer to an understanding of what it means for young people to flourish when it is viewed as a collective endeavour: responsibility is held within community and realised in the same manner. Likewise, the idea of flourishing is easier to hold onto when actual conditions are envisioned within which flourishing is possible – the types of relationships, experiences, resources and opportunities that would nurture young people beyond the bare minimum – than it is to think about each individual life, and associated set of experiences, impacted by EFRH.

Drawing together therefore what young people impacted by EFRH need alongside a wider commitment to creating conditions in which all young people flourish, Figure 10.1 illustrates those goals in relation to the reorientated system foundations, and reimagined relationships, presented in Parts I and II of this book, respectively. While the impact of negative life events cannot be ignored or diminished, the vision we set out in Figure 10.1, and the evidence underpinning it, provides us immense hope and energy, and we believe it may do so for many others too. Even where EFRH has not been prevented, a system can be imagined, planned for, curated and delivered that is attuned and responsive to young people affected by EFRH – who are themselves capable of flourishing, and likely to thrive.

Figure 10.1: Goal of needs and flourishing in a transformed safeguarding system

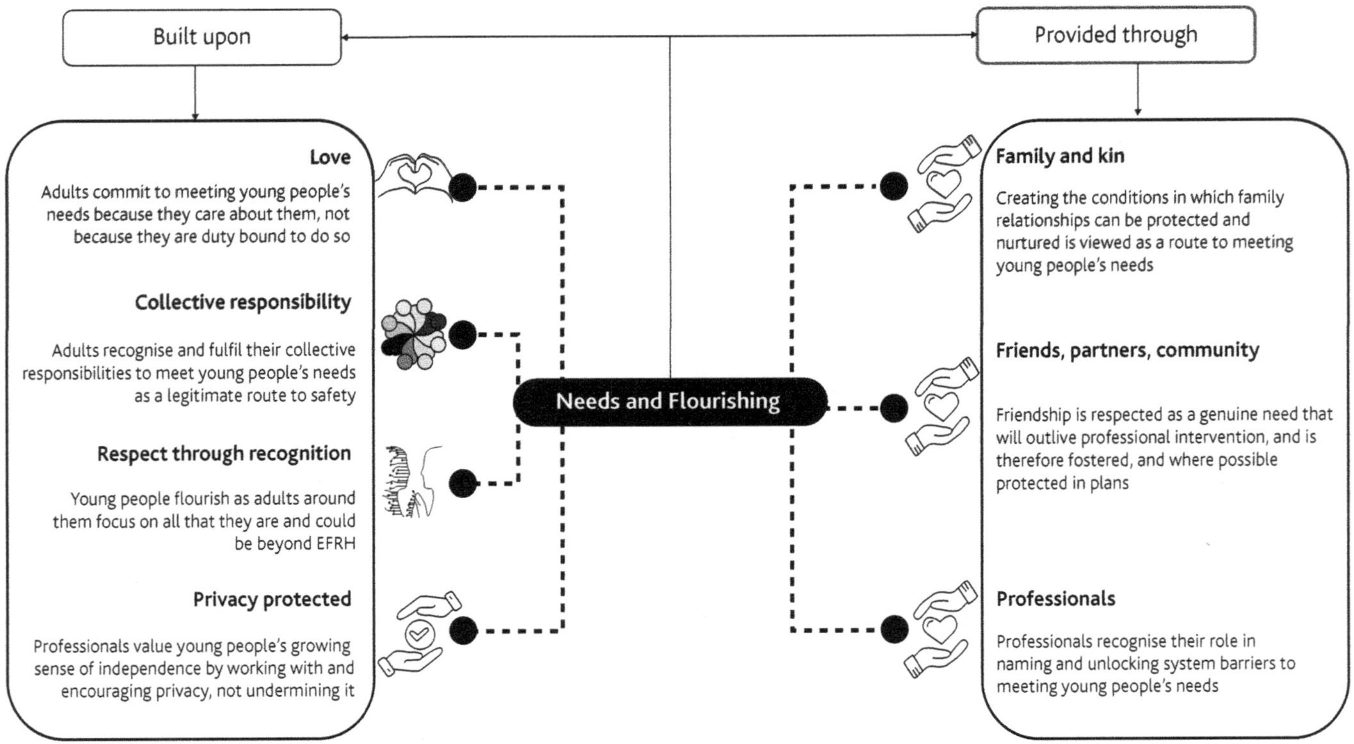

Box 10.1: Reflective questions for leaders and practitioners raised by Chapter 10

1. What might the goals of your organisation or system look like if young people's needs and preferences, and their opportunities to flourish, are prioritised from the outset?
2. How different would such reimagined goals be from the current priorities and objectives of your service?
3. What fundamental features of your systems would require modification or more radical transformation if these new youth-centred goals were to drive the practice approach?

Resources to support innovation

We suggest using the Roadmap tool, which was developed through the Innovate Project, as this can support you and your colleagues to determine where to start if you want to plan priority areas for action in your service. This tool and its guidance pack (Creating system conditions for ethical and effective innovation) can be freely downloaded at: www.theinnovateproject.co.uk/practice-tools/.

11

Conclusion: The realities of re-weighting safeguarding systems

In 2024 we drew a line in the sand. We wrote a paper in which we called for policy and practice responses to extra-familial risks and harms (EFRH) that moved beyond surface improvements and demonstrated commitment to a fundamental reimagining of the foundations of child welfare, child protection and wider safeguarding systems. Two years on we re-state here: a commitment to protecting young people from EFRH, and supporting them to have safe, full and happy lives, requires moving *beyond* current paradigms familiar to safeguarding and reimagining systems based on what young people need and want. This book offers that initial reimagining. We propose: a reorientating of the foundations upon which safeguarding systems are built; a transformation in how we view, support and engage the relationships that make up and interact with such systems; and a resetting of the goals such systems can realise.

In this chapter we conclude by proposing ways to turn the vision we offer in the book into a practical reality; building upon the reflective questions and visual representations offered at the end of Chapters 2 to 10. The vision we set out may take time to realise. Its feasibility lies in ongoing collaboration with those served by, delivering, resourcing, researching and guiding safeguarding systems. What we offer therefore is a place from which to start – a place grounded in interlocking theories and practice evidence far beyond the narrow scope of EFRH to both understand how things are and importantly what they could be.

The integrated vision

In combination, the three parts of this book offer a vision for safeguarding systems that would, if operationalised, do things differently.

Fundamentally, this would be systems that

- pursue and provide 'radical love' for all young people;
- offer 'recognition–respect' to all young people;
- hold a 'collective responsibility' for, and with, all young people;
- 'proportionately protect privacy' of all young people as a route to safety.

These four foundations then shape all relationships that characterise, or interact with, those systems.

In relationships with their parents, carers, wider family and kin, young people in this reimagined system would feel, and be, loved unconditionally. They would have the space to build such loving connections with their friends, romantic partners and wider communities, whose ways of expressing love and care would also be valued by the professionals around them. In interactions with professionals, young people would also feel, and be, cared about deeply, through reciprocal experiences of unconditional nurture, and protection through advocacy and humane practices.

Across all these relationships young people would be respected for who they are – in the fullness of their growing identities. This includes those that rub up against what may be most valued by family, friends or professionals at different points in time.

Through this, young people would experience a community in which professionals, peers, partners and parents/carers/family are connected with each other. Together this community would hold collective responsibility for the conditions in which young people might experience safety and be enabled to flourish, both recognising the contribution of each, and coming alongside each other to create mutually reinforcing contexts of care and protection.

Finally, these relationships would recognise, respect and protect privacy. Parents/carers and professionals would lead with a desire to maintain young people's privacy, creating conditions in which young people would feel able to approach them for support and advice. Likewise, privacy in young people's friendships and community relationships would largely be viewed as developmentally normal and expected. Working from this basis means relationships are not positioned as a vehicle for gathering information, nor as the subject of the information to be gathered, but instead interactions/relations through which safety and advice can be sought and provided.

The goals of this re-envisioned system would further ground the relationships within the system to their proposed foundations. These four foundations would be activated, through relationships, to build safety with and around young people, pursue social and epistemic justice, meet their needs and create conditions in which they can live full lives (Figure 11.1). As such, the foundations, relationships and goals we set out in this book interact with each other – and should do so at interpersonal, team, organisational, policy, commissioning, education and system-wide levels for change to be made visible. We now set out three ways that this vision could be made a practical reality in safeguarding responses to EFRH; ways that would provide us a litmus test on the extent to which safeguarding systems were nearing the radical transformation that we propose.

Figure 11.1: The three levels of transformed safeguarding systems

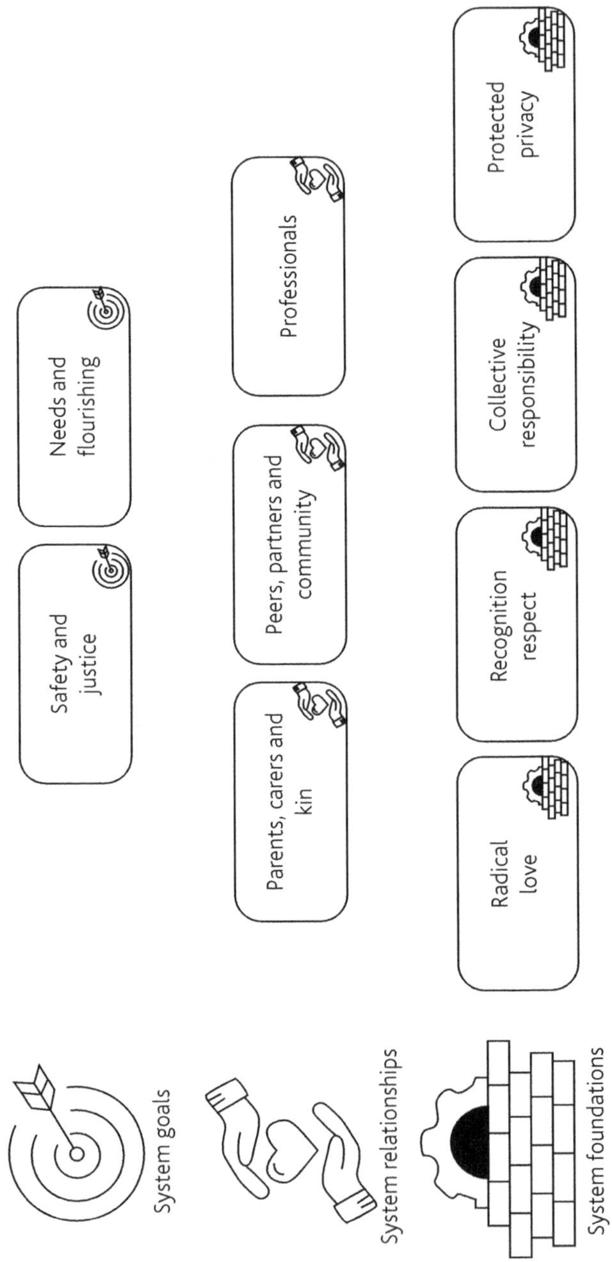

Beyond casework, towards collectivism

Nearly every chapter in this book proposed an approach to safeguarding young people that conventional casework models of system and service delivery would struggle to accommodate. The relationships and contexts central to our proposed system – including friendship groups, parks, social media platforms, schools and transport terminals – do not have parameters suited to casework.

We provide a fictional example of a group of four friends to illustrate this point. Two of them, Shaun and Robert, are being criminally exploited. They were first approached in their local shopping centre and have since been trafficked via trainlines to various parts of the UK. They have two friends from college, Micah and Nate, who are not being exploited but who provide them with emotional support, and with whom they socialise at times when they are not being trafficked to distribute drugs. Social workers and youth workers may want to engage with and understand the whole group but Micah and Nate, who are safe, do not need to be 'opened' via case work to statutory social work 'intervention'. Moreover, long-term support for Shaun and Robert may not only rest with youth workers but also with Micah and Nate, who are the people who will be alongside Shaun and Robert beyond the length of any 'case'.

The previously described approach, to step outside of 'casework', reflects the foundations of the system we propose – one in which responsibility is held collectively more than it is individualised. Collective responsibility, especially that which is targeted at the conditions in which young people are living their lives cannot be documented, tracked or fully expressed by 'case-working' those 'conditions'. Support for Shaun and Robert may include identifying places in their local neighbourhoods where they can spend time safely and identifying the 'community guardians' – people who are older than Shaun and Robert, are already in the places where they spend their time and whom they trust. Being provided with dongles for internet access is also something that Robert says is important to him as he doesn't have Wi-Fi at home; his parents cannot afford it. In one of the Innovate Project sites a social worker arranged time to go fishing with two boys like Shaun and Robert to explore an interest they had expressed and to give them a sense of peace. In our fictional example, some local shopkeepers, youth workers, social workers, the parents of Shaun, Micah, Nate and Robert, and a local fishing club are all playing a role in creating conditions for the boys to flourish, and the boys are part of that process.

Likewise, our calls in Chapter 5 for a Triple P approach to when and how it is appropriate to breach Privacy (Purposeful, Proportionate, Participatory), mean that young people like Shaun, Robert, Micah and Nate may tell social workers and youth workers things that they do not want to be formally recorded, such as who they fancy at the moment, a recurring dream one of them keeps having, a joke they made that didn't land well. These everyday self-disclosures help the boys to build rapport with the social worker and youth worker who are coordinating support for them, and they do not intend for multiple other people to know. In such situations, when the information is not relevant to a safeguarding assessment, but does help them to safeguard young people by getting to 'know them' better, then professionals supporting boys like Shaun and Robert need to be trusted to 'hold' information, rather than automatically share it through formal systems. Such holding does not compromise safety, rather it promotes it through building the kind of trusting relationships that mean a young person is subsequently more likely to share when they are experiencing vulnerability or threat (Lefevre et al, 2017). And should Shaun or Robert say something that their college tutor or someone else in the community with a safeguarding role *does* need to know, wherever possible their youth worker or social worker will discuss this with Shaun or Robert first; hence, how it is shared, and for what purpose, is something that all parties have had the chance to express a view on and shape.

At its most fundamental, the system we propose is a humane one in which safety is pursued through relationships of radical love and recognition-based respect. In such relationships Shaun and Robert are not 'cases' to manage; they are people to support, come alongside, advocate for and for whom there is hope and ambition. In Chapter 8, therefore, we proposed relationships between young people and professionals that are firmly positioned outside of casework framings or categorisations of certainty; this would shift away from a pattern where professional involvement with Shaun was shaped through scoring him as an '8' or an 'amber' on a risk matrix, or by the pursuit of 'school attendance' as a decontextualised outcome measure for Robert. Relationships are instead positioned to hold the unknown and uncertainty as characteristic of a full, changing, life during adolescence. In some ways, such uncertainty can be co-opted to hold onto hope: things are not all known, and they also are not all decided; there is always room to change the narrative.

Beyond risk, towards safety

In the systems we put forward in this book, researchers tracking local responses to EFRH could be observing a meeting where the plans for two girls, whom we will call Sasha and Lacey, were being agreed (as we did many times during the Innovate Project – see Lloyd and Peace, 2025 for more details) and hear conversations more weighted towards building safety for these young people, than assuming such safety will be achieved through risk mitigation alone. Social workers, youth workers, local library managers, a pastoral lead in education and Sasha and Lacey's parents would all be sat together to consider what the two girls have told them about where they feel safe. They would be seeking to understand what it is about the local library that helps Sasha and Lacey to feel safe, before identifying ways to replicate this when they are at school (a context in which they currently feel unsafe). The focus of such a meeting would not be an exception; it would be the rule. All safeguarding meetings would identify young people's access to safety and agree plans to increase this (and in the process mitigate risk), including by meeting young people's needs and wants. As such, plans would feature far fewer EFRH-focused, short-term interventions, and instead consider whether the conditions are in place for young people's needs and wants related to education, health, housing and employment to be safely met.

At a strategic level this would mean that at meetings, service managers and commissioners would discuss local area *safety profiles* ahead of, the 'hotspot mapping' *or* 'problem profiling' that are currently far more common across the studies we have completed. Senior leaders would know the places and spaces where young people feel safest in any local area and would seek to protect and replicate these spaces as far as possible. Such information would primarily come directly from young people and their communities, through relationships in which young people are truly known by the professionals and other adults in their lives, rather than through system datasets that do not always accurately reflect what young people feel or experience yet largely dominate how EFRH is strategically framed or discussed. It is interesting to us that the UK, like many other countries, has a crime survey which reports the levels of risk and harm young people face; yet, there is much less knowledge about the numbers of young people who have access to an adult they trust outside of family members, who have formed close friendships, and/or who feel safe and school, college, work or in their local communities. There are some well-being surveys that seek to do this, but this information features far less in shaping local and national responses to EFRH – which instead are largely driven by data on risks rather than knowledge of safety.

Systems that strategically and operationally prioritise safety-profiling are ones in which professionals would more readily look for the *presence* of things – such as love, care, privacy, respect, belonging – as opposed to prioritising the measurement of an absence of things such as risk, crime, information and so on. So, when professionals are discussing support plans with Sasha and Lacey, who are struggling with online peer-sexual harassment and abuse that has spilled out to some fights in their local neighbourhood, professionals are first looking to identify where and how these young women feel safe and benefit from positive experiences. In their friendship with each other, for example, Sasha and Lacey experience love and care. They also experience love and care from their parents; however, they are worried that their parents may want to keep them apart as each blames the other for their child's current predicament. Sasha and Lacey want their parents to recognise the care they provide to each other, and they want their school to do the same. Often in school they are separated to try to avoid flare-ups between students, but this leaves Sasha and Lacey isolated. They meet up in the library before they go home separately, as it is the only place they can spend time together. As such, professionals have a job to ensure both young women can safely spend time together at school and at home, avoiding experiences of social isolation or situations where they will be pushed into community spaces in order to connect. Such planning will not remove the risks that Sasha and Lacey have experienced online. However, it will demonstrate that they have been heard and understood, and the things that they will need beyond this moment in time are being provided/facilitated: friendship, the respect of their families and an educational provision they can access safely.

By providing these elements, a basis upon which Sasha and Lacey can feel held, trusted and cared for by the collective, the professional systems would then create the conditions in which these girls may also open up about the harms they have experienced and ask for help, for example, in tackling the sharing of indecent images. They may give an indication of the online platforms where they are bullied, creating opportunities for online youth work or bystander interventions that de-escalate harm. In systems reorientated as we recommend risk is not ignored. Rather risk is mitigated on the path to safety, or as a consequence of building safety, rather than being equated with it. This kind of safety can act as a buffer around risks that are beyond professional knowledge and control, with the result that safety, and its provision, are still within reach.

Beyond justice, towards care

Finally, we envisage a care-orientated system in which justice is a feature, as opposed to a justice-orientated system that we try to make more caring (Firmin et al, 2026). This may seem obvious given that love and care is the focus of Chapter 2. However, we encourage deep engagement by readers with the other chapters of this book to truly appreciate the implications of this injunction. Gilligan's original work to introduce a care ethic via a 'Different Voice' (1982) and latterly via a 'Human Voice' (2023) is very helpful here. Gilligan writes that introducing a care ethic requires us to be 'audacious' (Gilligan, 2023, p 97), as it reconnects what we *feel* to what we say we *know*, and to what we *do* in systems; this orients professionals to what is right, even when these things do not feel right within existing system expectations. For Gilligan, a care ethic introduces:

> A voice that joins thinking and feeling, self and relationship, mind and body. And with this realization comes the recognition that separations once hailed as milestones of progress (the separation of

> reason from emotion, mind from body, self from relationships) are, in fact, manifestations of injury or trauma. (2023, p 66)

Or as one young woman told Gilligan, it 'is an internal sort of knowing, like just has to do with like not your brain but more your mind' (2023, p 79).

In her work to apply Gilligan's care-ethic to organisations, Tronto (2005) reminds us that 'caring' organisations need to recognise the interdependent (rather than independent), contextual (rather than individual) and relational nature of human lives, in order to deliver care. This is not a neutral exercise; it is not about keeping everything fundamentally the same in organisations but delivering them in a kinder fashion. The approach moves us away from primarily seeing our lives as individual, rational and ordered. It goes beyond organising care in accordance with rules and duties. In this sense we provide care, because we do care, in communion with others as opposed to providing care because we are legally bound to do so.

This is potentially the hardest shift for us all to make. Many organisations that care for people impacted by violence find themselves engaging in adversarial, black-and-white, legal routes to unlocking protection. In the field of EFRH, this has led to national reviews that prioritise calls for new offences to better prosecute those who cause harm to young people, or recommendations that organise responses to violent incidents principally through a lens of police investigation, and measure system success in these situations via numbers of prosecutions and so on (see Casey, 2025 for an example). It is not that in some respects criminal–legal frameworks have not played a role in the protection of young people. The challenge is that (a) they have often also played a role in the criminalisation of, and harm caused to, young people, and (b) they are not geared to prioritise the relational, contextual, facets of human life that we amplify in this book. It is not only, therefore, in the way that individual meetings or services are organised that we see a justice ethic loom large – to the point that care is hard to come by; it is equally apparent via dominance of intelligence gathering exercises framed as 'protective' in their own right (Chapters 5 and 8), or through the push for legal duties to enact actions or hold professionals accountable for failures, silencing wider conditions in which they are largely set up to fail (Chapter 4). The predominant ethos in policy, practice and wider society currently is to frame EFRH as a criminal justice matter *first and foremost*, with good practice then orientated around enacting this justice orientation kindly.

For systems we call for in this book, a kind approach to justice will be insufficient; this approach remains weighted to justice (particularly criminal justice) first. Our evidence suggests a need for systems weighted towards a capacity to hold uncertainty, over pursuing certainty, to seek safety ahead of reducing risk, to protect privacy more often than usurping it. We are calling for work that sits in the discomfort of the grey, challenging systems that prefer black and white. We ourselves have struggled with how to land some of the points we make; as part of the systems we are reimagining, at times we found ourselves drawn to even more legal duties and system requirements to leverage the changes that are predominantly incompatible with these boundaries.

What then would be seen in a system that was care-orientated and in which 'justice', in its broadest sense, played a part? It is important to note that we are not calling for a complete removal of laws and duties. What we are recommending is a shift in emphasis – so that laws and duties would come secondary to, and sit within, the systems we envisage, rather than being the driving force behind them. As such, the relationships we outlined in Part II of the book come to the forefront of system delivery – with all their complexity and uncertainty, rather than the individuals who make up those relationships being considered largely independently of them. We envisage safeguarding systems in which these relationships are adequately resourced, respected and in community with each other.

If this care-ethic orientation is applied to Shaun, Robert, Sasha and Lacey, a reimagined approach comes into view that leverages systems who care about these young people principally because it is the culture of the system to recognise and respond to young people's intrinsic humanity and value as people who deserve happy and full lives, rather than out of duty alone. Here, young people are enabled to go on fishing trips, are helped to spend time together having fun, are respected for what they bring to the table and are encouraged to think about their futures and ambitions. In this reimagined system, practitioners will initially be encouraged to 'go the extra mile' for young people – as doing more than what is legally required will feel like that. However, over time, that extra mile will not feel like any distance at all, as it will be what safeguarding systems are newly geared up to do when the priority is for young people to live full lives rather than scrape the bare minimum. In multi-agency meetings professionals will discuss what these young people need or want to feel safe and reach their potential, in addition to what they need to survive the weekend. They can visualise futures for these young people in which professionals no longer play an active role in their lives but have contributed to conditions in which young people are continuing to grow and flourish. These practitioners can also hold a line when justice-orientated pursuits seek to overtake matters; for example, where criminal investigations are pursued at the expense of Lacey and Sasha rather to their benefit; or where information that Robert shares with a youth worker to inform his safety plan is later used to prosecute him: practices characteristic of current system weighting. In this sense, caring is not simply a provision of love, it is a push-back against punishment.

Who is with us?

Some readers might have travelled this far with us and think that what we have outlined over 11 chapters is a nice idea but idealist and impractical. We do not agree. In fact, everything we have suggested comes from the green shoots of innovation and progress we observed in the Innovate Project. What we propose is that safeguarding systems could be transformed if they were weighted towards these green shoots and consequently minimised other system characteristics that too often produce ineffective, or even detrimental, impacts for young people's safety. In our data there were glimmers of 'what could be' fighting through the weeds of 'what was'; we saw that such weeds were likely to suffocate the green shoots, if there was no one there to create a garden in which they could breathe. In this sense we visualise this book as a greenhouse: a space to incubate the potential we witnessed and articulate the conditions needed to cultivate that potential for it to grow and multiply.

In Figure 11.2 we illustrate what the re-weighting we propose in this chapter looks like. This illustration reflects our desire, as set out in Chapter 1 to move beyond binaries, and instead to work across spectrums; and when it comes to safeguarding systems, to tip the balance of these spectrums as a consequence of transformed system foundations, relationships and goals. Therefore, we commit to working towards places in which safeguarding is principally a practice of care, safety and collectivism – whereas these features are currently subdued within practices of justice, risk-management and individualism. Our proposals mean individuals would act, and take accountability within, collectives, risk would be mitigated via the provision of safety, and justice would be realised as a consequence of care. We argue that this rebalancing is essential. In the current status quo it is hard to realise the collective when we are principally concerned with individuals, a prioritisation of risk has compromised young people's safety and a pursuit of justice has dehumanised those who most need our care.

We are committed to taking the ideas laid out in this book and putting them to the test. We have all been involved in participatory action research projects before and can see the potential of the method for bringing this book to life: from the point at which young people are 'referred' into services for help; through to the approaches taken to assess what they need, plan how to meet those needs and deliver a response; from the work undertaken pre-referral; when relational responses to contexts and groups prevent harm from escalating and build in safety as a buffer; where wider interactions with young people in their schools, workplaces, families and communities are ones in which they are respected and cared-for by a collective; where leaders know where young people feel and are safe, understand why and remain committed to building upon and extending these experiences far-and-wide; and where social work and youth work educators are equipping practitioners

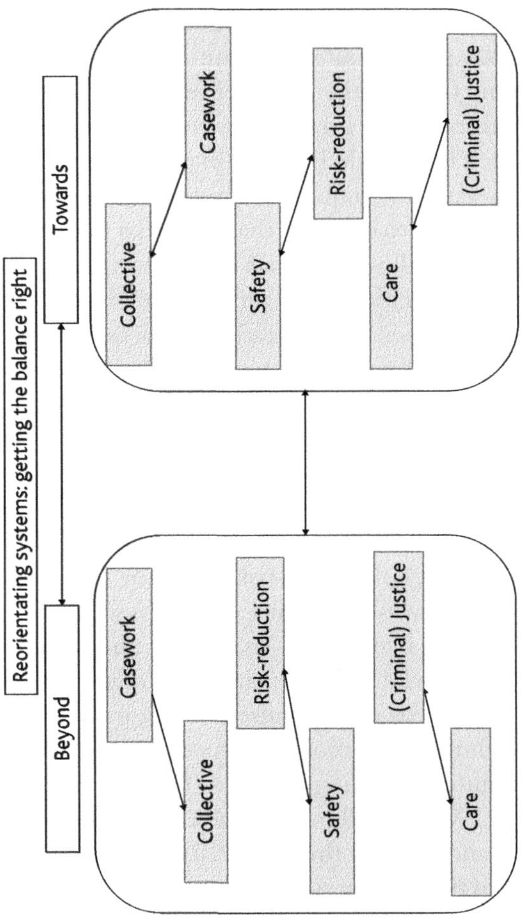

Figure 11.2: Safeguarding systems rebalanced

with new tools, rather than those that currently characterise our systems, so that safeguarding approaches can be reimagined from the ground-up.

So, we say to politicians, system leaders, practitioners – who is with us? We are ready to join with you to do the reimagining and innovation we propose at a practical level: to create systems with new foundations, through a set of re-envisioned relationships and in pursuit of a new set of goals; systems in which professionals care because we care, not because we are duty bound to do so; and in which young people feel, recognise and see that care when confronted with harms beyond their front doors.

Box 11.1: Reflective questions for leaders and practitioners raised by Chapter 11

1. How might your service principles and practice methods need to be reshaped to incorporate the system foundations and system relationships set out in this chapter?
2. How might service goals need to be rethought so that they are primarily care-orientated, with justice playing more of a secondary a part?
3. What are the practical steps that need to be taken to ensure there is a collective vision in your organisation for the radical transformation we propose?

Resources to support innovation

To prepare for innovation, we recommend beginning with the Diamond 9 tool, designed to help organisations exploring system conditions for innovation. You can download this tool, its guidance pack (Creating system conditions for ethical and effective innovation) and a range of other innovation resources developed through the Innovate Project at: www.theinnovateproject.co.uk/practice-tools/.

References

Abela, A., Devaney, C., Kojan, B.H., Kotzeva, T., Arsic, J. and Wilson, S. (2024) The meaningful participation of children in matters that affect them: Child participation in the context of child protection across five European countries. Children and *Youth Services Review*, *163*, 107746.

Action for Children (2024) Shattered lives, stolen futures: The Jay Review of Criminally Exploited Children. Action for Children. Available at: http://actionforchildren.org.uk/our-work-and-impact/policy-work-campaigns-and-research/policy-reports/the-jay-review-of-criminally-exploited-children/ (accessed 29 January 2026).

Adams, J., Lawrence, E.M., Goode, J.A., Schaefer, D.R. and Mollborn, S. (2022) Peer network processes in adolescents' health lifestyles. *Journal of Health and Social Behavior*, *63*(1), 125–41.

Agamben, G. (1998) *Homo Sacer: Sovereign power and bare life* (D. Heller-Roazen, Trans.). Stanford University Press.

Agostino, H. and Toulany, A. (2023) Considerations for privacy and confidentiality in adolescent health care service delivery. *Paediatrics & Child Health*, *28*(3), 172–77.

Alexander, C. (2008) (Re)thinking 'gangs'. Runnymede Trust. Available at: https://www.runnymedetrust.org/publications/rethinking-gangs (accessed 29 January 2026).

All-Party Parliamentary Group for Runaway and Missing Children and Adults (2016) *Inquiry into the safeguarding of 'absent' children: 'It is good when someone cares.' Final report*. Available at: https://tce.researchinpractice.org.uk/wp-content/uploads/2020/02/The-All-Party-Parliamentary-Group-for-Runaway-and-Missing-Children-and-Adults-Inquiry-into-the-safeguarding-of-%E2%80%98absent%E2%80%99-children-%E2%80%98It-is-good-when-someone-cares%E2%80 (accessed 13 March 2026).

Alliance for Youth Justice (2025) From exploited to exploiter? Preventing the unjust criminalisation of victims of child criminal exploitation in the transition to adulthood. Alliance for Youth Justice. Available at: https://t2a.org.uk/wp-content/uploads/2025/09/FINAL-AYJ-Exploited-to-Exploiter-CCE-Transition-to-Adulthood-Report-10.09.25-1.pdf (accessed 29 January 2026).

Allnock, D. and Atkinson, R. (2019) 'Snitches get stitches': School-specific barriers to victim disclosure and peer reporting of sexual harm committed by young people in school contexts. *Child Abuse & Neglect*, *89*, 7–17.

Arnot, M. and Swartz, S. (2018) Gender respect: Empirical insights for (moral) educators about women's struggles for respect in the Global South. *Journal of Moral Education*, *47*(4), 481–97.

Audley, S., Hsueh, Y. and Zhang, H. (2020) I'm respectful: Why don't they like me? Evaluator and gender effects of showing respect and children's social competence. *Social Development, 29*(1), 249–72.

Augusti, E.M. and Myhre, M.C. (2024) The barriers and facilitators to abuse disclosure and psychosocial support needs in children and adolescents around the time of disclosure. *Child Care in Practice, 30*(2), 187–202.

Augustyn, M.B., Ward, J.T. and Krohn, M.D. (2017) Exploring intergenerational continuity in gang membership. *Journal of Crime and Justice, 40*(3), 252–74.

Aussems, K., Muntinga, M., Addink, A. and Dedding, C. (2020) 'Call us by our name': Quality of care and wellbeing from the perspective of girls in residential care facilities who are commercially and sexually exploited by 'loverboys'. *Children and Youth Services Review, 116*, 105213.

Bancroft, K.H. (2012) Zones of exclusion: Urban spatial policies, social justice, and social services. *The Journal of Sociology & Social Welfare, 39*(3), 63–84.

Banyard, V., Waterman, E. and Edwards, K. (2021) Bystanders to prevent peer sexual violence: Understanding patterns of prosocial behavior over time from early to later adolescence. *Journal of Youth and Adolescence, 50*(10), 1982–94.

Barber, B.K. and Schluterman, J.M. (2008) Connectedness in the lives of children and adolescents: A call for greater conceptual clarity. *Journal of Adolescent Health, 43*(3), 209–16.

Barber, B.K., Stolz, H.E. and Olsen, J.A. (2005) Parental support, psychological control, and behavioral control: Assessing relevance across time, culture, and method. *Monographs of the Society for Research in Child Development, 70*(4), 1–137.

Barr, D. (2017) Friendship and belonging, in *Fostering Friendship*. Routledge, pp 19–30.

Barron, C. (2022) How exclusion from the public and private realm can negatively effect adolescents' sense of community belonging. *Irish Journal of Psychological Medicine, 39*(2), 155–62.

Barry, M. (2016) On the cusp of recognition: Using critical theory to promote desistance among young offenders, *Theoretical Criminology, 20*(1), 91–106.

Barter, C., McCarry, M., Berridge, D. and Evans, K. (2009) *Partner exploitation and violence in teenage intimate relationships*. NSPCC. Available at: https://www.nspcc.org.uk/globalassets/documents/research-reports/partner-exploitation-violence-teenage-intimate-relationships-report.pdf (accessed 12 March 2026).

Bason, C. (2018) *Leading public sector innovation: Co-creating for a better society* (2nd edn). Policy Press.

BBC (2005) Hoodies: good, bad or ugly? Available at: https://www.bbc.co.uk/threecounties/content/articles/2005/06/10/hannah_smith_hoodie_feature.shtml (accessed 13 March 2026).

BBC (2015) School sex crime reports in UK top 5,500 in three years. Available at: https://www.bbc.com/news/education-34138287 (accessed 2 October 2025).

BBC (2017) Two young Devon men die after 'taking drugs at Plymouth Pryzm nightclub'. Available at: https://www.bbc.com/news/uk-england-devon-42293096 (accessed 12 March 2026).

Beckett, H. (2011) *Not a world away: The sexual exploitation of children and young people in Northern Ireland* . Barnardos NI.

Beckett, H. (2019) Moving beyond discourses of agency, gain and blame: Reconceptuliasing young people's experiences of sexual exploitation, in J. Pearce (ed.) *Child sexual exploitation: Why theory matters*. Bristol Policy Press, pp 23–43.

Beckett, H. and Walker, J. (2017) Words matter: Reconceptualising the conceptualisation of child sexual exploitation. In *Understanding and responding to child sexual exploitation*, Routledge, pp 9–23.

Beiner, R. (1984) Walter Benjamin's philosophy of history. *Political Theory, 12*(3), 423–34.

Benavente, B., Díaz-Faes, D.A., Ballester, L. and Pereda, N. (2022) Commercial sexual exploitation of children and adolescents in Europe: A systematic review. *Trauma, Violence, & Abuse, 23*(5), 1529–48.

Benjamin, J. (1988) *The bonds of love: Psychoanalysis, feminism, and the problem of domination*. Pantheon.

Berelowitz, S., Clifton, J., Firmin, C., Gulyurtlu, S. and Edwards, G. (2013) *'If only someone had listened': Office of the Children's Commissioner's inquiry into child sexual exploitation in gangs and groups: Final report*. Office of the Children's Commissioner.

Bhadani, A., Kearns, E., Evans, J., Emden, J. and Mort, L. (2023) 'Editorial', *IPPR Progressive Review, 30*, 66–8.

Billingham, L. (2018) *Hackney wick through young eyes: What local young people value, the problems they face, and what they want to change*. Wick Award and Hackney Quest.

Billingham, L. and Irwin-Rogers, K. (2020) Mattering and the violence in our cities, in J. Dobson and R. Atkinson (eds) *Urban Crisis Urban Hope*. Anthem Press, pp 55–62.

Billingham, L. and Irwin-Rogers, K. (2022) *Against youth violence: A social harms perspective*. Bristol University Press.

Blakemore, S.J. (2018) Avoiding social risk in adolescence. *Current Directions in Psychological Science, 27*(2), 116–22.

Boddy, J. (2023) Engaging with uncertainty: Studying child and family welfare in precarious times. *Families, Relationships and Societies, 12*(1), 127–14.

Bostock, L. and Koprowska, J. (2022) 'I know how it sounds on paper' risk talk, the use of documents and epistemic justice in child protection assessment home visits. *Qualitative Social Work, 21*(6), 1147–66.

Bowlby, S. and McKie, L. (2019) 'Care and caring: An ecological framework', *Area 51*(3), 532–39.

Bracewell, K., Larkins, C., Radford, L. and Stanley, N. (2020) Educational opportunities and obstacles for teenagers living in domestic violence refuges. *Child Abuse Review, 29*(2), 130–43.

Brandon, M. Sidebotham, P., Bailey, S., Belderson, P., Hawley, C., Ellis, C. and Megson, M. (2012) *New learning from serious case reviews.* Department for Education, DFE-RR226. Available at: https://assets.publishing.service.gov.uk/media/5a7a0893ed915d6d99f5cab0/DFE-RR226_Report.pdf (accessed 29 January 2026).

Brennan, E. and McElvaney, R. (2020) What helps children tell? A qualitative meta-analysis of child sexual abuse disclosure. *Child Abuse Review, 29*(2), 97–113.

Butler, A., Willetts, G. and Copnell, B. (2017) Nurses' perceptions of working with families in the paediatric intensive care unit. *Nursing in Critical Care, 22*(4), 195–202.

Bywaters, P., Scourfield, J., Jones, C., Sparks, T., Elliott, M., Hooper, J. et al (2020) Child welfare inequalities in the four nations of the UK. *Journal of Social Work, 20*(2), 193–215.

Cairney, P. and Toomey, C. (2025) Systems leadership: A qualitative systematic review of advice for policymakers. *Open Research Europe, 5*, 6.

Campbell, J.R. (2022) Why 'the best interests' of unaccompanied asylum-seeking children are left at the border: Structural violence and British asylum policies. *Journal of Borderlands Studies, 37*(4), 847–64.

Care Act 2014, c. 23 (UK) Available at: https://www.legislation.gov.uk/ukpga/2014/23/contents (accessed 12 March 2026).

Carmeli, R. (2022) The grammar of paradox: Deciphering Winnicott's language theory. *The International Journal of Psychoanalysis, 103*(1), 89–107.

Carr, D. and Springer, K.W. (2010) Advances in families and health research in the 21st century. *Journal of Marriage and Family, 72*(3), 743–61.

Casey, L. (2025) National audit on group-based child sexual exploitation and abuse. Available at: www.gov.uk/government/publications/national-audit-on-group-based-child-sexual-exploitation-and-abuse (accessed 9 March 2026).

Chabot, S. (2008) Love and revolution. *Critical Sociology, 34*(6), 803–28.

Chapman, R. and Carel, H. (2022) Neurodiversity, epistemic injustice, and the good human life. *Journal of Social Philosophy, 53*(4), 614–31.

Chase, E. (2010) Agency and silence: Young people seeking asylum alone in the UK. *British Journal of Social Work, 40*(7), 2050–68.

Chief Secretary to the Treasury (2003) *Every Child Matters*. Cm 5860. The Stationary Office.

Child Safeguarding Practice Review Panel (2020) *It was hard to escape: safeguarding children at risk from criminal exploitation.* Available at: https://assets.publishing.service.gov.uk/media/67cb0a9d5993d41513a45c5b/Race_Racism_Safeguarding_March_2025.pdf (accessed 11 March 2026).

Child Safeguarding Practice Review Panel (2024) *Annual report 2023–2024.* Available at: https://www.gov.uk/government/publications/child-safeguarding-practice-review-panel-annual-report-2023-to-2024 (accessed 13 March 2026).

Child Safeguarding Practice Review Panel (2025) 'It's silent': Race, racism and safeguarding children. Available at: https://assets.publishing.service.gov.uk/media/67cb0a9d5993d41513a45c5b/Race_Racism_Safeguarding_March_2025.pdf (accessed 29 January 2026).

Children Act 1989, c. 41 (UK). Available at: https://www.legislation.gov.uk/ukpga/1989/41 (accessed 11 March 2026).

Children's Commissioner (2022) *A head start: Early support for children's mental health*. Children's Commissioner.

Children's Commissioner (2025) *Register, regulate and raise standards: The Children's Commissioner's view on unregistered alternative provision.* The Children's Commissioner for England.

Children's Commissioner for Wales (2020) No wrong door: Bringing services together to meet children's needs. Available at: https://www.childcomwales.org.uk/wp-content/uploads/2020/06/NoWrongDoor_FINAL_EN230620.pdf (accessed 7 October 2025).

Children's Society (2022) *The good childhood report 2022*. Available at: www.childrenssociety.org.uk/information/professionals/resources/good-childhood-report-2022 (accessed 9 March 2026).

Christie, C. (2018) *A trauma-informed health and care approach for responding to child sexual abuse and exploitation current knowledge report.* Available at: https://assets.publishing.service.gov.uk/government/uploads/system/uploads/attachment_data/file/712725/trauma-informed-health-and-care-approach-report.pdf (accessed 8 October 2025).

Cicchetti, D. (2016) Socioemotional, personality, and biological development: Illustrations from a multilevel developmental psychopathology perspective on child maltreatment. *Annual Review of Psychology*. *67*(1), 187–211.

Clarke, J. (2005) New Labour's citizens: Activated, empowered, responsibilized, abandoned? *Critical Social Policy, 25*(4), 447–63.

Clawson, H.J., Dutch, N., Solomon, A. and Grace, L.G. (2009) *Human trafficking into and within the United States: A review of the literature.* Office of the Assistant Secretary for Planning and Evaluation, US Department of Human and Health Services. Available at: https://aspe.hhs.gov/reports/human-trafficking-within-united-states-review-literature-0 (accessed 23 January 2026).

Cockbain, E. and Brayley, H. (2012) Child sexual exploitation and youth offending: A research note. *European Journal of Criminology, 9*(6), 689–700.

Cocker, C., Holmes, D. and Cooper, A. (2024) *Transitional safeguarding.* Policy Press.

Coleman, J. (2011) *The nature of adolescence* (4th edn). Routledge.

Connolly, J., Pepler, D., Craig, W. and Taradash, A. (2000) Dating experiences of bullies in early adolescence. *Child Maltreatment, 5*(4), 299–310.

Coote, A. (2023) Rebuilding the UK's social contract. *IPPR Progressive Review, 30*, 69–76.

Cossar, J., Brandon, M., Bailey, S., Belderson, P. and Biggart, L. (2013) *'It takes a lot to build trust': Recognition and telling: Developing earlier routes to help for children and young people.* Office of the Children's Commissioner.

Crossley, S. and Leigh, J. (2017) The 'troubled' case of Rotherham. *Critical and Radical Social Work, 5*(1), 23–40.

D'Andrea, W., Ford, J., Stolbach, B., Spinazzola, J. and van der Kolk, B.A. (2012) Understanding interpersonal trauma in children: Why we need a developmentally appropriate trauma diagnosis. *American Journal of Orthopsychiatry, 82*(2), 187–200.

Darwall, S.L. (1977) Two kinds of respect. *Ethics, 88*(1), 36–49.

Davies, B. (2018) *Austerity, youth policy and the deconstruction of the youth service in England.* Springer.

Davis, J. (2022) Adultification bias within child protection and safeguarding. HM Inspectorate of Probation. Available at: https://hmiprobation.justiceinspectorates.gov.uk/document/adultification-bias-within-child-protection-and-safeguarding/ (accessed 23 January 2026).

Davis, J. and Marsh, N. (2020) Boys to men: the cost of 'adultification' in safeguarding responses to Black boys. *Critical and Radical Social Work, 8*(2), 255–9.

de Vries, I., Ebrahem, S., Donninger, D., van der Meer, B. and van Bemmel, S. (2025) Social contexts of isolation, vulnerability, and resilience among minors with experiences of commercial sexual exploitation in the Netherlands. *Child Abuse & Neglect, 164*, 107439.

Deakin, J., Fox, C. and Matos, R. (2022) Labelled as 'risky' in an era of control: How young people experience and respond to the stigma of criminalized identities. *European Journal of Criminology, 19*(4), 653–73.

DeCandia, C. and Guarino, K. (2015) Trauma-informed care: An ecological response. *Journal of Child and Youth Care Work, 25*, 7–32.

DeLisi, M., Vaughn, M.G., Gentile, D.A., Anderson, C.A. and Shook, J.J. (2013) Violent video games, delinquency, and youth violence: New evidence. *Youth Violence and Juvenile Justice*, *11*(2), 132–42.

Department for Children, Schools and Families (2009) *Safeguarding children and young people from sexual exploitation*. HMSO.

Department for Education (2018) Applying corporate parenting principles to looked-after children and care leavers: Statutory guidance for local authorities. Available at: https://assets.publishing.service.gov.uk/media/5a93eb3ae5274a5b87c2fde4/Applying_corporate_parenting_principles_to_looked-after_children_and_care_leavers.pdf (accessed 7 October 2025).

Department for Education (2022) Children's social care innovation programme: insights and evaluation. Available at: https://www.gov.uk/guidance/childrens-social-care-innovation-programme-insights-and-evaluation (accessed 9 January 2026).

Department for Education (2023a) State of the nation 2022: Children and young people's wellbeing. Available at: https://www.gov.uk/government/publications/state-of-the-nation-2022-children-and-young-peoples-wellbeing (accessed 7 October 2025).

Department for Education (2023b) Children's social care national framework statutory guidance on the purpose, principles for practice and expected outcomes of children's social care. Available at: https://assets.publishing.service.gov.uk/media/657c538495bf650010719097/Children_s_Social_Care_National_Framework__December_2023.pdf (accessed 7 October 2025).

Department for Education (2024) Information sharing: Advice for practitioners providing safeguarding services for children, young people, parents and carers. Available at: https://www.gov.uk/government/publications/safeguarding-practitioners-information-sharing-advice (accessed 7 October 2025).

Department for Education (2025) Children's Wellbeing and Schools Bill: Policy summary notes. Available at: https://assets.publishing.service.gov.uk/media/67dd2b17a18f580c277f7887/CWS_Bill_Policy__Summary__notes_as_amended_in_the_House_of__Commons.pdf (accessed 7 October 2025).

Department for Education and Skills (2007) *Care matters: Time for change*. The Stationery Office.

Deutsch, N.L. and Jones, J.N. (2008) 'Show me an ounce of respect': Respect and authority in adult-youth relationships in after-school programs. *Journal of Adolescent Research*, *23*(6), 667–88.

Dickens, J., Taylor, J., Cook, L., Cossar, J., Garstang, J., Hallett, N. et al (2022) *Learning for the future: Final analysis of Serious Case Reviews, 2017–19*. Department for Education.

Dillon, J. (2021) 'Wishes and feelings': Misunderstandings and missed opportunities for participation in child protection proceedings. *Child & Family Social Work, 26*(4), 664–76.

Dore, I. (2019) Doing knowing ethically: Where social work values meet critical realism. *Ethics and Social Welfare, 13*(4), 377–91.

Economist Impact (2022) *Out of the shadows index 2022*. Economist Impact. Available at: https://outoftheshadows.nyc3.cdn.digitaloceanspaces.com/uploads/documents/OOS_Index_Global_Report_2022_EN_V2_2023-02-08-174957_kmfz.pdf (accessed 13 March 2026).

Egan, M., Neary, J., Keenan, P.J. and Bond, L. (2013) Perceptions of antisocial behaviour and negative attitudes towards young people: Focus group evidence from adult residents of disadvantaged urban neighbourhoods (Glasgow, UK). *Journal of Youth Studies, 16*(5), 612–27.

Elliott, G.C., Colangelo, M.F. and Gelles, R.J. (2005) Mattering and suicide ideation: Establishing and elaborating a relationship. *Social Psychology Quarterly, 68*(3), 223–38.

Ellis, K. (2018) Contested vulnerability: A case study of girls in secure care. *Children and Youth Services Review, 88*, 156–63.

Enns, C.Z. (2004) *Feminist theories and feminist psychotherapies: Origins, themes, and diversity*. Routledge.

Enright, R.D., Wang Xu, J., Rapp, H., Evans, M. and Song, J.Y. (2022) The philosophy and social science of agape love. *Journal of Theoretical and Philosophical Psychology, 42*(4), 220–37.

Estyn (2021) *'We don't tell our teachers' Experiences of peer-on-peer sexual harassment among secondary school pupils in Wales*. Available at: https://estyn.gov.wales/improvement-resources/we-dont-tell-our-teachers-experiences-of-peer-on-peer-sexual-harassment-among-secondary-school-pupils-in-wales-2/ (accessed 13 March 2026).

EVAW (2017) Written evidence from End Violence Against Women Coalition (CMH0124) to the Health Select Committee. Available at: https://www.endviolenceagainstwomen.org.uk/select-committee-submission-links-young-peoples-mental-health-to-sexual-harassment/#:~:text=Select%20Committee%20submission%20links%20girls'%20mental%20health%20to%20sexual%20harassment,-EVAW&text=Written%20evidence%20submitted%20by%20the,services%20and%20specialist%20support%20organisations (accessed 2 October 2025).

Ewell Foster, C., Horwitz, A., Thomas, A., Opperman, K., Gipson, P., Burnside, A. et al (2017) Connectedness to family, school, peers, and community in socially vulnerable adolescents. *Children and Youth Services Review, 81*, 321–31.

Fanon, F. (1952) *Black skin, white mask*. Grove Press.

Featherstone, B., Gupta, A. and Morris, L. (2018) *Protecting children: A social model*. Policy Press.

Finkelhor, D., Turner, H. and Colburn, D. (2023) Which dynamics make online child sexual abuse and cyberstalking more emotionally impactful: Perpetrator identity and images? *Child Abuse & Neglect, 137*, Article 106020.

Firmin, C. (2018) Contextual risk, individualised responses: An assessment of safeguarding responses to nine cases of peer-on-peer abuse. *Child Abuse Review, 27*(1), 42–57.

Firmin, C. (2020) *Contextual safeguarding and child protection: Rewriting the rules*. Routledge. https://doi.org/10.4324/9780429283314

Firmin, C. (2024) Binaries and blurred lines: The ethical stress of child protection social work in the grey of extra-familial harm. *Ethics and Social Welfare, 18*(4), 404–21.

Firmin, C. and Knowles, R. (2020) *The legal and policy framework for contextual safeguarding approaches: A 2020 update on the 2018 legal briefing*. Contextual Safeguarding Network, University of Bedfordshire. Available at: https://researchportal.beds.ac.uk/en/publications/the-legal-and-policy-framework-for-contextual-safeguarding-approa-3/?utm_source=chatgpt.com (accessed 12 March 2026).

Firmin, C. and Wroe, L. (2021) *Building safety safeguarding black young men and boys in Lambeth*. Lambeth Safeguarding Children's Partnership. Available at: https://www.contextualsafeguarding.org.uk/resources/toolkit-overview/building-safety-safeguarding-black-young-men-and-boys-in-lambeth/ (accessed 13 March 2026).

Firmin, C. and Knowles, R. (2022) Has the purpose outgrown the design?, in D. Holmes (ed.) *Safeguarding young people: Risk, rights, resilience and relationships*. Jessica Kingsley Publishers, pp 129–56.

Firmin, C. and Owens, R. (2022) Holding it together? Professional perspectives on the role of relationships when relocating young people due to extra-familial harm. *International Journal on Child Maltreatment: Research, Policy and Practice, 5*(2), 231–55.

Firmin, C. and King, H. (2026) *Prioritising protection: The role of children's services and wider safeguarding partnerships in protecting young people impacted by extra-familial harm*. Youth Endowment Fund.

Firmin, C., Peace, D. and Wroe, L. (2026) Why 'common-sense' is complicated: Unearthing the cultural facilitators of contextual safeguarding structures. *Journal of Social Work*, 14680173251409263.

Firmin, C., Lefevre, M., Huegler, N. and Peace, D. (2022) *Safeguarding young people beyond the family home: Responding to extra-familial risks and harms*. Policy Press.

Firmin, C., Lefevre, M., Langhoff, K. and Ruch, G. (2024) A line in the sand: Moving from surface improvement to foundational shifts to develop effective responses to extra-familial risks and harms. *British Journal of Social Work, 55*(3), 1296–316.

Firmin, C., Langhoff, K., Eyal-Lubling, R., Maglajlic, R.A. and Lefevre, M. (2024) 'Known to services' or 'Known by professionals': Relationality at the core of trauma-informed responses to extra-familial harm. *Children and Youth Services Review*, *160*, 107595.

Flett, G. (2018) *The psychology of mattering: Understanding the human need to be significant*. Academic Press.

Fong, R. and Cardoso, J.B. (2010) Child human trafficking victims: Challenges for the child welfare system. *Evaluation and Program Planning*, *33*(3), 311–16.

Foshee, V.A., McNaughton Reyes, L., Agnew-Brune, C.B., Simon, T.R., Vaji, K.V., Lee, R.D. et al (2014) The effects of the evidence-based Safe Dates dating abuse prevention program on other youth violence outcomes. *Prevention Science*, *15*(6), 907–16.

Foucault, M. (1982) The subject and power. *Critical Inquiry*, *8*(4), 777–95.

Fox, C.L., Corr, M.L., Gadd, D. and Butler, I. (2014) Young teenagers' experiences of domestic abuse. *Journal of Youth Studies*, *17*(4), 510–26.

Franklin, A., Brown, S. and Brady, G. (2018) The use of tools and checklists to assess the risk of child sexual exploitation: Lessons from UK practice. *Journal of Child Sexual Abuse*, *27*(8), 978–97.

Franklin, A., Bradley, L., Greenaway, J., Goff, S., Atkins, S. and Rylatt, L. (2024) *Internal trafficking and exploitation of children and young people with special educational needs and disabilities (SEND) within England and Wales: Understanding identification and responses to inform effective policy and practice*. Modern Slavery and Human Rights Policy and Evidence Centre. Available at: https://proceduresonline.com/trixcms2/media/23276/ms-and-send-full-report-2024.pdf (accessed 23 January 2026).

Fricker, M. (2007) *Epistemic injustice: Power and the ethics of knowing*. Oxford University Press.

Frost, L. (2016) Exploring the concepts of recognition and shame for social work. *Journal of Social Work Practice*, *30*(4), 431–46.

Gamble, J. and McCallum, R. (2022) *Local child safeguarding practice review: Child Q*, City & Hackney Safeguarding Children Partnership. Available at: https://chscp.org.uk/wp-content/uploads/2022/03/Child-Q-PUBLISHED-14-March-22.pdf (accessed 7 October 2025).

Gaskell, C. (2008) 'But they just don't respect us': Young people's experiences of (dis)respected citizenship and the New Labour Respect Agenda. *Children's Geographies*, *6*(3), 223–38.

Gibbs, A., Jewkes, R., Sikweyiya, Y. and Willan, S. (2015) Reconstructing masculinity? A qualitative evaluation of the Stepping Stones and Creating Futures interventions in urban informal settlements in South Africa. *Culture, Health & Sexuality*, *17*(2), 208–22.

Gilligan, C. (1982) *In a different voice: Psychological theory and women's development*. Harvard University Press.

Gilligan, C. (2014) Moral injury and the ethic of care: Reframing the conversation about differences. *Journal of Social Philosophy*, *45*(1), 89–106.

Gilligan, R. (2023) *In a human voice*. Polity Press.

Giselsson, K. (2012) *Grounds for respect: Particularism, universalism, and communal accountability*. Lexington Books.

Givens, T.E. (2021) *Radical empathy: Finding a path to bridging racial divides*. Policy Press.

Golombok, S. and Tasker, F. (2015) Socioemotional development in changing families, in M.E. Lamb and R.M. Lerner (eds) *Handbook of child psychology and developmental science, Vol. 3. Socioemotional processes* (7th edn). John Wiley & Sons, pp 419–63.

Gorin, S. and Jobe, A. (2013) Young people who have been maltreated: Different needs—different responses? *British Journal of Social Work*, *43*(7), 1330–46.

Graham, B., White, C., Edwards, A., Potter, S. and Street, C. (2019) *School exclusion: A literature review on the continued disproportionate exclusion of certain children*. Department for Education.

Greenfield, P.M., Keller, H., Fuligni, A. and Maynard, A. (2003) Cultural pathways through universal development. *Annual Review of Psychology*, *54*(1), 461–90.

Gregorowski, C. and Seedat, S. (2013) Addressing childhood trauma in a developmental context. *Journal of Child and Adolescent Mental Health*, *25*(2), 105–18.

Gupta, A., Blumhardt, H. and ATD Fourth World. (2018) Poverty, exclusion and child protection practice: The contribution of 'the politics of recognition & respect'. *European Journal of Social Work*, *21*(2), 247–59.

Hallett, S. (2016) 'An uncomfortable comfortableness': 'Care', child protection and child sexual exploitation. *British Journal of Social Work*, *46*(7), 2137–52.

Hallett, S. (2017) *Making sense of child sexual exploitation: Exchange, abuse and young people*. Policy Press (2), 175–95.

Hallsworth, S. and Young, T. (2008) Gang talk and gang talkers: A critique. *Crime, Media, Culture*, *4*(2), 175–95.

Hamilton, C.J., Rodgers, A., Howard, K. and Warrington, C. (2019) From the ground up: Young research advisors' perspectives on relationships between participation and protection. *Journal of Children's Services*, *14*(3), 228–34.

Hanlon, N. (2022) Relational justice and relational pedagogy in professional social care work. *Social Work Education*, *43*(3), 570–87.

Hanson, E. and Holmes, D. (2014) *That difficult age: Developing a more effective response to risks in adolescence: Evidence scope*. Research in Practice.

Hardin, H.K., Bender, A.E., Hermann, C.P. and Speck, B.J. (2020) An integrative review of adolescent trust in the healthcare provider relationship. *Journal of Advanced Nursing*, 77(4), 1645–55.

Harju, A., Bernedo Muñoz, I.M. and Tofteng, D. (2024) Tensions and dilemmas in participatory youth projects working within institutional frameworks. *International Journal of Adolescence and Youth, 29*(1), 2312855.

Hart, P. (2017) Disguised compliance – Or undisguised nonsense?. *Family Law Week*, 10 April 2017. Available at: www.familylawweek.co.uk/articles/disguised-compliance-or-undisguised-nonsense/ (accessed 9 March 2026).

Heaven, P.C., Newbury, K. and Wilson, V. (2004) The Eysenck psychoticism dimension and delinquent behaviours among non-criminals: Changes across the lifespan?. *Personality and Individual Differences, 36*(8), 1817–25.

Heimer, K. and DeCoster, S.D. (1999) The gendering of violent delinquency. *Criminology, 37*(2), 277–318.

Henriksen, A.K., Bengtsson, T.T. and Henriksen, T.D. (2024) Crime prevention, support or punishment? Introducing an ambiguous system of youth justice in Denmark. *Youth Justice, 24*(3), 463–79.

Henry, K.L. (2008) Low prosocial attachment, involvement with drug-using peers, and adolescent drug use: A longitudinal examination of mediational mechanisms. *Psychology of Addictive Behaviors, 22*(2), 302.

Hernandez, R. and Ebersole, D. (2022) Parents' and children's privacy management about sensitive topics: A dyadic study. *Journal of Family Issues, 43*(1), 73–95.

Hickle, K. (2016) *A trauma-informed approach: Policing responses to child sexual exploitation*. Briefing Report. University of Sussex. Available at: https://www.uobcsepolicinghub.org.uk/assets/documents/Trauma-Informed-Approach-Briefing-Final.pdf (accessed 23 January 2026).

Hickle, K. (2020) Introducing a trauma-informed capability approach in youth services. *Children & Society, 34*(6), 537–51.

Hickle, K. and Lefevre, M. (2022) Learning to love and trust again: a relational approach to developmental trauma, in D. Holmes (ed.) *Safeguarding young people: Risk, rights, relationships and resilience*. Jessica Kingsley, pp 159–76.

Hill, T. (1998) Respect for persons in Kant's ethics, in The *Routledge encyclopedia of philosophy*. Taylor and Francis. Available at: https://www.rep.routledge.com/articles/thematic/respect-for-persons/v-1/sections/respect-for-persons-in-kants-ethics (accessed 7 October 2025).

HM Government (2018) *Working together to safeguard children: A guide to inter-agency working to safeguard and promote the welfare of children*. Department for Education.

HM Government (2023) Official statistics modern slavery: National referral mechanism and duty to notify statistics UK, end of year summary 2022. Available at: https://www.gov.uk/government/statistics/modern-slavery-national-referral-mechanism-and-duty-to-notify-statistics-uk-end-of-year-summary-2022/modern-slavery-national-referral-mechanism-and-duty-to-notify-statistics-uk-end-of-year-summary-2022#:~:text=Thr (accessed 7 October 2025).

Holmes, D. (2022) Transitional safeguarding: The case for change. *Practice, 34*(1), 7–23.

Holmes, D. and Smale, E. (2018) *Transitional safeguarding – adolescence to adulthood: Strategic briefing*. Research in Practice.

Holmes, L. and Lefevre, M. (2024) Value for whom? Rethinking cost-effectiveness from young people's perspective. *Health Education Journal, 84*(4), 446–58.

Honneth, A. (1996) *The struggle for recognition: The moral grammar of social conflicts*. The MIT Press.

Hood, A.N. (2023) Dual status and adultification: Black girls' lives in context. *Journal of Family Strengths, 23*(1), 3.

Hopper, E.K., Bassuk, E.L. and Olivet, J. (2010) Shelter from the storm: Trauma-informed care in homelessness services settings. *The Open Health Services and Policy Journal, 3*(2), 80–100.

Horgan, D. and Ní Raghallaigh, M. (2019) The social care needs of unaccompanied minors: The Irish experience. *European Journal of Social Work, 22*(1), 95–106.

Hsueh, Y., Zhou, Z., Cohen, R., Hundley, R.J. and Deptula, D.P. (2005) Knowing and showing respect: Chinese and US children's understanding of respect and its association to their friendships. *Journal of Psychology in Chinese Societies, 6*(2), 229–60.

Huegler, N. and Ruch, G. (2022) Risk, vulnerability and complexity: transitional safeguarding as a reframing of binary perspectives. *Practice, 34*(1), 25–39.

Huegler, N., Damman, J.L., Ruch, G. and Bowyer, S. (2024) 'We were persistently othering them out': Reconceptualising 'safeguarding' for young people experiencing extra-familial risks and harms during transition to adulthood. *Health Education Journal, 84*(4), 432–45.

Hunt, G.R., Higgins, D.J., Willis, M.L., Mathews, B., Lawrence, D., Meinck, F. et al (2024) The prevalence of peer sexual harassment during childhood in Australia. *Journal of Interpersonal Violence, 39*(23–4), 5108–30.

Hunter, R., Burton, M. and Trinder, L. (2020) *Assessing risk of harm to children and parents in private law children cases: Final report*. Ministry of Justice. Available at: https://kar.kent.ac.uk/81894/ (accessed 13 March 2026).

Huo, Y.J., Binning, K.R. and Molina, L.E. (2010) Testing an integrative model of respect: Implications for social engagement and well-being. *Personality and Social Psychology Bulletin, 36*(2), 200–12.

Huppert, F.A. and So, T.T. (2013) Flourishing across Europe: Application of a new conceptual framework for defining well-being. *Social Indicators Research, 110*(3), 837–61.

Ikomi, S. (2023) Child Q: A case study of the adultification of Black girls in schools. In *The European Conference on Education 2023: Official Conference Proceedings*. The International Academic Forum. Available at: https://papers.iafor.org/submission67668/ (accessed 23 January 2026).

Independent Care Review (2020) *The promise*. Available at: www.carereview.scot (accessed 25 February 2026).

Jay, A. (2014) *Independent inquiry into child sexual exploitation in Rotherham (1997–2013)*. Rotherham Metropolitan Borough Council.

Johnson, F. (2013) *Redacted overview report on the serious case review relating to Tom and Vic*. Kingston LSCB.

Jones, C., Stalker, K., Franklin, A., Fry, D., Cameron, A. and Taylor, J. (2017) Enablers of help-seeking for deaf and disabled children following abuse and barriers to protection: a qualitative study. *Child & Family Social Work*, *22*(2), 762–71.

Jones, R. (2015) The end game: The marketisation and privatisation of children's social work and child protection. *Critical Social Policy*, *35*(4), 447–69.

Juhila, K., Raitakari, S. and Hansen Löfstrand, C. (2016) Responsibilization in governmentality literature, in K. Juhila, S. Raitakari and C. Hall (eds) *Responsibilisation at the margins of welfare services*. Routledge, pp 11–34.

King, H., Crossley, S. and Smith, R. (2021) Responsibility, resilience and symbolic power. *The Sociological Review*, *69*(5), 920–36.

King, V., Boyd, L.M. and Pragg, B. (2018) Parent–adolescent closeness, family belonging, and adolescent well-being across family structures. *Journal of Family Issues*, *39*(7), 2007–36.

Knijn, T. and Van Nijnatten, C.H.C.J. (2011) Child welfare in the Netherlands: Between privacy and protection. *Child Protection Systems: International Trends and Orientations*, 223–42.

Koch, I., Williams, P. and Wroe, L. (2024) 'County lines': Racism, safeguarding and statecraft in Britain. *Race & Class*, *65*(3), 3–26.

Laird, R.D. and Hawk, S.T. (2024) Adolescents' perceptions of privacy violations by parents, siblings, and friends. *Journal of Research on Adolescence*, *34*(4), 1378–90.

Lammy, D. (2017) *The Lammy Review: An independent review into the treatment of, and outcomes for, Black, Asian and minority ethnic individuals in the criminal justice system*. Ministry of Justice. Available at: https://www.gov.uk/government/publications/lammy-review-final-report (accessed 13 March 2026).

Langhoff, K., Lefevre, M. and Larkin, R. (2024) Shipping containers and speed boats: exploring the contexts and relational spaces professionals navigate to safeguard young people from criminal exploitation. *Journal of Children's Services*, *19*(1), 74–87.

Lapsley, I. (2009) New public management: The cruellest invention of the human spirit? 1. *Abacus*, *45*(1), 1–21.

Latimer, K., Adams Elias, C. and Firmin, C.E. (2020) *Opportunities for peer safeguarding intervention: A briefing following fieldwork with safer London*. University of Bedfordshire.

Laursen, B. (2018) Peer influence, in W.M. Bukowski, B. Laursen and K.H. Rubin (eds) *Handbook of peer interactions, relationships, and groups*. Guildford Press, pp 447–69.

Leckey, R., Schmieder-Gropen, R., Nnebe, C. and Clouthier, M. (2022) Indigenous parents and child welfare: Mistrust, epistemic injustice, and training. *Social & Legal Studies*, *31*(4), 559–79.

Lefevre, M. (2018) *Communicating and engaging with children and young people: making a difference* (2nd edn). Policy Press.

Lefevre, M., Tanner, K. and Luckock, B. (2008) Developing social work students' communication skills with children and young people: A model for the qualifying level curriculum, *Child and Family Social Work*, *13*, 166–76.

Lefevre, M., Hickle, K. and Luckock, B. (2019) 'Both/and' not 'either/or': Reconciling rights to protection and participation in working with child sexual exploitation. *British Journal of Social Work, 49*(7), 1837–55.

Lefevre, M., Hickle, K., Luckock, B. and Ruch, G. (2017) Building trust with children and young people at risk of child sexual exploitation: The professional challenge. *British Journal of Social Work*, *47*(8), 2456–73.

Lefevre, M., Temperley, J., Goldsmith, C. and Hampson, M. (2025) Creating a conducive zone for innovation in children's social care. *Health & Social Care in the Community*, *2025*(1), 3599333.

Lefevre, M., Huegler, N., Lloyd, J., Owens, R., Damman, J., Ruch, G. et al (2024) Innovation in social care: New approaches for young people affected by extra-familial risks and harms, in *Innovation in social care*. Policy Press.

Leigh, J., Beddoe, L. and Keddell, E. (2020) Disguised compliance or undisguised nonsense? A critical discourse analysis of compliance and resistance in social work practice. *Families, Relationships and Societies*, *9*(2), 269–85.

Levitas, R. (2005) *The inclusive society: Social exclusion and New Labour*. Palgrave Macmillan.

Lindsay, B (2022) *Towards culturally sensitive schools part 2*. Power The Fight. Available at: https://www.powerthefight.org.uk/wp-content/uploads/2022/06/towards-culturally-sensitive-schools-part-2.pdf (accessed 13 March 2026).

Lines, L.E., Hunter, S., Marshall, A., Johnson, T. and Aston, M. (2025) How can we talk about child protection without talking about child protection? *Child Protection and Practice*, *4*, 100121.

Lloyd, J. and Firmin, C. (2019) No further action: Contextualising social care decisions for children victimised in extra-familial settings. *Youth Justice*, *20*(1–2), 79–92.

Lloyd, J. and Peace, D. (2025) Subverting the gaze: Using fictional videos and reaction videos as a participatory method to create practice change in social care systems. *International Journal of Social Research Methodology*, 1–18. https://doi.org/10.1080/13645579.2025.2606944

Lloyd, J., Manister, M. and Wroe, L. (2023) Social care responses to children who experience criminal exploitation and violence: The conditions for a welfare response. *The British Journal of Social Work*, *53*(8), 3725–43.

Lloyd, J., Balci, M., Firmin, C. and Owens, R. (2019) *Peer group assessment guidance*. University of Bedfordshire.

Lloyd, J., Hickle, K., Owens, R. and Peace, D. (2024) Relationship-based practice and contextual safeguarding: Approaches to working with young people experiencing extra-familial risk and harm. *Children & Society*, *38*(4), 1113–29.

Lloyd, S. (2022) 'She doesn't have to get in the car … ': Exploring social workers' understandings of sexually exploited girls as agents and choice-makers. *Children's Geographies*, *20*(5), 536–48.

Local Government Association (2013) *Making safeguarding personal: Sector-led improvement*. Available at: https://www.local.gov.uk/sites/default/files/documents/Making%20Safeguarding%20Personal%202012-13%20full%20report.pdf (accessed 12 March 2026).

Long, R., Roberts, N. and Foster, D. (2025) *Children's wellbeing and schools bill 2024–25: Research briefing*. House of Commons Library.

Lynch, K., Baker, J. and Lyons, M. (2016) *Affective equality: Love, care and injustice*. Springer.

Mabuvira, V. (2020) Making sense of African thought in social work practice in Zimbabwe: Towards professional decolonisation, *International Journal of Social Work*, *63*(4), 419–30.

Malone, K. (2002) Street life: Youth, culture and competing uses of public space. *Environment and Urbanization*, *14*(2), 157–68.

Malti, T., Peplak, J. and Zhang, L. (2020) The development of respect in children and adolescents. *Monographs of the Society for Research in Child Development*, *85*(3), 7–99.

Mansouri, F., Beaman, L. and Hussain, S. (2025) The everyday transnational practices of migrant youth: A transcultural perspective. *Journal of International Migration and Integration*. Advance online publication. https://doi.org/10.1007/s12134-025-01283-9

Mapes, A.R. and Cavell, T.A. (2021) Perceived barriers, relationship quality, and informal mentors: Adolescents' preference for disclosing about dating violence. *Journal of Community Psychology*, *49*(7), 2719–37.

Marsh, N. (2024) *An exploratory study: Investigating the socio-political and personal factors influencing social work decision-making in child exploitation cases in England* (Doctoral dissertation, University of East London).

Marshall, H. (2023) Victims first? Examining the place of 'child criminal exploitation' within 'child first' youth justice. *Children & Society*, *37*(4), 1156–70.

Marshall, H. (2024) Child criminal exploitation and the interactional emergence of victim status. *The British Journal of Criminology*, *64*(5), 1011–27.

Mason-Jones, A.J. and Loggie, J. (2019) Child sexual exploitation. An analysis of serious case reviews in England: Poor communication, incorrect assumptions and adolescent neglect. *Journal of Public Health, 42*(1), 62–8.

Mathews, B., Pacella, R., Scott, J.G., Finkelhor, D., Meinck, F., Higgins, D.J. et al (2023) The prevalence of child maltreatment in Australia: Findings from a national survey. *Medical Journal of Australia, 218*, S13–S18.

McAllister, J. (2022) *The independent review of children's social care: Final report*. Department for Education.

McGuinness, T. (2016) *The age of criminal responsibility*. UK Parliament Briefing Paper. House of Commons Library. Available at: https://researchbriefings.files.parliament.uk/documents/CBP-7687/CBP-7687.pdf (accessed 7 October 2025).

McKibbin, G. and Humphreys, C. (2019) The perceptions of Australian workers about caring for sexually exploited children in residential care. *Child Abuse Review, 28*(6), 418–30.

McKie, L., Gregory, S. and Bowlby, S. (2002) Shadow times: the temporal and spatial frameworks and experiences of caring and working, *Sociology, 36*(4), 897–924.

McKinney, C. and Renk, K. (2008) Multivariate models of parent-late adolescent gender dyads: The importance of parenting processes in predicting adjustment. *Child Psychiatry and Human Development, 39*(2), 147–70.

Meehan, T.C. (2003) Careful nursing: A model for contemporary nursing practice. *Journal of Advanced Nursing, 44*, 99–107.

Melrose, M. and Pearce, J. (2013) Introduction: Critical perspectives on child sexual exploitation and related trafficking, in *Critical perspectives on child sexual exploitation and related trafficking*, Palgrave Macmillan UK, pp 1–8.

Merkel-Holquin, L., Fluke, J. and Krugman, R. (2019) *National systems of child protection*. Springer.

Meysen, T. and Kelly, L. (2018) Child protection systems between professional cooperation and trustful relationships: A comparison of professional practical and ethical dilemmas in England/Wales, Germany, Portugal, and Slovenia. *Child & Family Social Work, 23*(2), 222–9.

Miller, S.M. and Savoie, A.J. (2002) *Respect and rights: Class, race, and gender today*. Bloomsbury Publishing PLC.

Miller-Perrin, C. and Wurtele, S.K. (2017) Sex trafficking and the commercial sexual exploitation of children. *Women & Therapy, 40*(1–2), 123–51.

Millie, A. (2014) The aesthetics of anti-social behaviour, in *Anti-Social Behaviour in Britain: Victorian and Contemporary Perspectives*, Palgrave Macmillan UK, pp 102–11.

Moore, K. and Miles, S. (2004) Young people, dance and the sub-cultural consumption of drugs. *Addiction Research & Theory, 12*(6), 507–23.

Morris, J. (2003) Including all children: Finding out about the experiences of children with communication and/or cognitive impairments. *Children & Society*, *17*(5), 337–48.

Munford, R. and Sanders, J. (2020) Shame and recognition: Social work practice with vulnerable young people. *Child & Family Social Work*, *25*(1), 53–61.

Munro, E. (2011) *The Munro review of child protection. Final report: A child-centred system*, Department for Education. Available at: https://www.gov.uk/government/publications/munro-review-of-child-protection-final-report-a-child-centred-system (accessed 29 January 2026).

Munro, E. (2019) Decision-making under uncertainty in child protection: Creating a just and learning culture. *Child & Family Social Work*, *24*(1), 123–30.

Murphy, C. (2023) How learning from the lived experiences of child protection social workers can help us understand the factors underpinning workforce instability within the English child protection system. *Journal of Social Work Practice*, *37*(2), 263–76.

Musto, J.L. (2022) The afterlife of decriminalisation: Anti-trafficking, child protection, and the limits of trauma-informed efforts. *Ethics and Social Welfare*, *16*(2), 169–92.

Nagy, É. and Horkai, A. (2021) Parental caringscapes – the analyses of mothering practices in local community contexts. *Acta Medicinae Et Sociologica*, *12*(33), 125–43.

Nakkan, C. (2025) *A growing divide: Two decades of intergenerational unfairness.* Intergenerational Foundation. Available at: https://www.if.org.uk/wp-content/uploads/2025/05/A-growing-divide-two-decades-of-intergenerational-unfairness-interactive.pdf (accessed 7 October 2025).

National Audit Office (2022) *Support for vulnerable adolescents.* National Audit Office Cross Government Session 2022–23, 11 November 2022 HC 800, ISBN: 978-1-78604-452-5.

National Safeguarding Panel and Davies (2025) *'It's silent': Race, racism and safeguarding children.* Child Safeguarding Practice Review Panel.

Noddings, N. (1984) *Caring: A feminine approach to ethics and moral education.* University of California Press.

Noddings, N. (2004) Foreword, in C.W. Bingham and A.M. Sidorkin (eds) *No education without relation* (Vol *259*) Peter Lang.

Noller, P. and Atkin, S. (2014) *Family life in adolescence.* Walter de Gruyter GmbH & Co KG.

Nuffield Family Justice Observatory (2025) *New data shows rise in the number of children aged 12 and under deprived of their liberty under the authority of the High Court.* Nuffield Family Justice Observatory. Available at: https://www.nuffieldfjo.org.uk/news/data-released-by-the-ministry-of-justice-shows-rise-in-number-of-children-under-12-deprived-of-their-liberty (accessed 29 January 2026).

Nyamu, I.K. and Wamahiu, S.P. (2022) What might a decolonial perspective on child protection look like? Lessons from Kenya. *Childhood, 29*(3), 423–38.

Oates, F. and Malthouse, K. (2021) Working for the welfare: Support and supervision needs of Indigenous Australian child protection practitioners. *Social Sciences, 10*(8), 277.

Oberle, E., Ji, X.R., Alkawaja, M., Molyneux, T.M., Kerai, S., Thomson, K.C. et al (2024) Connections matter: Adolescent social connectedness profiles and mental well-being over time. *Journal of Adolescence, 96*(1), 31–48.

Office for National Statistics (2018) The nature of violent crime in England and Wales: Year ending March 2018. Available at: https://www.ons.gov.uk/peoplepopulationandcommunity/crimeandjustice/articles/thenatureofviolentcrimeinenglandandwales/yearendingmarch2018#:~:text=Violent%20crimes%20against%20children,or%20in%20Appendix%20Table%2011 (accessed 1 October 2025).

Ofsted (2015) *Sexual exploitation of children: Ofsted thematic report.* Available at: https://www.gov.uk/government/publications/sexual-exploitation-of-children-ofsted-thematic-report (accessed 23 January 2026).

Ofsted (2018) *Protecting children from criminal exploitation, human trafficking and modern slavery: an addendum.* Available at: Protecting children from criminal exploitation, human trafficking and modern slavery: addendum (accessed 1 October 2025).

Ofsted (2021) *Review of sexual abuse in schools and colleges.* Available at: https://www.gov.uk/government/publications/review-of-sexual-abuse-in-schools-and-colleges (accessed 1 October 2025).

OSCE (2019) *2018–2019 report of the special representative and co-ordinator for combating trafficking in human beings.* Organization for Security and Co-Operation in Europe. Available at: 2018-2019 Report of the Special Representative and Co-ordinator for Combating Trafficking in Human Beings | Office of the Special Representative and Co-ordinator for Combating Trafficking in Human Beings (accessed 12 March 2026).

Owens, P.E. (2002) No teens allowed: The exclusion of adolescents from public spaces. *Landscape Journal, 21*(1), 156–63.

Owens, R., Walker, J. and Bradbury-Leather, V. (2024) Relational epistemic safety: What young people facing harm in their communities want and need from professionals tasked with helping them. *Journal of Youth Studies, 28*(8), 1247–66.

Palmer, E. (2019) Trafficked children and child protection systems in the European Union. *European Journal of Social Work, 22*(4), 551–62.

Pantazis, C., Carver, N., Karlsen, S., Mogilnicka, M. and White, R. (2025) Pre-crime, hyper-vigilance and the over-surveillance of migrant-heritage families in 'FGM-safeguarding' in England and Wales. *Critical and Radical Social Work, 13*(2), 176–94.

Parton, N. (2011) Child protection and safeguarding in England: Changing and competing conceptions of risk and their implications for social work. *British Journal of Social Work, 41*(5), 854–75.

Parton, N. (2014) *The politics of child protection: Contemporary developments and future directions.* Bloomsbury Publishing.

Peace, D. (2023) Contextual safeguarding beyond the UK, in C. Firmin and J. Lloyd (eds) *Contextual safeguarding: The next chapter.* Policy Press, pp 77–88.

Peace, D., Wroe, L. and Huegler, N. (2025) Harm, safety and belonging: exploring 'contextual safeguarding' with refugee youth in Europe. *European Journal of Social Work, 28*(5), 957–71.

Pearce, J.J. (2009) *Young people and sexual exploitation: 'It's not hidden, you just aren't looking'.* Routledge.

Pearce, J.J. (2013) 'What's going on' to safeguard children and young people from child sexual exploitation: A review of local safeguarding children boards' work to protect children from sexual exploitation. *Child Abuse Review, 23*(3), 159–70.

Pease, B., Vreugdenhil, A. and Stanford, S. (2017) *Critical ethics of care in social work.* Taylor & Francis.

Peplak, J. and Malti, T. (2017) 'That really hurt, Charlie!' Investigating the role of sympathy and moral respect in children's aggressive behavior. *The Journal of Genetic Psychology, 178*(2), 89–101.

Peter, J. and Valkenburg, P.M. (2011) Adolescents' online privacy: Toward a developmental perspective, in S. Trepte and L. Reinecke (eds) *Privacy online: Perspectives on privacy and self-disclosure in the social web.* Springer, pp 221–34.

Phillips, C. (2025) 'Lifestyle' as the new wayward: Child welfare, sexual exploitation and young people. *European Social Work Research*, 1–14.

Piaget, J. (1965) *The moral judgment of the child.* Harcourt Brace.

Pierpoint, H. (2020) *Age of criminal responsibility.* British Academy. Available at: https://medium.com/reframing-childhood-past-and-present/age-of-criminal-responsibility-1e7714db9c1c (accessed 7 October 2025).

Pike, N., Langham, M. and Lloyd, S. (2019) *Parents' experiences of the children's social care system when a child is sexually exploited.* Pace. Available at: https://ivisontrust.org.uk/wp-content/uploads/2020/01/Parents%E2%80%99-experiences-of-Children%E2%80%99s-Social-Care-Report-digital.pdf (accessed 23 January 2026).

Pimm-Smith, R. (2026) Child protection intersectionality: Disparities in racially minoritised and asylum-seeking backgrounds, in R. Akhtar (ed.) *Diverse voices in family law.* Bristol University Press, pp 137–60.

Porto, M. (2025) *Agape* in teaching: revolutionary love for a volatile, uncertain, complex and ambiguous (VUCA) world. *Pedagogies: An International Journal, 21*(1), 80–99.

Prime Minister's Office (2015) PM unveils tough new measures to tackle child sexual exploitation. Department of Health and Social Care. Available at: https://www.gov.uk/government/news/pm-unveils-tough-new-measures-to-tackle-child-sexual-exploitation (accessed 8 October 2025).

Public Accounts Committee (2025) *Support for children and young people with special educational needs. First report of session 2024–25.* HC 353, House of Commons. Available at: https://committees.parliament.uk/publications/46238/documents/231788/default/ (accessed 12 March 2026).

Pullmann, M.D., Roberts, N., Parker, E.M., Mangiaracina, K.J., Briner, L., Silverman, M. et al (2020) Residential instability, running away, and juvenile detention characterizes commercially sexually exploited youth involved in Washington State's child welfare system. *Child Abuse & Neglect, 102*, 104423.

Purcell, M.E. (2024) 'It's why young people choose to come here': Professional love and the ethic of care in UK youth work practice. *Ethics and Social Welfare, 18*(2), 149–63.

Radford, L., Corral, S., Bradley, C., Fisher, H., Bassett, C., Howat, N. et al (2011) *Child abuse and neglect in the UK today*. National Society for the Prevention of Cruelty to Children (NSPCC). Available at: https://learning.nspcc.org.uk/research-resources/pre-2013/child-abuse-neglect-uk-today (accessed 13 March 2026).

Ramey, H.L., Lawford, H.L., Pancer, S.M., Matsuba, M.K. and Pratt, M.W. (2022) Trajectories of youth's helping from adolescence into adulthood: The importance of social relations and values. *American Journal of Community Psychology, 69*(1–2), 134–44.

Rankopo, M.J. and Osei-Hwedie, K. (2011) Globalization and culturally relevant social work: African perspectives on indigenization. *International Social Work, 54*(1), 137–47.

Rannala, I.E., Gorman, J., Tierney, H., Guðmundsson, Á., Hickey, J. and Corney, T. (2024) Ethical practice in professional youth work: Perspectives from four countries. *Ethics and Social Welfare, 18*(2), 195–210.

Rees, G. (2017) Friends and peers, in G. Rees, *Children's views on their lives and well-being: Findings from the Children's Worlds Project.* Springer International Publishing, pp 99–107.

Repetti, R.L., Taylor, S.E. and Seeman, T.E. (2002) Risky families: family social environments and the mental and physical health of offspring. *Psychological Bulletin, 128*(2), 330.

Richardson, J.W. and Scott, K.A. (2002) Rap music and its violent progeny: America's culture of violence in context. *Journal of Negro Education, 71*(3), 175–92.

Ringrose, J. (2016) Postfeminist media panics over girls' 'sexualisation': implications for UK sex and relationship guidance and curriculum, in V. Sundaram and H. Sauntson (eds) *Global perspectives and key debates in sex and relationships education: Addressing issues of gender, sexuality, plurality and power.* Palgrave Pivot.

Roberts, D.F., Christenson, P.G. and Gentile, D.A. (2003) The effects of violent music on children and adolescents. *Media Violence and Children, 8*, 153–70.

Robinson, J. (2009) The social construction of deviant identities: The devil wears a hoodie, in *Key issues in childhood and youth studies*, Routledge, pp 137–47.

Rogowski, S. (2012) Social work with children and families: Challenges and possibilities in the neo-liberal world. *British Journal of Social Work, 42*(5), 921–40.

Royal College of Paediatrics and Child Health (2020) *State of child health*. RCPCH. Available at: https://stateofchildhealth.rcpch.ac.uk (accessed 7 October 2025).

Russell, D.H. and Higgins, D.J. (2023) Friends and safeguarding: Young people's views about safety and to whom they would share safety concerns. *Child Abuse Review, 32*(3), e2825.

Rustin, M. (2005) Conceptual analysis of critical moments in Victoria Climbié's life. *Child & Family Social Work, 10*(1), 11–19.

Schmid, J. (2021) A reinterrogation of South African child welfare discourse: A case for decolonisation?. *The British Journal of Social Work, 52*(5), 2437–54.

Schotanus-Dijkstra, M., Pieterse, M.E., Drossaert, C.H., Westerhof, G.J., De Graaf, R., Ten Have, M. et al (2016) What factors are associated with flourishing? Results from a large representative national sample. *Journal of Happiness Studies, 17*(4), 1351–70.

Scottish Government (2021) *National guidance for child protection in Scotland 2021*. Available at: https://hub.careinspectorate.com/media/4577/national-guidance-for-child-protection-in-scotland-2021.pdf (accessed 12 March 2026).

Scottish Government (2024) *Keeping the promise to our children, young people and families: Update on progress 2024*. The Scottish Government.

Segal, M. (2023) The conflict between maintaining confidentiality in social work and protecting a minor from harm. *Journal of Family Social Work, 26*(1), 31–44.

Shawar, Y.R., Truong, P.P. and Shiffman, J. (2022) The emergence of political priority for addressing child sexual abuse in the United Kingdom. *Child Abuse & Neglect, 128*, 105601.

Sheehan, K., Walsh, C. and Cusack, A. (2024) 'It's group-on-one': Social disconnection as a tool of and defence against child criminal exploitation in the Republic of Ireland. *Crime Prevention and Community Safety, 26*(3), 266–84.

Shuker, L. (2013) Constructs of safety for children in care affected by sexual exploitation, in M. Melrose and L. Pearce (eds) *Critical perspectives on child sexual exploitation and related trafficking*. Palgrave Macmillan, pp 125–38.

Shuker, L. and Ackerley, E. (2017) *Empowering parents: Evaluation of parents as partners in safeguarding children and young people in Lancashire project 2014–2017*. University of Bedfordshire. Available at: https://researchportal.beds.ac.uk/en/publications/empowering-parents-evaluation-of-parents-as-partners-in-safeguard-3/ (accessed 23 January 2026).

Simons, L.G. and Conger, R.D. (2007) Linking mother–father differences in parenting to a typology of family parenting styles and adolescent outcomes. *Journal of Family Issues*, *28*(2), 212–41.

Simpson, J.E. (2025) The panopticon effect: The use of surveillance and monitoring by foster carers and social work practitioners to minimise unmediated contact. *Critical and Radical Social Work*, *13*(1), 24–40.

Smetana, J.G. (2010) *Adolescents, families, and social development: How teens construct their worlds*. John Wiley & Sons.

Smith, D.E. (2005) *Institutional ethnography: A sociology for people*. Bloomsbury Publishing PLC.

Smithson, H., Ralphs, R. and Williams, P. (2013) Used and abused: The problematic usage of gang terminology in the United Kingdom and its implications for ethnic minority youth. *British Journal of Criminology*, *53*(1), 113–28.

Smithson, R. and Gibson, M. (2017) Less than human: A qualitative study into the experience of parents involved in the child protection system. *Child & Family Social Work*, *22*(2), 565–74.

Sprecher, S. and Fehr, B. (2005) Compassionate love for close others and humanity. *Journal of Social and Personal Relationships*, *22*(5), 629–51.

Sroufe, L.A., Egeland, B., Carlson E.A. and Collins, W.A. (2005) *The development of the person: The Minnesota study of risk and adaptation from birth to adulthood*. Guilford Press.

Stabler, L., Cunningham, E., Mannay, D., Boffey, M., Cummings, A., Davies, B. et al (2023) 'I probably wouldn't want to talk about anything too personal': A qualitative exploration of how issues of privacy, confidentiality and surveillance in the home impact on access and engagement with online services and spaces for care-experienced young people. *Adoption & Fostering*, *47*(3), 277–94.

Stalker, K. and McArthur, K. (2012) Child abuse, child protection and disabled children: A review of recent research. *Child Abuse Review*, *21*(1), 24–40.

Steckley, L. and Smith, M. (2011) Care ethics in residential child care: A different voice. *Ethics and Social Welfare*, *5*(2), 181–95.

Stevens, A., Schreeche-Powell, E., Billingham, L. and Irwing-Rogers, K. (2025) Interventionitis in the criminal justice system: Three English cases. *Critical Criminology*, *33*, 171–87.

Thomas, R., Lynch, A. and Ruch, G. (2025) Creating a containing space for analysing data: roles and responsibilities in the Many Minds process. *Journal of Psychosocial Studies*, *18*(2), 138–55.

Thornhill, L. (2023) Parents as partners: Destigmatising the role of parents of children affected by extra familial harm, in C. Firmin and J. Lloyd (eds) *Contextual safeguarding: The next chapter*. Policy Press, pp 77–88.

Todorovic, D., van der Linden, J., Sieckelinck, S. and Timmerman, M.C. (2025) From likes to lifeworlds: The contributions of youth work practice in the online lifeworld to young people's development. *Social Sciences*, *14*(10), 618.

Trnka, S. and Trundle, C. (2014) Competing responsibilities: Moving beyond neoliberal responsibilisation. *Anthropological Forum*, *24*(2), 136–53.

Tronto, J.C. (2005) An ethic of care, in A.E. Cudd, and R.O. Andreasen (eds) *Feminist theory: A philosophical anthology*. Blackwell Publishing, pp 251–63.

UNDOC (2022) Global report on trafficking in persons 2022. United Nations publications. Available at: https://www.unodc.org/documents/data-and-analysis/glotip/2022/GLOTiP_2022_web.pdf (accessed 7 October 2025).

UNICEF (2019) *An everyday lesson: #ENDviolence in schools*. UNICEF. Available at: https://www.unicef.org/documents/everyday-lesson-endviolence-schools (accessed 12 March 2026).

Van Bijleveld, G.G., Dedding, C.W. and Bunders-Aelen, J.F. (2015) Children's and young people's participation within child welfare and child protection services: A state-of-the-art review. *Child & Family Social Work*, *20*(2), 129–38.

van Dijk, M., Eichelsheim, V., Kleemans, E., Soudijn, M. and Van de Weijer, S. (2022) Intergenerational continuity of crime among children of organized crime offenders in the Netherlands. *Crime, Law and Social Change*, 77(2), 207–27.

Vespoli, G., Taddei, B., Imbimbo, E., De Luca, L. and Nocentini, A. (2025) The concept of privacy in the digital world according to teenagers. *Journal of Public Health*, *33*(12), 2731–42.

Villa, C. (2024) *The effects of youth clubs on education and crime*. IFS. Available at: https://ifs.org.uk/sites/default/files/2025-06/WP202451-The-effects-of-youth-clubs-on-education-and-crime.pdf (accessed 13 March 2026).

Vittersø, J. (2004) Subjective well-being versus self-actualization: Using the flow-simplex to promote a conceptual clarification of subjective quality of life. *Social Indicators Research*, *65*(3), 299–331.

Wall, I. and Johnsdotter, S. (2024) Sex as self-injury: The appearance of a new diagnostic category in Sweden. *Sexualities*, *27*(1–2), 206–23.

Warnick, B.R. (2013) *Understanding student rights in schools: Speech, religion, and privacy in educational settings*. Teachers College Press.

Warr, M. (2002) *Companions in crime: The social aspects of criminal conduct*. Cambridge University Press.

Warrington, C. (2013) 'Helping me find my own way': Sexually exploited young people's involvement in decision-making about their care. Doctoral thesis. University of Bedfordshire.

Warrington, C. and Larkins, C. (2019) Children at the centre of safety: Challenging the false juxtaposition of protection and participation. *Journal of Children's Services*, *14*(3), 133–42.

Warrington, C., Langhoff, K. and Warnock, B. (2024) The role of arts-based methods in supporting safe and participatory research addressing sexual violence with young people. *Health Education Journal*, *84*(4), 385–98 (Original work published 2025).

Welsh Government (2021) *Working together to safeguard people volume 7 – Safeguarding children from child sexual exploitation*. Available at: https://www.gov.wales/sites/default/files/publications/2021-02/safeguarding-children-from-child-sexual-exploitation.pdf (accessed 12 March 2026).

Westin, A.F. (1967) Special report: legal safeguards to insure privacy in a computer society. *Communications of the ACM*, *10*(9), 533–7.

Weston, S. and Mythen, G. (2020) Working with and negotiating 'risk': Examining the effects of awareness raising interventions designed to prevent child sexual exploitation. *The British Journal of Criminology*, *60*(2), 323–42.

Wilkins, D. and Whittaker, C. (2018) Doing child-protection social work with parents: What are the barriers in practice?. *The British Journal of Social Work*, *48*(7), 2003–19.

Williams, D.P. (2018) *Being matrixed: The (over)policing of gang suspects in London*. StopWatch.

Wilson, A.V. and Mueller-Johnson, K. (2024) Discovering a predictive mechanism to identify risk and harm in extra-familial child exploitation: Time to reconsider the Multi-agency Child Exploitation (MACE) Response?. *Cambridge Journal of Evidence-Based Policing*, *8*(1), 3.

Winnicott, D.W. (1971) *Playing and reality*. Routledge.

Wisniewski, P.J., Vitak, J. and Hartikainen, H. (2022) Privacy in adolescence, in B.P. Knijnenburg, X. Page, P.J. Wisniewski, H.R. Lipford, N. Proferes and J. Romano (eds) *Modern socio-technical perspectives on privacy*. Springer, pp 315–36.

Witten, H., Savahl, S. and Adams, S. (2019) Adolescent flourishing: A systematic review. *Cogent Psychology*, *6*(1), 1640341.

Wolfram, H.J., Mohr, G. and Schyns, B. (2007) Professional respect for female and male leaders: influential gender-relevant factors. *Women in Management Review*, *22*(1), 19–32.

World Health Organization (2002) World report on violence and health. Available at: https://www.who.int/publications/i/item/9241545615 (accessed 7 October 2025).

World Health Organization (2017) The violence prevention alliance approach. Available at: https://www.who.int/groups/violence-prevention-alliance/approach (accessed 8 October 2025).

World Health Organization (2024) Youth violence. Available at: https://www.who.int/news-room/fact-sheets/detail/youth-violence (accessed 23 January 2026).

Wroe, L.E. (2021) Young people and "county lines": A contextual and social account. *Journal of children's services*, *16*(1), 39–55.

Wroe, L.E. (2022) When helping hurts: a zemiological analysis of a child protection intervention in adolescence – implications for a critical child protection studies. *Social Sciences*, *11*(6), 263.

Wroe, L.E. and Lloyd, J. (2020) 'Watching over or working with? Understanding social work innovation in response to extra-familial harm', *Social Sciences*, *9*(4), 37, 1–16.

Wroe, L.E., Peace, D. and Firmin, C. (2023) 'Relocating' adolescents from risk beyond the home: What do we learn when we ask about safety? *The British Journal of Social Work*, *53*(5), 2958–78.

Wroe, L., Owens, R., Lloyd, J. and Firmin, C. (2025) From 'risky choices' to 'risky contexts'? The state of play of UK child welfare responses to adolescent 'extra-familial harm'. National and international implications. *The British Journal of Social Work*, *55*(7), 3414–34.

Young, T., Fitzgibbon, W. and Silverstone, D. (2014) A question of family? Youth and gangs. *Youth Justice*, *14*(2), 171–85.

Index

References to figures appear in *italic* type; those in **bold** type refer to tables.

M

N

O

P

R

Printed and bound by CPI Group (UK) Ltd, Croydon, CR0 4YY
14/09/2026
14961992-0001